Kundalini
the evolutionary energy in man

Kundalini

the evolutionary
energy in man

Gopi Krishna

with a psychological
commentary by James Hillman

foreword by Gene Kieffer

Shambhala
Boston & London
1997

Shambhala Publications, Inc.
Horticultural Hall
300 Massachusetts Avenue
Boston, Massachusetts 02115
www.shambhala.com

Commentary © 1967, 1970 by James Hillman
Foreword © 1997 by Gene Kieffer
Book totally revised and reset 1970
Revised edition © 1970 in Great Britain by Vincent Stuart &
John M. Watkins Ltd., London

For information about the work and publications of Gopi
Krishna, contact The Kundalini Research Foundation, P.O. Box
2248, Darien, CT 06820, U.S.A. In Canada, books by Gopi
Krishna may be ordered from F.I.N.D. Research Trust, R.R. 5,
Flesherton, Ontario N0C 1E0.

13   12   11   10   9   8   7

Printed in the United States of America

∞ This edition is printed on acid-free paper that meets the
American National Standards Institute Z39.48 Standard.

Distributed in the United States by Random House, Inc.,
and in Canada by Random House of Canada Ltd

Library of Congress Cataloging-in-Publication Data

Gopi Krishna, 1903–
    Kundalini: the evolutionary energy in man / Gopi
Krishna; foreword by Gene Kieffer; psychological
commentary by James Hillman.
        p.   cm.
    ISBN-13 978-1-57062-280-9 (alk. paper)
    ISBN-10 1-57062-280-9
    1. Gopi Krishna, 1903–   .   2. Kuṇḍalinī.
    3. Hindus—India—Biography.   I. Title.
BL1175.G62A3   1997   96-9602
294.5'43—dc20   CIP

Foreword

Not e'en a shadow of the thought
Of Victory should cross your mind,
When with the inner changes wrought
The coiled-up power starts to unwind.
　　　　　—Gopi Krishna, *The Way to Self-Knowledge*

W HEN this book was first published in 1970, the author's descriptions of his experiences caught everyone by surprise. Nothing in the literature, neither in the ancient texts on Yoga nor in the comparatively recent reports by Western saints and mystics, was remotely similar. They were so at odds with the preconceived ideas at the time that Frederic Spiegelberg, the eminent historian of world religions and professor emeritus of comparative religion and Indology at Stanford University, was moved to write in an introduction to the first edition of the book: "We have here, in this wholly unintellectual personality, a classical example of a simple man, uneducated in Yoga, who yet through intense labor and persistent enthusiasm, succeeds in achieving, if not Samadhi, yet some very high state in Yoga perfection, based entirely on his inner feeling development and not at all on ideas and traditions. Gopi Krishna is an extremely honest reporter, to the point of humbleness." Professor Spiegelberg could not have known in 1967 that Pandit Gopi Krishna would go on to write more than a dozen other books, numerous articles, and many thousands of pages of unpublished works, some in verse, some in prose, and almost all in English, over the course of the next decade and a half.

He had decided to begin work on yet another new book when he fell gravely ill with a lung infection. He was still

recovering from a previous illness, brought on by fatigue and
the intense heat in New Delhi, where he had been staying.
When the temperature soared above 115 degrees Fahrenheit,
it was decided that he would be more comfortable at his
home in Srinagar, Kashmir. His condition improved rapidly,
but he developed a lung infection, and within a week or so
succumbed. He was awake, resting in the arms of his wife,
when he took his last breath. It was on the morning of July
31, 1984, and he was eighty-one years of age.

If this present work leaves the reader with the impression
that Gopi Krishna was a frail man, it would be incorrect.
Generally speaking, he enjoyed excellent health. But he often
said that due to the experiences described herein, his mental
and physical condition was such that he had to be extremely
careful with his diet and make certain never to overtax his
mental strength. He would sometimes remark that his life
hung by a slender thread, or that he lived on a razor's edge.

Just ten days before his death, he had written in a letter that
he believed the earlier crisis had passed and he was rapidly
regaining his strength. Soon, he said, he would begin work
on yet another book. Many friends had urged him to write
more about his inner experiences, and this would fulfill their
desire. It was a very upbeat letter, from a man who couldn't
wait to get back to work after a debilitating illness.

There were several friends who, early on, wondered why
Gopi Krishna didn't just invent something new, discover a
cure for cancer, or work a miracle or two, in order to impress
the public and win support for his research. His response to
such suggestions was to remind them that there wasn't a single mention of miracles in the Upanishads—the fountainhead
of all metaphysical and spiritual thought in India—nor in the
dialogues of Buddha. In fact, there isn't a word in favor of
miracles in the dialogues of Buddha, he said, nor in the *Bhagavad Gita,* or the sayings of Ramakrishna, or of Ramana
Maharshi.

In a conversation he once said that when he sometimes had
visions they were "more real, more solid," than the coffee

table standing in front of him, which he struck with his hand to emphasize the point. He explained that the ecstatic trance could be of two kinds, one visionary, the other without form. The reason he refrained from describing his visions—except for what he has written here, and in *The Riddle of Consciousness*—was that they would seem too fantastic to believe. So the book that he had in mind to write just before he passed away might have turned out to be sensational.

Perhaps he felt that it was time for such a book. He had always maintained that his mission was to convince scientists to investigate Kundalini. Writing about his visionary experiences might have lessened his credibility. There would be plenty of fantastic discoveries in the mind and consciousness—and in physiology, also—once empirical research was seriously under way.

One of the scientists who was greatly interested in this research was Carl Fredrich von Weizsäcker, the astrophysicist and author, who had his own Max Planck Institute for the Life Sciences in Starnberg, Germany. Professor Weizsäcker had visited Gopi Krishna in Kashmir on three occasions and wrote an introduction to a small book the Pandit had written in 1970, entitled *The Biological Basis of Religion and Genius* (New York: Harper & Row, 1972). In the introduction, Professor Weizsäcker showed that Gopi Krishna's views about the physiological basis of Kundalini were entirely compatible with modern quantum physics.

Probably almost everyone familiar with the concept of Kundalini agreed with the Pandit that Kundalini would be the target of intense investigation sooner or later. But he was infused with a feeling of urgency that could only be compared to what we know about the Old Testament prophets. This was the result of a book he had written in verse in 1967, entitled *The Shape of Events to Come,* reflecting the tensions of the Cold War. His main preoccupation ever since was the world's rapidly expanding arsenals of nuclear weapons.

A pragmatist as well as an enlightened visionary, he thought as far back as the 1970s that serious research on Kundalini would not get under way before the decade of the 1990s. But in a world in which writers routinely go on tours to promote their books on radio and television, and sign autographs in bookstores, he lived quietly with his wife, Bhabi, in their home in Srinagar. In the winter months, they would move in with their eldest son, Jagdish, and his family in New Delhi, because it got much too cold in Kashmir, where few if any homes had central heating.

Gopi Krishna was always glad to discuss his ideas with anyone who came to visit, not only because it afforded him the opportunity to pass along his message but to learn firsthand what was happening around the world. He read the newspapers daily, and one of his few desires was to have a telex machine so that he could communicate quickly with his friends in Europe and America. Due to the expense, no telex machine was ever installed. Today, if he were living, he would undoubtedly have an Internet address and a home page on the World Wide Web.

According to Gopi Krishna, the next step in human evolution is not beyond our imagination, nor is it very far off. In conversations, he would sometimes compare the mind of an intelligent animal, such as a dog, with that of a human being by way of attempting to illustrate the difference between ordinary consciousness and superconsciousness. Try to imagine, he would say, what it would be like if your pet dog were to awaken from a nap with a human brain in place of the one it was born with. Flooded by thoughts, impressions, emotions, and information, it would be overwhelmed. A sudden awakening of Kundalini produces the same bewilderment, although the difference may not be quite so great.

In a typical day, Gopi Krishna would write for a few hours in the morning, tend to his correspondence, meet with visitors, and take care of the usual tasks of a householder. When he wrote, it was almost always in English, which he learned in school at an early age.

The Pandit never owned a car but rode in taxis and buses. He had none of the modern conveniences we take for granted and consider indispensable, except for a telephone, which was often unreliable in Kashmir. It wasn't until 1972, after he had made two trips to Europe that, at the urging of friends, running water and electricity were installed in his ancestral home in Srinagar. Even then, his meals were still cooked over a kerosene burner or in an open oven in the kitchen wall.

Gopi Krishna visited the United States three times and Canada twice, the first time in 1978, when he was invited to speak at a conference in New York on Consciousness Research. He returned the following year for a conference in Philadelphia, after which he spent several weeks in Connecticut. Before returning home, he visited a new group of friends in Toronto who had become excited about his research.

Their interest grew to the extent that at one point they chartered a 747 to India, where they spent several weeks at his Institute at Nishat, on Dal Lake near Srinagar. Many who were on that trip continue to promote his ideas, but the property of the Institute was lost a few years later when the dispute between Pakistan and India, over the political fate of Kashmir, upset the stability of the region.

Gopi Krishna's last visit to North America was in October 1983, when he was invited to speak at the United Nations in New York at a conference of Native Americans. He broke up the return flight by remaining in Zurich for several months, where he began writing his last work, *The Way to Self-Knowledge*. He said that it was in response to the many requests he had received for just such a book.

Professor Spiegelberg wrote in his introduction, "In view of [Gopi Kirshna's] detailed testimony it becomes clearly impossible to treat the whole realm of Kundalini-experience as something belonging to the concept of either biology or psychology. . . . The vocabulary of the Kundalini-Yoga system refers neither to those facts which in the West are considered to be psychological nor to anything within the realm of inner body feelings which are so elaborately described in Yoga texts. . . ."

And yet in spite of this seemingly insurmountable hurdle, Gopi Krishna succeeded in changing the way many people think about Yoga and enlightenment. The idea that enlightenment has a biological basis is growing in acceptance as scientists discover more about the brain and consciousness.

> Incredible though it seems, it is a fact
> That Prana and pure consciousness react
> On one another to produce the myth
> Of this stupendous world we battle with.
>
> Then consciousness a wondrous aspect wears,
> So lofty and sublime that all our fears
> And doubts about ourselves dissolve at once,
> As if illumined by a hundred suns
> Of knowledge to be assured the Vision seen
> Is That which will be, is and e'er has been;
> The Source Eternal of all that is known.
>
> The world of that too by which it is shown
> The mind and process by which this is done:
> The whole scheme of creation in but One.
>
> In this amazing radiant Presence all
> The staggering worlds, which awe us and enthrall,
> Become a ghostly shadow seen at night;
> A far-off melting cloud in sunshine bright,
> While mind, with ego vastly whittled down,
> In mute astonishment sees itself drown
> Into one all-enfolding Life sublime,
> Only pure consciousness, devoid of time
> And space, one all-embracing world of love
> And joy not found on earth or heaven above.
>
> —Gopi Krishna, *The Riddle of Consciousness*

GENE KIEFFER
July 10, 1996

Chapter One

ONE morning during the Christmas of 1937 I sat cross-legged in a small room in a little house on the outskirts of the town of Jammu, the winter capital of the Jammu and Kashmir State in northern India. I was meditating with my face towards the window on the east through which the first grey streaks of the slowly brightening dawn fell into the room. Long practice had accustomed me to sit in the same posture for hours at a time without the least discomfort, and I sat breathing slowly and rhythmically, my attention drawn towards the crown of my head, contemplating an imaginary lotus in full bloom, radiating light.

I sat steadily, unmoving and erect, my thoughts uninterruptedly centered on the shining lotus, intent on keeping my attention from wandering and bringing it back again and again whenever it moved in any other direction. The intensity of concentration interrupted my breathing; gradually it slowed down to such an extent that at times it was barely perceptible. My whole being was so engrossed in the contemplation of the lotus that for several minutes at a time I lost touch with my body and surroundings. During such intervals I used to feel as if I were poised in mid-air, without any feeling of a body around me. The only object of which I was aware was a lotus of brilliant colour, emitting rays of light. This experience has happened to many people who practise meditation in any form regularly for a sufficient length of time, but what followed on that fateful morning in my case, changing the whole course of my life and outlook, has happened to few.

During one such spell of intense concentration I suddenly felt a strange sensation below the base of the spine, at the place touching the seat, while I sat cross-legged on a folded blanket spread on the floor. The sensation was so extraordinary and so pleasing that my attention was forcibly drawn towards it. The moment my attention was thus unexpectedly withdrawn from the point on which it was focused, the sensation ceased. Thinking it to be a trick played by my imagination to relax the tension, I dismissed the matter from my mind and brought my attention back to the point from which it had wandered. Again I fixed it on the lotus, and as the image grew clear and distinct at the top of my head, again the sensation occurred. This time I tried to maintain the fixity of my attention and succeeded for a few seconds, but the sensation extending up-wards grew so intense and was so extraordinary, as compared to anything I had experienced before, that in spite of myself my mind went towards it, and at that very moment it again disappear-ed. I was now convinced that something unusual had happened for which my daily practice of concentration was probably responsible.

I had read glowing accounts, written by learned men, of great benefits resulting from concentration, and of the miraculous powers acquired by yogis through such exercises. My heart began to beat wildly, and I found it difficult to bring my attention to the required degree of fixity. After a while I grew composed and was soon as deep in meditation as before. When completely immersed I again experienced the sensation, but this time, instead of allow-ing my mind to leave the point where I had fixed it, I maintained a rigidity of attention throughout. The sensation again extended upwards, growing in intensity, and I felt myself wavering; but with a great effort I kept my attention centered round the lotus. Suddenly, with a roar like that of a waterfall, I felt a stream of liquid light entering my brain through the spinal cord.

Entirely unprepared for such a development, I was completely taken by surprise; but regaining self-control instantaneously, I remained sitting in the same posture, keeping my mind on the point of concentration. The illumination grew brighter and brighter, the roaring louder, I experienced a rocking sensation and then felt myself slipping out of my body, entirely enveloped in a halo of light. It is impossible to describe the experience accurately. I felt the point of consciousness that was myself growing wider, surrounded by waves of light. It grew wider and wider, spreading outward while the body, normally the immediate object of its perception, appeared to have receded into the distance until I became entirely unconscious of it. I was now all consciousness, without any outline, without any idea of a corporeal appendage, without any feeling or sensation coming from the senses, immersed in a sea of light simultaneously conscious and aware of every point, spread out, as it were, in all directions without any barrier or material obstruction. I was no longer myself, or to be more accurate, no longer as I knew myself to be, a small point of awareness confined in a body, but instead was a vast circle of consciousness in which the body was but a point, bathed in light and in a state of exaltation and happiness impossible to describe.

After some time, the duration of which I could not judge, the circle began to narrow down; I felt myself contracting, becoming smaller and smaller, until I again became dimly conscious of the outline of my body, then more clearly; and as I slipped back to my old condition, I became suddenly aware of the noises in the street, felt again my arms and legs and head, and once more became my narrow self in touch with body and surroundings. When I opened my eyes and looked about, I felt a little dazed and bewildered, as if coming back from a strange land completely foreign to me. The sun had risen and was shining full on my face, warm and soothing. I tried to lift my hands, which always rested in my lap, one upon the other, during meditation. My arms felt limp and lifeless. With an effort I raised them up and stretched them to enable the blood to flow freely. Then I tried to free my legs from the posture in which I was sitting and to place them in a more comfortable position but could not. They were heavy and stiff. With the help of my hands I freed them and stretched them out, then put my back against the wall, reclining in a position of ease and comfort.

What had happened to me? Was I the victim of a hallucination? Or had I by some strange vagary of fate succeeded in experiencing the Transcendental? Had I really succeeded where millions of others had failed? Was there, after all, really some truth in the oft-repeated claim of the sages and ascetics of India, made for thousands of years and verified and repeated generation after generation, that it was possible to apprehend reality in this life if one followed certain rules of conduct and practised meditation in a certain way? My thoughts were in a daze. I could hardly believe that I had a vision of divinity. There had been an expansion of my own self, my own consciousness, and the transformation had been brought about by the vital current that had started from below the spine and found access to my brain through the backbone. I recalled that I had read long ago in books on Yoga of a certain vital mechanism called Kundalini, connected with the lower end of the spine, which becomes active by means of certain exercises, and when once roused carries the limited human consciousness to transcendental heights, endowing the individual with incredible psychic and mental powers. Had I been lucky enough to find the key to this wonderful mechanism, which was wrapped up in the legendary mist of ages, about which people talked and whispered without having once seen it in action in themselves or in others? I tried once again to repeat the experience, but was so weak and flabbergasted that I could not collect my thoughts sufficiently enough to induce a state of concentration. My mind was in a ferment. I looked at the sun. Could it be that in my condition of extreme concentration I had mistaken it for the effulgent halo that had surrounded me in the superconscious state? I closed my eyes again, allowing the rays of the sun to play upon my face. No, the glow that I could perceive across my closed eyelids was quite different. It was external and had not that splendour. The light I had experienced was internal, an integral part of enlarged consciousness, a part of my self.

I stood up. My legs felt weak and tottered under me. It seemed as if my vitality had been drained out. My arms were no better. I massaged my thighs and legs gently, and, feeling a little better, slowly walked downstairs. Saying nothing to my wife, I took my meal in silence and left for work. My appetite was not as keen as usual, my mouth appeared dry, and I could not put my thoughts into my work in the office. I was in a state of exhaustion and lassitude, disinclined to talk. After a while, feeling suffocated and ill at ease, I left for a short walk in the street with the idea of finding diversion for my thoughts. My mind reverted again and again to the experience of the morning, trying to recreate in imagination the marvellous phenomenon I had witnessed, but without success. My body, especially the legs, still felt weak, and I could not walk for long. I took no interest in the people whom I met, and walked with a sense of detachment and indifference to my surroundings quite foreign to me. I returned to my desk sooner than I had intended, and passed the remaining hours toying with my pen and papers, unable to compose my thoughts sufficiently to work.

When I returned home in the afternoon I felt no better. I could not bring myself to sit down and read, my usual habit in the evening. I ate supper in silence, without appetite or relish, and retired to bed. Usually I was asleep within minutes of putting my head to the pillow, but this night I felt strangely restless and disturbed. I could not reconcile the exaltation of the morning with the depression that sat heavily on me while I tossed from side to side on the bed. I had an unaccountable feeling of fear and uncertainty. At last in the midst of misgivings I fell asleep. I slept fitfully, dreaming strange dreams, and woke up after short intervals in sharp contrast to my usual deep, uninterrupted sleep. After about 3 a.m. sleep refused to come. I sat up in bed for some time. Sleep had not refreshed me. I still felt fatigued and my thoughts lacked clarity. The usual time for my meditation was approaching. I decided to begin earlier so that I would not have the sun on my hands and face, and without disturbing my wife, went upstairs to my study. I spread the blanket, and sitting cross-legged as usual, began to meditate.

I could not concentrate with the same intensity as on the previous day, though I tried my best. My thoughts wandered, and instead of being in a state of happy expectancy I felt strangely nervous and uneasy. At last, after repeated efforts, I held my attention at the usual point for some time, waiting for results. Nothing happened and I began to feel doubts about the validity of my previous experience. I tried again, this time with better success. Pulling myself together, I steadied my wandering thoughts, and fixing my attention on the crown, tried to visualize a lotus in full bloom as was my custom. As soon as I arrived at the usual pitch of mental fixity, I again felt the current moving upward. I did not allow my attention to waver, and again with a rush and a roaring noise in my ears the stream of effulgent light entered my brain, filling me with power and vitality, and I felt myself expanding in all directions, spreading beyond the boundaries of flesh, entirely absorbed in the contemplation of a brilliant conscious glow, one with it and yet not entirely merged in it. The condition lasted for a shorter duration than it had done yesterday. The feeling of exaltation was not so strong. When I came back to normal, I felt my heart thumping wildly and there was a bitter taste in my mouth. It seemed as if a scorching blast of hot air had passed through my body. The feeling of exhaustion and weariness was more pronounced than it had been yesterday.

I rested for some time to recover my strength and poise. It was still dark. I had now no doubts that the experience was real and that the sun had nothing to do with the internal lustre that I saw. But, why did I feel uneasy and depressed? Instead of feeling exceedingly happy at my luck and blessing my stars, why had despondency overtaken me? I felt as if I were in imminent danger of something beyond my understanding and power, something intangible and mysterious, which I could neither grasp nor analyse. A heavy cloud of depression and gloom seemed to hang round me, rising from my own internal depths without relation to external circumstances, I did not feel I was the same man I had been but a few days before, and a condition of horror, on account of the inexplicable change, began to settle on me, from which, try as I might, I could not make myself free by any effort of my will. Little did I realize that from that day onwards I was never to be my old normal self again, that I had unwittingly and without preparation or even adequate knowledge of it roused to activity the most wonderful and stern power in man, that I had stepped unknowingly upon the key to the most guarded secret of the ancients, and that thenceforth for a long time I had to live suspended by a thread, swinging between life on the one hand and death on the other, between sanity and insanity, between light and darkness, between heaven and earth.

I began the practice of meditation at the age of seventeen. Failure in a house examination at the College, which prevented me from appearing in the University that year, created a revolution in my young mind. I was not so much worried by the failure and the loss of one year as by the thoughts of the extreme pain it would cause my mother, whom I loved dearly. For days and nights I racked my brain for a plausible excuse to mitigate the effect of the painful news on her. She was so confident of my success that I simply had not the courage to disillusion her. I was a merit scholarship holder, occupying a distinguished position in College, but instead of devoting time to the study of assigned texts, I busied myself in reading irrelevant books borrowed from the library. Too late I realized that I knew next to nothing about some of the subjects, and had no chance whatever of passing the test. Having never suffered the ignominy of a failure in my school life, and always highly spoken of by the teachers, I felt crestfallen, pierced to the quick by the thought that my mother, proud of my distinction and sure of my ability to get through the examination with merit, would be deeply hurt at this avowal of my negligence.

Born, in a village, of a family of hard-working and God-fearing peasants, fate had destined her as a partner to a man considerably senior to her in age, hailing from Amritsar, at that time no less than six days' journey by rail and cart from the place of her birth. Insecurity and lawlessness in the country had forced one of my forefathers to bid adieu to his cool native soil and to seek his fortune in the torrid plains of distant Punjab. There, changed in dress and speaking a different tongue, my grandfather and great-grandfather lived and prospered like other exiles of their kind, altered in all save their religious rites and customs and the unmistakable physiognomy of Kashmiri Brahmins. My father, with a deep mystical vein in him, returned to the land of his ancestors

when almost past his prime, to marry and settle there. Even
during the most active period of his worldly life he was always on
the look-out for Yogis and ascetics reputed to possess occult
powers, and never tired of serving them and sitting in their company to learn the secret of their marvellous gifts.

He was a firm believer in the traditional schools of religious
discipline and Yoga, extant in India from the earliest times, which
among all the numerous factors contributing to success allot the
place of honour to renunciation, to the voluntary relinquishment
of all worldly pursuits and possessions, to enable the mind, released from the heavy chains binding it to the earth, to plumb its
own ethereal depths undisturbed by desire and passion. The
authority for such conduct emanates from the Vedas, nay, from
the examples themselves set by the inspired authors of the Vedic
hymns and the celebrated seers of the Upanishads, who conforming
to an established practice prevailing in the ancient society of
Indo-Aryans, retired from the busy life of householders at the
ripe age of fifty and above, sometimes accompanied by their
consorts, to spend the rest of their lives in forest hermitages in
uninterrupted meditation and preaching, the prelude to a grand
and peaceful exit.

This unusual mode of passing the eve of life has exercised a
deep fascination over countless spiritually inclined men and
women in India and even now hundreds of accomplished and,
from the worldly point of view, happily circumstanced family
men of advanced age, bidding farewell to their otherwise comfortable homes and dutiful progeny, betake themselves to distant
retreats to pass their remaining days peacefully in spiritual pursuits, away from the fret and fever of the world. My father, an
ardent admirer of this ancient ideal, which provides for many a
refreshing contrast to the 'dead-to-heaven and wed-to-earth' old
age of today, chose for himself a recluse's life, about twelve years
after marriage, his gradually formed decision hastened by the
tragic death of his first-born son at the age of five. Retiring
voluntarily from a lucrative Government post, before he was even
fifty, he gave up all the pleasures and cares of life and shut himself
in seclusion with his books, leaving the entire responsibility of

managing the household on the inexperienced shoulders of his young wife.

She had suffered terribly. My father renounced the world when she was in her twenty-eighth year, the mother of three children, two daughters and a son. How she brought us up, with what devotion she attended to the simple needs of our austere father, who cut himself off completely from the world, never even exchanging a word with any of us, and by what ceaseless labour and colossal self-sacrifice she managed to maintain the good name and honour of the family would make fit themes for a great story of matchless heroism, unflinching regard to duty, chastity, and supreme self-abnegation. I felt guilty and mortified. How could I face her with an admission of my weakness? Realizing that by my lack of self-control I had betrayed the trust reposed in me, I determined to make up for the lost opportunity in other ways. At no other time in my life should I be guilty of the same offence again. But in order to curb the vagrant element in my nature and to regulate my conduct it was necessary that I should make a conquest of my mind, which by following unhindered its own inclinations to the neglect of duty had brought me to such a sorry plight, a prey to poignant grief and remorse, fallen low in my own eyes.

Having made the resolve, I looked around for a means to carry it into effect. In order to succeed it was necessary to have at least some knowledge of the methods to bring one's rebellious self into subjugation. Accordingly, I read a few books of the usual kind on the development of personality and mind control. Out of the huge mass of material contained in these writings, I devoted my attention to only two things: concentration of mind and cultivation of will. I took up the practice of both with youthful enthusiasm, directing all my energies and subordinating all my desires to the acquisition of this one object within the shortest possible period of time. Sick with mortification at my lack of self-restraint, which made me yield passively to the dictates of desire to substitute absorbing story books and other light literature for the dry and difficult college texts, I made it a point to assert my will in all things, beginning with smaller ones and gradually extending its application to bigger and more difficult issues, forcing myself as a penance to do irksome and rigorous tasks, against which my ease-loving nature recoiled in dismay, until I began to feel a sense of mastery over myself, a growing conviction that I would not again fall an easy prey to ordinary temptations.

From mind control it was but a step to Yoga and occultism. I passed almost imperceptibly from a study of books on the former to a scrutiny of spiritualistic literature, combined with a cursory reading of some of the scriptures. Smarting under the disgrace of my first failure in life, and stung by a guilty conscience, I felt a growing aversion to the world and its hopelessly tangled affairs that had exposed me to this humiliation; and gradually the fire of renunciation began to burn fiercely in me, seeking knowledge of an honourable way of escape from the tension and turmoil of life to the peace and quietude of a consecrated existence. At this time of acute mental conflict, the sublime message of the Bhagavad Gita had a most profound and salutary effect on me, allaying the burning mental fever by holding before me the promise of a perennially peaceful life in tune with the Infinite Reality behind the phenomenal world of mingled joy and pain. In this way, from the original idea to achieve success in wordly enterprise by eliminating the possibility of failure owing to flaccid determination, I imperceptibly went to the other extreme: I was soon exercising my will and practising meditation not for temporal ends, but with the sole object of gaining success in Yoga even if that necessitated the sacrifice of all my earthly prospects.

My worldly ambition died down. At that young age, when one is more influenced by ideals and dreams than by practical consider-ations and is apt to look at the world through golden glasses, the sorrow and misery visible on every side by accentuating the con-trast between what is and what ought to be tend to modify the direction of thought in particularly susceptible natures. The effect on me was twofold: it made me more realistic, roughly shaking me out of unwarranted optimism based on the dream of a pain-less, easy existence, and at the same time it steeled my determina-tion to find a happiness that would endure, and had not to be purchased at the cost of the happiness of others. Often in the solitude of a secluded place or alone in my room I debated within myself on the merits and demerits of the different courses open to me. Only a few months before, my ambition had been to prepare myself for a successful career in order to enjoy a life of plenty and comfort, surrounded by all the luxuries available to the affluent class of our society. Now I wanted to lead a life of peace, immune from wordly fervour and free of contentious strife. Why set my heart on things, I told myself, which I must ultimately relinquish, often most reluctantly at the point of the sword wielded by death, with great pain and torture of the mind? Why should I not live in contentment with just enough to fulfil reasonably the few needs imposed by nature, devoting the time I could save thereby to the acquirement of assets of a permanent nature, which would be mine for ever, a lasting ornament to the unchanging eternal self in me instead of serving merely to glorify the flesh?

The more I thought about the matter, the more strongly I was drawn towards a simple, unostentatious life, free from thirst for worldly greatness, which I had pictured for myself. The only obstacle to the otherwise easy achievement of my purpose which I felt was rather hard to overcome lay in winning the consent of my mother, whose hopes, already blasted once by the sudden resolve of my father to relinquish the world, were now centred in me. She wished to see me a man of position and substance, risen high above want and able to lift her economically ruined family out of the poverty and drudgery into which it had fallen by the renunciation of my father, who had given away freely whatever my thrifty mother could save from their income, leaving no reserve to fall back upon in time of need. I knew that the least knowledge of my plans would cause her pain, and this I wanted to avoid at any cost. At the same time the urge to devote myself to the search for reality was too strong to be suppressed. I was on the horns of a dilemma, torn between my filial duty and my own natural desire to retrieve the decayed fortune of the family on the one hand, and my distaste for the world on the other.

But the thought of giving up my home and family never oc-

curred to me. I should have surrendered everything, not excepting even the path I had selected for myself, rather than be parted
from my parents or deviate in any way from the duty I owed to
them. Apart from this consideration, my whole being revolted at
the idea of becoming a homeless ascetic, depending on the labour
of others for my sustenance. If God is the embodiment of all that
is good, noble, and pure, I argued within myself, how can He
decree that those who have a burning desire to find Him, surrendering themselves to His will, should leave their families, to whom
they owe various obligations by virtue of the ties He has Himself
forged in the human heart, and should wander from place to
place depending on the charity and beneficence of those who
honour those ties? The mere thought of such an existence was
repugnant to me. I could never reconcile myself to a life which,
in any way, directly or indirectly, cast a reflection on my manhood, on my ability to make use of my limbs and my talents to
maintain myself and those dependent on me, reducing me practically to the deplorable state of a paralytic, forced to make his
basic needs the concern of other people.

I was determined to live a family life, simple and clean, devoid
of luxury, free from the fever of social rivalry and display, permitting me to fulfil my obligations and to live peacefully on the
fruit of my labour, restraining my desires and reducing my needs,
in order to have ample time and the essentially required serenity
of mind to pursue calmly the path I had chosen for myself. At that
young age it was not my intellect but something deeper and more
far-seeing, which, building on the reverse suffered by me and
triumphing at the end over the conflict raging in me, chalked out
the course of life I was to follow ever after. I was ignorant at the
time of the awful maelstrom of superphysical forces into which I
was to plunge blindly many years later to fish out from its fearsome depths an answer to the riddle which has confronted mankind for many thousands of years, perhaps waiting for an opportunity, dependent on a rare combination of circumstances to
come in harmony with modern scientific trend of human thought,
in order to bridge the gulf existing between ingenuous faith on
one side and critical reason on the other. I can assign no other

reason for the apparent anachronism I displayed at an unripe age, when I was not shrewd enough to weigh correctly all the implications of the step I proposed to take in adopting an abstemious mode of existence, to strive for self-realization while leading a family life, instead of tearing asunder the bonds of love, as is done by hundreds of frustrated youths in my country every year in emulation of highly honoured precedent and in consonance with scriptural and traditional authority.

We lived in Lahore in those days, occupying the top part of a small three-storied house in a narrow lane on the fringe of the city. The area was terribly congested, but fortunately the surrounding buildings were lower than ours, allowing us enough sun and air and a fine unobstructed view of the distant fields. I selected a corner in one of the two small rooms at our disposal for my practice and went to it every day with the first glimmer of dawn, for meditation. Beginning with a small duration, I extended the period gradually until in the course of a few years I was able to sit in the same posture, erect and steady, with my mind well under control and bent firmly on the object contemplated for hours without any sign of fatigue or restlessness. With hard determination I tried to follow all the rules of conduct prescribed for the students of Yoga. It was not an easy task for a college youth of my age, without the personal guidance of a revered teacher, to live up to the standard of sobriety, rectitude, and self-restraint necessary for success in Yoga, amidst the gaiety and glamour of a modern city in the constant company of happy-go-lucky, boisterous fellow-students and friends. But I persisted, adhering tenaciously to my decision, each failure spurring me on to a more powerful effort, resolved to tame the unruly mind instead of allowing it to dominate me. How far I succeeded, considering my natural disposition and circumstances, I cannot say, but save for the vigorous restraint I exercised upon myself for many years, curbing the impetuosity and exuberance of riotous youth with an iron hand, I think I should never have survived the ordeal which awaited me in my thirty-fifth year.

My mother understood from my suddenly altered demeanour and subdued manner that a far-reaching change had taken place in me. I never felt the need of explaining my point of view to prepare her for the resolution I had taken. Reluctant to cause her the least pain, I kept my counsel to myself, avoiding any mention of my choice when we discussed our future plans, considering it premature, when I had not even completed my college term, to anticipate a contingency due to arise only at the time of selection of a career. But circumstances so transpired that I was spared the unpleasant task of making my determination known to my mother. I stood second in a competitive test held for the selection of candidates for a superior Government service, but due to a change in the procedure I was finally not accepted. Similarly the disapproval of my brother-in-law had the effect of annulling a proposal for my joining the medical profession.

Meanwhile a sudden breakdown in my health due to heat created such an anxiety in the heart of my mother that she insisted on my immediate departure to Kashmir, attaching no importance to my studies when a question of my health was involved. Receiving at this juncture an offer of appointment to a low-salaried clerical post in the Public Works Department of the State, I accepted it readily with her consent and left for the beautiful valley, with no regrets, to take part for the first time in the mechanical drudgery of a small office. Within a year my parents followed me to Srinagar and soon after my mother busied herself in finding a matrimonial alliance for me. Next summer, in the twenty-third year of my life, I was joined in wedlock in the traditional manner to my wife, seven years my junior in age, belonging to a Pandit family of Baramulla.

I startled her on our very first meeting by leaving the nuptial chamber at three o'clock in the morning for a bath under the copiously flowing water tap in the nearby riverside temple, returning after an hour to sit in meditation without a word until it was time to leave for work. She admirably adjusted herself to what must have seemed to her unsophisticated mind an eccentric streak in her husband, ready with a warm kangri* when I re-

---

* A kangri is a small earthenware bowl encased in wicker in which burning charcoal is kept for heating the body. It is usually kept next to the skin under the long robe used by Kashmiris.

turned from the temple numb with winter cold. About a year after I was transferred to Jammu to serve my term in that Province. She followed me after a few months with my parents, to both of whom she endeared herself by her sense of duty and unremitting attention to their comfort. Years passed, not without lapses on my part and interruptions due to circumstances beyond my control; but I never lost sight of the goal I had set before myself and never swerved from the path I had chosen, decreed in this manner to prepare myself to some extent, without having the least knowledge of the crisis I had to face in the great trial ahead.

At the time of the extraordinary episode in 1937, I was serving as a clerk under the Director of Education in our State. Prior to that I had been working in the same capacity in the office of the Chief Engineer, from which I had been transferred for having the temerity to question an unjust directive from the Minister-in-charge, who often took morbid pleasure in bullying subordinates. I had no liking for the work in either office, although from the point of view of my other colleagues I held enviable positions. I was required to maintain the classified lists and service records of senior-grade employees, to formulate proposals for their promotion and transfer, to dispose of their petitions and appeals, and to attend to their requests. In this way I had to deal with a large section of the personnel in both departments, many of whom, detecting chances of undeserved favours at the cost of unsuspecting fellow employees, frequented the offices regularly, hunting for easy gains, obliging colleagues to do likewise to save themselves from a possible loss.

By the very nature of my duties it was utterly impossible for me to escape comment and criticism of my acts, which influenced the life and career of someone or other. But some of these acts had also the reverse effect of confronting me with my own conscience on behalf of a poor and supportless, but deserving candidate. Because of a desire to deal equal justice in all cases, I was frequently brought in conflict with hidden influences surreptitiously at work behind the apparently spotless façade of Government offices, which every now and then created insoluble problems and odious situations for me. I had a strange partiality for the underdog, and this trait in my character worked equally against my own interests, and on at least two occasions impelled me to refuse chances of promotion, out of turn, in preference to senior colleagues.

Temperamentally I was not suited for a profession of this kind, but possessing neither the qualifications for another, nor means nor inclination to equip myself for a better one, I continued to move in the rut in which I had placed myself on the first day. Although I worked hard and to the best of my ability, I was more interested in the study and practice of Yoga than in my official career. The latter I treated merely as a means to earn a livelihood, just sufficient to meet our simplest needs. Beyond that it had no value or significance for me. I had a positive dislike for being drawn into controversies with crowds of disputing contestants on every side as happened almost every day, creating at times disquieting ripples in my otherwise placid mental pool, which I strove to keep unruffled and calm, indispensable to my Yoga practices.

Only a few years after my joining the Public Works Department, clouds of intrigue began to gather round the then Chief Engineer, whose attempts to put a curb on the shady acts of corrupt officers landed him in difficulties, and a plot was woven round him by his subordinates in collusion with officials of the Ministry, all of whom had suffered deprivation of many wonted facilities at his hands. The conspiracy ended in his compulsory retirement from service much before his time amid expressions of amazement at such an act of injustice from those who were in the know of the affair. With his retirement I was left defenceless against a host of powerful and vindictive enemies who poisoned the Minister against me and resorted to devious ways to cause me harassment and harm. The last straw was furnished by my own criticism under the new Chief Engineer of a defective order received from the Ministry which, to my great relief, culminated in my transfer from a place whose atmosphere had become much too vitiated for my liking.

In the Education Directorate the conditions were more reassuring for me. There were no chances of corruption on the scale that had existed in the Public Works Department. Conse-quently the distracting play of plot and counter-plot, which had been a regular feature of the former office, was also absent. Here my path ran more or less smoothly until 1947. It was in no small measure due to the sense of security and the congenial atmo-sphere in the new office that I was able to retain my link with it in spite of the ordeals I had to face and the suspense I had to bear for a long period, while attending to the day-to-day work at my table.

Chapter Two

I WAS born in 1903 in the small village of Gairoo, about 20 miles from Srinagar, the capital of Kashmir. It was the parental home of my mother, and she went to stay there at the time of my birth to have the care and attention of her elder sister and brothers during her confinement. My father had constructed a small, two-storeyed hut of his own in their big compound. It was a humble structure, built of sun-dried bricks with a thatched roof and served as our residence for a long time; for the years of my childhood and afterwards at intervals, whenever tired of the city we yearned for a breath of country air.

My first faint recollections of childhood circle round a medium sized house in a quiet sector of the city of Srinagar. I can still recall a scene in which I was held tight in the arms of my oldest maternal uncle, who comforted me with soft, endearing words after a fit of prolonged weeping caused by the anger of my mother for having stayed out too long playing with the children. As I was the only son she never dressed me in fine clothes, to guard against the evil eye, nor allowed me long out of her sight for fear of mishaps. Another indelible childhood memory is of a moonlit night with my mother and one of my maternal uncles, sleeping on an open-from-the-sides but roofed top of a small wooden cabin, used as a granary, a common structure in rural habitations in Kashmir. We had travelled all day on horseback on the way to the distant abode of a reputed hermit, but failing to reach our destination at nightfall had sought shelter in the house of a farmer, who accommodated us thus for the night. I cannot recall the appearance of the saint, except that his long, matted hair fell on his shoulders as he sat cross-legged against one of the walls of his small room directly facing the door. I remember him taking me in his lap and stroking my hair, which my mother had allowed to grow long in conformity with a solemn vow she had taken not to apply scissors or razor to it except at the time of the sacred thread ceremony.

Years later, when I had grown intelligent enough to understand her, my mother revealed to me the purpose of her visit to the saint. She said that years before he had appeared to her in a dream at a most anxious time. She had passed the preceding day in an extremely perturbed frame of mind caused by my inability to swallow anything owing to a swollen and badly inflamed throat. In the dream the holy personage, of whose miraculous deeds she had heard astounding accounts from innumerable eyewitnesses, opened my mouth gently with his hand and touched its interior down to the throat softly with his finger; then making a sign to her to feed me vanished from sight. Awakening with a start, my mother pressed me close to her and to her immense relief felt me sucking and swallowing the milk without difficulty. Overjoyed at the sudden cure, which she attributed to the miraculous power of the saint, she then and there made a vow that she would go on a pilgrimage to his place of residence to thank him personally for the favour. Owing to household worries and other engagements she could not make the pilgrimage for some years and undertook it at a time when I was sufficiently grown up to retain a faint impression of the journey and the visit. The most surprising part of the story is that, as my mother affirmed afterwards repeatedly, the hermit, at the very moment of our approach after entering the room, casually inquired whether I had been able to suck and swallow my milk after his visit to her in the dream. Wonderstruck, my mother had fallen prostrate at his feet, humbly invoking his blessings upon me.

I cannot vouch for the miraculous part of the episode. All I can say is that my mother was veracious and critically observant in other things. I have related the episode merely as a faintly remembered incident of early childhood. Since then I have come across innumerable accounts of similar and even more incredible feats, narrated by trustworthy, highly intelligent eyewitnesses; but on closer investigation the bulk of the material was found to be too weakly supported to stand the force of rigid scientific inquiry. For a long time I lent no credence to such stories, and I can emphatically assert even today that a real Yogi in touch with the other world, capable of producing genuine psychical phenomena at will, is one of the rarest beings on earth.

Another remarkable event of my childhood at the age of eight which I remember more vividly occurred one day as I walked along a road in Srinagar in early spring on my way to the house of our religious preceptor. The sky was overcast and the road muddy, which made walking difficult. All at once, with the speed of lightning, a sudden question, never thought of before, shot across my mind. I stood stockstill in the middle of the road confronted within to the depths of my being with the insistent inquiry, 'What am I?', coupled with the pressing interrogation from every object without, 'What does all this mean?' My whole being as well as the world around appeared to have assumed the aspect of an everlasting inquiry, an insistent, unanswerable interrogation, which struck me dumb and helpless, groping for a reply with all my strength until my head swam and the surrounding objects began to whirl and dance round me. I felt giddy and confused, hardly able to restrain myself from falling on the slimy road in a faint. Steadying myself, I proceeded on my way, my childish mind in a ferment over the incident of which, at that age, I could not in the least understand the significance. A few days later I had a remarkable dream in which I was given a glimpse of another existence, not as a child or as an adult but with a dream personality utterly unlike my usual one. I saw a heavenly spot, peopled by god-like, celestial beings, and myself bodiless, something quite different—diffused, ethereal—a stranger belonging to a different order and yet distinctly resembling and intimately close to me, my own self transfigured, in a gloriously bright and peaceful environment, the very opposite of the shabby, noisy surroundings in which I lived. Because of its unique and extraordinarily vivid nature the dream was so indelibly imprinted upon my memory that I can recall it distinctly even today. The recollection of the scene in later years was invariably accompanied by a feeling of wonder at and a deep yearning for the exotic, inexpressible happiness enjoyed for a brief interval. The dream was probably the answer to the overwhelming, unavoidable question that had arisen from my depths a few days before, the first irresistible call from the invisible other world which, as I came to know later, awaits our attention close at hand, always intimately near, yet, for those with their backs to it, farther away than the farthest star in the firmament.

In the year 1914 we journeyed to Lahore where my father was required to present himself personally at the Treasury to receive his pension. From that day to the time of my appointment in 1923 we lived there summer and winter. It was there that I received my high school and two years of college education, even at that young age oppressed by unfavourable and trying circumstances. We lived poorly and I had not the advantage of a private coach or guide; it was with great difficulty that my mother could find enough money to purchase even my essentially needed books and clothes. Denied the possibility of purchasing extra books, my study was confined to school classics, but I soon had the chance to read a slightly abridged translation in Urdu of the Arabian Nights at the age of about twelve, which I came upon accidentally in the house of my aunt. The book for the first time created in me a burning thirst for fairy tales, stories of adventure and travel, and other romantic literature which continued undiminished for several years. At the age of fourteen, starting with easy stories, I turned from Urdu to English, devouring hungrily every story book and romance that came into my hands. From novels and other light material I gradually passed on to popular elementary books on science and philosophy available in our small school library. I read avidly, my developing mind eager for satisfactory replies to the questions which cropped up as the result of my own survey of the narrow world in which I lived, and the

stray glimpses of the broader one of which I came to know more
and more from the graphic accounts contained in the books.

I was brought up in a strictly religious atmosphere by my
mother, whose faith rested unshakably on each of the innumerable gods and goddesses in her crowded pantheon. She used to go
to the temple long before the first faint glimmer of dawn streaked
the horizon, returning at daybreak to attend to the needs of the
household, in particular to keep our frugal morning meal ready
for me. In early childhood I followed implicitly the direction of
her simple faith, sometimes to the extent of forgoing the sweet
last hours of sleep towards dawn in order to go with her to the
temple. With rapt attention I listened to the superhuman exploits
of Krishna, which my maternal uncle read aloud every evening
until almost midnight from his favourite translation of Bhagavad
Purana, a famous book of Hindu mythology, containing the story
of the incarnations of the god Vishnu in human form. According
to popular belief, Krishna imparted the lofty teaching of Bhagavad Gita to the warrior, Arjuna, on the battlefield before the
commencement of action in the epic war, Mahabharata. Wondering at the prodigious, supernatural feats of valour and strength recounted in the narrative with a wealth of detail, which carried my
childish imagination into fantastic realms, I unquestioningly
accepted every impossible and unbelievable incident with which
the story abounds as truth, filled with a desire to grow into a
superman of identical powers myself.

The information I now accumulated from my high school texts
and more extensively from the study of other literature acted as a
cathartic and had the effect of purging my mind gradually of
irrational and fantastic notions I had gathered in childhood, replacing them with a rational and realistic picture of the world.
Occasionally, noticing an exact identity of thought between what
I felt but could not articulate and the clearly expressed idea of a
writer, I was so carried away by emotion that, dropping the book,
I would stand up and pace the room for a while to compose myself before continuing to read. In this way my mind was moulded
by degrees as much by my own inborn ideas about the nature of
things, developed by the exercise of reason in the healthy atmo-

sphere of literature, as by the influence of the great thinkers whose ideas I imbibed from their works. By the time I had completed my first year at college, the impact of the books, especially elementary treatises on astronomy and natural science to which I had access in the college library, as well as my ideas, formed or confirmed by continued study, had become powerful enough to start me on a path contrary to the one I had followed in childhood, and it did not take me long to emerge a full-fledged agnostic, full of doubts and questions about the extravagant notions and irrational beliefs of my own religion, to which I had lent complete credence only a few years before.

Dislodged from the safe harbour which my mother's simple faith had provided for me, my still unanchored mind was tossed here and there, clinging to one idea for a time and then replacing it with another, found to be equally untenable after a period. I became restless and reckless, too, unable to assuage the fire of uncertainty and doubt lit by my own desultory studies. Without reading any standard book on religion or any spiritual literature to counterbalance the effect of the admittedly materialistic tendency of the scientific works I had gone through, I took up cudgels on behalf of the latter, wielding my weapons with such dexterity that in the college debates as well as in private discussion few adherents of the former could defend their points of view. Although until that time I had not studied religion or tried any method of direct spiritual experience, or acquired systematic knowledge of any science or philosophy beyond that provided by a few elementary volumes, the questions and problems which agitated my mind at that young age never found a satisfactory solution in any book on science, philosophy or religion. More intent on demolition than construction, I read ravenously until in my second year I began to neglect my prescribed studies to the extent of giving preference to the library over the classroom. I was brought to an abrupt halt by my failure in the college examination towards the end of 1920. The shock demolished with one blow the seemingly invincible fortification of intellectual scepticism my immature judgment had created around myself.

Instead of yielding or collapsing, I turned determinedly towards a path, actually aligned for me by nature, as it is at the moment for thousands of other men and women all over the world. I could not have visualized at that time what transpired afterwards, just as by no exercise of fancy can even an intelligent man form the least conception of what awaits one on the superconscious plane. Deceived and disillusioned, I turned finally to the practice of Yoga, not as an expedient to save myself from the consequences of my own dereliction, but as a practicable method available to thirsty minds to verify individually the undemonstrable central truths of religion. When nothing tangible happened for nearly seventeen years, from the age of seventeen to thirty-four, I began to despair, at times led to doubt the method adopted and at others to suspect the whole science.

Even after the change from the chaotic to the more or less spiritual trend of mind, the critical element in my nature never left me completely. I was not one to be satisfied with shadowy appearances and cloudy manifestations, with cryptic symbols and mystic signs. Flashes of light before the eyes followed by darkness, humming in the ears due to pressure on the tympanic membrane, peculiar sensations in the body caused by fatigued nerves, semi-hypnotic conditions resulting from protracted concentration, appearances and phantoms due to tricky imagination in a state of tense expectancy, and other similar phenomena had absolutely no effect on me. By continued practice I had no doubt acquired a high degree of proficiency in the art of keeping the mind in a state of fixity for a long time and in maintaining a condition of absorption for long periods without discomfort; but that in itself was not proof of supernormal development or evidence of success in the enterprise I had undertaken.

Study of the scriptures and also of the literature of the other religions did not suffice to quiet the restless element in my nature or to appease the hungry spirit of critical inquiry. Stray passages from the teachings of prophets and the expressions of sages found an echo in the depths of my being without carrying conviction to my uncompromising intellect. The very fact that the existing world religions, descended from prophets or inspired sages, while tracing their origin to revelation from the Creator, differ radically in their cosmogony, mode of worship, observances, ritual, and even in some basic tenets was enough to raise serious doubts in my mind about the authenticity of the claim that the revealed material was a direct communication from God, the infallible source of all wisdom, and not merely the creation of more advanced brains in occasional touch with a higher but sometimes still fallible plane of consciousness. The total demolition by science in its very infancy of some of the citadels of antiquated religions, especially on the cosmogonical side, was sufficient in my view to expose the vulnerability of its other fronts as well to the attacks of its now robust opponent at any time. But science itself, though extremely useful in other ways and serviceable as a battering ram to smash religion, if not out of existence at least out of shape, was not in my view fit to rule the domain where faith holds sway. It had no satisfactory explanation to offer for my individual existence or for the infinitely complex creation around me. Confronted by a mystery, which grows deeper with the advance of knowledge, it was not yet in a position to be a source of illumination to one on issues admittedly beyond its present sphere of inquiry.

I thirsted for rationality in religion, for the worship of truth, whatever and wherever that might be. There was no spectacle more painful for me than the sight of a conscientious and intelligent man defending an absurdity which even a child could see through, simply because it formed an article of his faith to which he must hold at any cost, even if that cost included the sacrifice of reason and truth. On the other side, the irrationality of those who attempted to squeeze the universe within the narrow compass of reason was no less deplorable. They were ignorant about the nature of their own consciousness. The unknown entity that inhabits human bodies is still enveloped in mystery, and the rational faculty, one of its inseparable possessions, is no less an enigma than the owner itself. As such, the attempt to explain the cosmos purely in terms of human experience, as interpreted by reason, is as irrational an endeavour to solve the riddle of the universe as it would be to judge the appearance of an object with the aid of a mirror which, for all we know, might be blurring, multiplying, or distorting the image in a manner that misrepresents the original.

The conflicts and controversies going on between faith and faith on the one side and between faith and philosophy on the other made me wonder whether it would ever be possible to have a religion that possessed an appeal for all mankind, that would be as acceptable to the philosopher as to the peasant, and as welcome to the rationalist as to the priest. But could this question be answered in a way other than the negative so long as the pivotal truths of such a world religion are not empirically demonstrated, like other universally accepted laws and phenomena of nature? Obviously not. In order to persuade reason to rise above itself, it is essential to arrange its ascent in a manner not repugnant to it by violating any of its own jealously guarded principles. But as none of the existing religions are prepared to allow this kind of approach, even in the strictly temporal realm, much less the spiritual, there appears no possibility of a compromise between the two and consequently no likelihood of the efflorescence of a universal faith.

In spite of the phenomenal increase in human knowledge during the last two centuries in all other fields, the basic facts of religion are still subjects of dispute and controversy. It could not be otherwise, considering the fact that in this particular case the spirit of open inquiry had generally been curbed in the past. Viewed in the context of a rigidly lawbound universe, as revealed by science, the miracles and supernatural manifestations associated with faiths appeared to me to be but isolated and as yet not correctly interpreted phenomena of a cosmic law, still shrouded in mystery, which had to be understood first to explain satisfactorily the apparent obscurities and anomalies of religions and religious experience.

Even the accounts of the carefully observed and to all appearances supernatural manifestations and extraordinary phenomena exhibited by mediums and psychics all over Europe, although most startling and absorbing, often left me unconvinced, unable to reconcile the otherwise ordered harmony of nature with the erratic displays sometimes noticed at mediumistic seances. I could not bring myself to believe that law-abiding nature, at the peak of her glory in the beauty and perfection of the marvellous human organism, could be so inconsistent in the case of a few specially constituted men and women, themselves as ignorant about the nature of the power manifesting itself through them as the spectators of their extraordinary feats, as to take a sudden plunge from perfect order in the material universe to freakish sport in the spiritual realm.

That some, at least, of the manifestations were genuine there could be no doubt. But how were they to be accounted for? It was only after many years that I was able to locate the source of the bewildering phenomena and trace it to a marvellous super-intelligent power in man, which is both illuminating and mystifying—illuminating in the revealing flashes of genius and mystifying in the baffling masquerades of spirits and demons in mediums and the possessed; which is both blissful and awful—blissful in the en-rapturing visions of ecstatics and awful in the appalling shadows of insanity.

My interest in the study and practice of Yoga was not the outcome of any deep desire to possess psychic gifts. The tricks and deception sometimes practised by men of this class, the exhortations against the exhibition and abuse of spiritual powers contained in the scriptures, and above all the utter futility of an effort useless as a means to secure lasting benefits either for one's own self or for other men were all, to my mind, sufficient reasons to rise above the temptation for acquiring the powers to flout the laws of Matter without possessing at the same time the necessary strength of will to obey the laws of the spirit. The emphasis laid in some of the books on Yoga, both of the East and the West, on the development of psychic powers merely for the sake of gaining success in worldly enterprise invariably made me wonder at the incongruity in human nature, which, even in the case of a system designed to develop the spiritual side of man, focusses the attention more on the acquisition of visible, wonder-exciting properties of the body or mind than on the invisible but tranquil possessions of the soul.

The target I had in mind was far higher and nobler than what in the most attractive form I could expect, from the acquirement of the much coveted supernormal gifts. I longed to attain the condition of consciousness, said to be the ultimate goal of Yoga, which carries the embodied spirit to regions of unspeakable glory and bliss, beyond the sphere of opposites, free from the desire for life and fear of death. This extraordinary state of consciousness, internally aware of its own surpassing nature, was the supreme prize for which the true aspirants of Yoga had to strive. The possession of supernormal powers of the usual kind, whether of the body or mind, which kept a man still floundering in the stormy sea of existence without carrying him any nearer to the solution of the great mystery, seemed to me to be of no greater consequence than the possession of other earthly treasures, all bound to vanish with life. The achievements of science had brought astounding possibilities within the reach of man, possibilities no less amazing than what is related of even the most wonderful performances of the supernatural type with but one supreme exception—the miracle of transcendental experience and revelation, periodically vouchsafed to specially constituted individuals, which by accelerating ethical progress necessary for a peaceful and productive social order, has not only contributed the largest share in raising mankind to her present materially high pedestal but also made the miracles of science possible and profitable. It was towards this surpassing state of pure cognition, free from the limitations of time and space, about which the ancient ages of India had sung in rapturous terms, treating it as the highest objective of human life and endeavour, that I desired with all my heart to soar.

Commentary to Chapters One and Two

(*On a hot day in the early summer of 1952, I remember going to the house of Gopi Krishna in Srinagar with my wife and two friends, Gerald Hanley and F. J. Hopman who has done so much to see that this book finally reached the public. We were all living in Kashmir and had come upon the work of Gopi Krishna at a local fair where a pamphlet of his poetry with a brief account of his experiences was distributed by one of his followers. I went on the visit out of curiosity, sceptically, critically, expecting a mountebank, ready to argue, disprove, and later perhaps laugh.*

I recall the heat, the flies, and my shirt stuck with sweat to the back of an old leather arm-chair. He sat on a cot, reposed, round-bodied, in white, smiling. The look of his skin seemed different from others I had met during the past year in Kashmir; then I thought he looked healthy, now I might say he glowed. I remember the simplicity in which our conversation took place. Above all, I remember the eyes of the man: friendly, luminous, huge, softly focussed. They attracted and held my attention and somehow convinced me that what was happening in this room and with this man was genuine. I visited him several times for talks before we left on a pony-trek to Shishnag and then the return to Europe. Because one or two unusual events occurred to me in the high mountains after meeting with Gopi Krishna, I tend to regard him as an initiator and a signal person in my life. Our meeting went deeper than I then realized. His eyes first led me to trust my own sight, my own convictions, beyond my trained sceptical Western mind. This was itself an initiation into actual psychological work which I only later took up.

So it is with reverence to him and to the culture from which he has risen that I add these short comments as an act of gratitude. It is my intention neither to explain nor defend what Gopi Krishna has written, but only to relate where I am able some of his experiences to Western depth psychology, especially to the process of individuation as described in the Analytical Psychology of C. G. Jung.)

Our text opens with a classic example of the meditative technique. Whether for Eastern or Western psychology, the prerequisite of any human accomplishment is *attention*. The ability to concentrate consciousness is what we call in Western psychology a sign of ego-strength. Disturbances of attention can be measured by the association experiment which Jung developed to show how the ability of the ego to focus upon a relatively simple task (the association of words) can be impaired by unconscious complexes.

The assiduous, prolonged discipline of attention to a single image (the full-blooming, light-radiating lotus) is as difficult as any concentration upon a learning task in an extraverted manner. Whether introverted or extraverted, whether Eastern or Western, we may note at the beginning the significance of the ego, that which focusses, concentrates, attends.

The many-petalled lotus at the crown of the head is a traditional symbol of the Kundalini yoga. In the language of analytical psychology, the attention of the ego is fixed upon a self-image in mandala form. The ego has chosen its image according to the spiritual discipline, just as in Christian meditation there is the Sacred Heart, the Cross, the images of Christ, Mary, the Saints, etc. Rather than discuss the objects of concentration (comparative symbolism), let us note briefly in passing the difference of technique between *active imagination* and *yoga discipline*. In spiritual disciplines, as a rule, the attention is focussed upon already given or known images (in Zen Buddhism, there may be no images but a koan, a task, or a thing). In each case the focus of attention is prescribed, and one knows when one is wavering or 'off'. In active imagination as described by C. G. Jung, attention is given to whatever images or emotions, or body parts, etc., that 'pop into the mind'. Rather than suppressing the distractions, they are followed attentively. The method is half-way between the free-association of the Freudians, where one leaps freely from one image, word, thought to the next with no idea of the goal, and the traditional spiritual discipline of rigid fixity upon a given image. Active imagination develops a more personal psychological fantasy. (The lotus is after all a highly impersonal image which any adept anywhere could focus upon unrelated to his own personal psychological make-up. It is not 'his' lotus, but 'the' lotus.) Active imagination is concerned with the ego's relation with and personal reactions to the mental images. The emotional involvement with these images and their spontaneous reactions back are as important as the nature of the images themselves. If the quality of a free-association can be judged by its uninhibitedness (lack of suppression) and the quality of a disciplined meditation can be judged by its unwavering fixity and undistractedness, the quality of active imagination can be judged by its emotional intensity, which intensity is given by the opposition between the ego position of the conscious mind and the various figures, images, and intentions of the unconscious psyche. Hence, it is called *active* imagination in that the ego not only attends, not only suppresses what does not belong (as in a spiritual exercise), but actively takes part in the drama or dialogue which unfolds by asking questions, experiencing emotions, pressing towards solutions.

Furthermore, one aim of active imagination is often rather extraverted. I mean by this that one seeks through the meditation the counsel of inner figures concerning practical personal problems, whereas spiritual disciplines attempt to surmount (crown of the head) a world which gives rise to such personal problems and in which no permanent solutions can truly exist. In active imagination the counsel is sought not in terms of should I do this or that action, but rather what attitude is correct, what complex is constellated. Spiritual discipline on the other hand aims towards the divine and the transcendence of attitudes and complexes.

He desires 'the surpassing state of pure cognition' for which meditation is the way. This goal contrasts sharply with those of analysis. Because the goals differ, the methods for achieving these goals follow different tracks. Thus the methods of free-association and active imagination are not paths to liberation or illumination in the traditional sense. Sometimes these differences are forgotten in depth psychology so that we expect more from its methods than described in its goals. Then free-association has behind it a hope of gaining one supreme curative revelation into the root trauma—the 'pure cognition' to set one free of neurosis. But methods of psychology do not lead to goals of yoga. After all, active imagination is not a method of pure cognition; to seek through it the transcendence of space and time with a prophetic insight into tomorrow is mistaken. The value and genuineness of an active imagination is proved neither by synchronistic events nor by uncanny break-throughs. Active imagination is a technique of self-regulation and circulation. It serves the aim of psychological connection with the archetypal dominants.

The traditional goal of the sages is also to be differentiated from patho-psychological and para-psychological phenomena. Our author makes this quite clear. He would not be deflected by phantoms, by tricky light experiences and sounds. Nor would he be content with pre-cognitive visions and telepathic insights, nor even by achieving 'wonder-exciting properties of the body or mind'. He aimed for the source of both natural and such super-natural events, to know with the knowledge that knows him and through which he knows (pure cognition), rather than being a freakish medium of that knowledge with an occult gift and helter-skelter access to it. To serve that knowledge he would have to know it, not be merely a victim of it. Therefore, there is such stress in his account on the theoretical structure of his experience. The knowledge of what is going on is as important as the events themselves. From this point of view it is not enough to call the source of these phenomena the unconscious, which means only that we are unconscious of their true background. Psychological accounts for him do not really give an account since the word 'unconscious' admits defeat of the cognitive drive. As he is not willing to rest with secondary phenomena of the spirit (occult powers, special sensations, sporadic enlightenment, etc.), so too is he not willing to accept secondary accounts of their origins. From his viewpoint the insufficiencies of our Western explanations (in terms of patho- and para-psychology) go hand in hand with inferior kinds of experience. These experiences and explanations would depict a Kundalini stirred but stuck, risen but not accomplished. For his traditional point of view, there flows from the pure cognition of accomplished Kundalini both adequate experience and adequate explanation.

All of which should help us to remember the extreme importance of concepts and theory for the movement of psychological consciousness. The psyche needs a psychology that gives it room to move. It requires careful but intuitive thinking to support its adventures and give them sufficient frameworks. Psyche and psychology too closely reflect each other to have the radical development of the one without a corresponding theoretical radicalisation of the other. Where they fail to keep pace, we call those psychic events for which our theory is inadequate, 'alien', placing them in patho- or para-psychology. Furthermore, we call radical theories (like those of Kundalini yoga) 'mystical speculation' when the poverty of our psychic life fails to produce the empirical data on which the psychological theories have been erected.

Again and again we shall come to passages in the text which emphasize the enormous *physical cost* of the experience. It is important to realize, and we can be grateful to our author for never letting this fact slip, that transformation of personality is exhausting. Consciousness alone consumes hundreds of calories a day, and the intensity of introverted discipline requires as much energy as extensive extraverted mental activity. Outstanding in the work as we go through it is the importance of the body. In spite of the seventeen long years of discipline, the author suffered a severe disorientation of consciousness. We cannot put this down to a neurasthenic constitution or a neurotic hypochondriasis. It is as if the one thing he did not expect was the degree of physical cost, the actual organic events. In this our author is a modern man, for it is the problem of us modern men to connect the body again with the spirit, rather than identifying spirit with soul or mind, to the detriment of body. The emphasis upon the body in what follows is nothing else than a description of the meaning of incarnation of the spirit in a modern example.

From the personal, analytical point of view there are certain observations one could make concerning the *family* constellation of the author which may have had some bearing upon the archetypal eruption. From the beginning there was a spiritual ambition. His old father led the way in this direction and our author's desire to prove himself to his mother is a dominant theme. He was the only son, carrying the psychological burdens from both parents.

His own recollections of *childhood* bring out two facts which belong to his own 'personal myth'. The first is the experience of having almost died and having been saved by a wonder. The child-in-danger motif is part of the mythologem of the saviour-hero. It establishes chosenness; one has in childhood met the powers of darkness and been rescued from them by supernatural forces. The Gods single out at an early age those who are to carry consciousness further. The miracle of consciousness is frail at the beginning and can easily be snuffed out. Moses, Christ, Dionysius, Hercules are examples of the child-in-danger.

As a child he had the experience of questioning himself in that utter overwhelming way that we find in the Buddha (when he was considerably older). Or, in modern times, Jung's description of his early years in his autobiography, *Memories, Dreams, Reflections* iterates this motif of sudden devastating awareness. This same question lies at the root of all philosophy and it had the same shattering effect upon Descartes, but again at a later age.

Gopi Krishna's early dream can be reduced in banal terms to a wish-fulfillment. He found in his dream a world 'the very opposite of the shabby, noisy surroundings in which I lived'. Yet how little this sort of interpretation tells us! It is a compensatory wish-fulfilment surely, but it transcends the personal. It is archetypally compensatory, completing the world picture of earthly reality by an equally powerful reality of the unearthly. It is a wish-fulfilment not in the language of the world, but of a '*weltanschauung*'. As such it is a statement: 'Look! You are not what you think you are. You are not only what your surroundings make you. There is more to reality than what is given socially and externally. You have another personality altogether different from the one you take for granted as "you".' (I refer the reader again to the number one and number two personalities Jung writes of in his own life in *Memories, Dreams, Reflections.*)

It is therefore little wonder that with this archetypal background to his life (the father/mother constellation, being saved from early death, the childhood awareness of self, the dreamvision) that he could not read enough of symbolic, mythic material. *The Arabian Nights* and fairy tales connect personalities number one and number two. Fairy tales tell universal truths; they are archetypal accounts of how the personality meets and overcomes its own dangers. They speak in the language of symbols directly to the soul. The fairy tale is not a substitution for reality but is a necessary nourishment for the world of psychic reality.

Lastly, in regard to the *author's personal psychology*, we find two further rather typical facts. The failed examinations cut Gopi Krishna off from a substitute career in which his spiritual aims could have become an intellectual or academic ambition. This sort of failure is often to be found in biographies of unusual people. It is signal, preventing the personality from developing along collectively approved lines. After the examination failure, there was only one way to go: his own. Failure as such does not give logic to this decision; rather the failure is symbolized into a parting of the ways, a fateful annunciation, so that it became clear to him what his call really was. The call was then finally announced in the author's thirty-fifth year, that is, at the midpoint of life, after having discharged his extraverted duties (education, work, parents, marriage, children, society) and the introverted obligations of the ego (to establish a living contact with the unconscious, the development of a subjective point of view, a *weltanschauung*). Too often in the West we fail to realize that even in Eastern disciplines the spiritual life is not meant as an escape from the worldly life. There is a karma to be fulfilled on earth, within the dharma of necessity. In fact, it would seem that the development of awareness requires a very solid basis in reality: an embodied personality in the daily world and an ego that can submit to its own unconsciousness. We can be grateful to our author for showing us in careful detail the ordinary outer context and inner milieu in which these extraordinary events took place.

Chapter Three

THE sudden awakening of Kundalini in one whose nervous system has reached the ripe stage of development as a result of favourable heredity, correct mode of living, and proper mental application, is often liable to create a most bewildering effect on the mind. The reason for it, though extremely simple, may not be easily acceptable to the present-day intellect, which treats the human mind as a finally sealed product, dependent, according to some, exclusively on the activity of the brain cells, beginning and ending with the body; according to others, on the responsiveness of the bone-shielded grey and white matter to the extremely subtle all-pervading cosmic mind or Universal spirit; and according to still others, on the existence of an immortal individual soul in the body. Without entering into a discussion of the correctness of these hypotheses advanced to account for the existence of mind, it is sufficient for our purpose to say that according to the authorities on Yoga, the activity of the brain and the nervous system, irrespective of whether it proceeds from an eternal self-existing spiritual source or from an embodied soul, depends on the existence in the body of a subtle life element known as *prana*, which pervades each cell of every tissue and fluid in the organism, much in the same way that electricity pervades each atom of a battery.

This vital element has a biological counterpart as thought has a biological complement in the brain, in the shape of an extremely fine biochemical essence of a highly delicate and volatile nature, extracted by the nerves from the surrounding organic mass. After extraction, this vital essence resides in the brain and the nervous system, and is capable of generating a subtle radiation impossible to isolate by laboratory analysis. It circulates in the organism as motor impulse and sensation, conducting all the organic functions of the body, permeated and worked by the super-intelligent cosmic life energy, or *prana*, by which it is continuously affected, just as the sensitive chemical layer on a photographic plate is affected by light. The term *prana*, as used by authorities on Yoga, signifies both the cosmic life energy and its subtle biological conductor in the body, the two being inseparable. At the very moment the body dies, the rare organic essence immediately undergoes chemical changes, ceasing to serve as a channel for the former in the previous capacity. Normally, the work of extraction of *prana* to feed the brain is done by a limited group of nerves, operating in a circumscribed area of the organism, with the result that the consciousness of an individual displays no variation in its nature or extent during the span of his life, exhibiting a constancy which is in sharp contrast to the continuously changing appearance of his body. With the awakening of Kundalini, the arrangement suffers a radical alteration affecting the entire nervous system, as a result of which other and more extensive groups of nerves are stirred to activity, leading to the transmission of an enormously enhanced supply of a more concentrated form of *pranic* radiation into the brain drawn from a vastly increased area of the body. The far-reaching effects of this immensely augmented flow of a new form of vital current into the cephalic cavity through the spinal cord before the system becomes fully accustomed to it may be visualized by considering the effects of a sudden increase in the flow of blood to the brain such as faintness, complete insensibility, excitement, irritability, or in extreme cases, delirium, paralysis, death.

The awakening may be gradual or sudden, varying in intensity and effect according to the development, constitution, and temperament of different individuals; but in most cases it results in a

greater instability of the emotional nature and a greater liability
to aberrant mental conditions in the subject, mainly owing to
tainted heredity, faulty modes of conduct, or immoderation in
any shape or form. Leaving out the extreme cases, which end in
madness, this generalization applies to all the categories of men in
whom Kundalini is congenitally more or less active, comprising
mystics, mediums, men of genius, and those of an exceptionally
high intellectual or artistic development only a shade removed
from genius. In the case of those in whom the awakening occurs
all at once as the result of Yoga or other spiritual practices, the
sudden impact of powerful vital currents on the brain and other
organs is often attended with grave risk and strange mental conditions, varying from moment to moment, exhibiting in the
beginning the abnormal peculiarities of a medium, mystic,
genius, and madman all rolled into one.

I had absolutely no knowledge of the technicalities of the
science or the mode of operation of the great energy or of the
spheres of its activity, as vast and as varied as humanity itself. I did
not know that I had dug down to the very roots of my being and
that my whole life was at stake. Like the vast majority of men
interested in Yoga I had no idea that a system designed to develop
the latent possibilities and nobler qualities in man could be fraught
with such danger at times as to destroy the sanity or crush life out
of one by the sheer weight of entirely foreign and uncontrollable
conditions of the mind.

On the third day of the awakening I did not feel myself in a
mood for meditation and passed the time in bed, not a little uneasy about the abnormal state of my mind and the exhausted
condition of my body. The next day when I sat for meditation,
after a practically sleepless night, I found to my consternation that
I completely lacked the power to concentrate my attention on any
point for even a brief interval and that a thin stream of the radiant
essence, which had impinged on my brain with such vivifying
and elevating effect on the first two occasions, was now pouring
into it automatically with a sinister light that instead of uplifting
had a most depressing influence on me.

The days that followed had all the appearance of a prolonged nightmare. It seemed as if I had abruptly precipitated myself from the steady rock of normality into a madly racing whirlpool of abnormal existence. The keen desire to sit and meditate, which had always been present during the preceding days, disappeared suddenly and was replaced by a feeling of horror of the supernatural. I wanted to fly from even the thought of it. At the same time I felt a sudden distaste for work and conversation, with the inevitable result that being left with nothing to keep myself engaged, time hung heavily on me, adding to the already distraught condition of my mind. The nights were even more terrible. I could not bear to have a light in my room after I had retired to bed. The moment my head touched the pillow a large tongue of flame sped across the spine into the interior of my head. It appeared as if the stream of living light continuously rushing through the spinal cord into the cranium gathered greater speed and volume during the hours of darkness. Whenever I closed my eyes I found myself looking into a weird circle of light, in which luminous currents swirled and eddied, moving rapidly from side to side. The spectacle was fascinating but awful, invested with a supernatural awe which sometimes chilled the very marrow in my bones.

Only a few days before it had been my habit, when in bed at night, to invite sleep by pursuing a pleasant chain of thoughts which often led me, without revealing the exact moment when it happened, from the waking state into the fantastic realm of dreams. Now everything was altered. I tossed restlessly from side to side without being able for hours to bring my agitated mind to the degree of composure needed to bring sleep. After extinguishing the lights, instead of seeing myself in darkness wafted gradually to a delicious state of rest preparatory to sleep, I found myself staring fearfully into a vast internal glow, disquieting and threatening at times, always in rapid motion as if the particles of an ethereal luminous stuff crossed and recrossed each other, resembling the ceaseless movement of wildly leaping lustrous clouds of spray rising from a waterfall which, lighted by the sun, rushes down foaming into a seething pool.

Sometimes it seemed as if a jet of molten copper, mounting up through the spine, dashed against my crown and fell in a scintillating shower of vast dimensions all around me. I gazed at it fascinated, with fear gripping my heart. Occasionally it resembled a fireworks display of great magnitude. As far as I could look inwardly with my mental eye, I saw only a brilliant shower or a glowing pool of light. I seemed to shrink in size when compared to the gigantic halo that surrounded me, stretching out on every side in undulating waves of copper colour distinctly perceptible in the surrounding darkness, as if the optic centre in the brain was now in direct contact with an extremely subtle, luminous substance in perpetual motion, flooding the brain and nervous system, without the intervention of the intermediary channels of the retina and the optic nerve.

I seemed to have touched accidentally the lever of an unknown mechanism, hidden in the extremely intricate and yet unexplored nervous structure in the body, releasing a hitherto held up torrent which, impinging upon the auditory and optic regions, created the sensation of roaring sounds and weirdly moving lights, introducing an entirely new and unexpected feature in the normal working of the mind that gave to all my thoughts and actions the semblance of unreality and abnormality. For a few days I thought I was suffering from hallucinations, hoping that my condition would become normal again after some time. But instead of disappearing or even diminishing as the days went by, the abnormality became more and more pronounced, assuming gradually the state of an obsession, which grew in intensity as the luminous appearances became wilder and more fantastic and the noises louder and more uncanny. The dreadful thought began to take hold of my mind that I was irretrievably heading towards a disaster from which I was powerless to save myself.

To one uninitiated in the esoteric science of Kundalini, as I was at that time, all that transpired afterwards presented such an abnormal and unnatural appearance that I became extremely nervous about the outcome. I passed every minute of the time in a state of acute anxiety and tension, at a loss to know what had happened to me and why my system was functioning in such an entirely abnormal manner. I felt exhausted and spent. The day after the experience I suffered loss of appetite, and food tasted like ash in my mouth. My tongue was coated white, and there was a redness in the eyes never noticed before. My face wore a haggard and anxious expression, and there were acute disturbances in the digestive and excretory organs. I lost my regularity and found myself at the mercy of a newly released force about which I knew nothing, creating a tumultuous and agitated condition of the mind as the sweep of a tempest creates an agitation in the placid waters of a lake.

There was no remission in the current rising from the seat of Kundalini. I could feel it leaping across the nerves in my back and even across those lining the front part of my body from the loins upward. But most alarming was the way in which my mind acted and behaved after the incident. I felt as if I were looking at the world from a higher elevation than that from which I saw it before. It is very difficult to express my mental condition accurately. All I can say is that it seemed as if my cognitive faculty had undergone a transformation and that I had, as it were, mentally expanded. What was more startling and terrifying was the fact that the point of consciousness in me was not as invariable nor its condition as stable as it had been before. It expanded and contracted, regulated in a mysterious way by the radiant current that was flowing up from the lowest plexus. This widening and narrowing were accompanied by a host of terrors for me. At times I felt slightly elated with a transient morbid sense of well-being and achievement, forgetting for the time being the abnormal state I was in, but soon after was made acutely conscious of my critical condition and again oppressed by a tormenting cloud of fear. The few brief intervals of mental elation were followed by fits of depression much more prolonged and so acute that I had to muster all my strength and will-power to keep myself from succumbing completely to their influence. I sometimes gagged my mouth to keep from crying and fled from the solitude of my room to the crowded street to prevent myself from doing some desperate act.

For weeks I had no respite. Each morning heralded for me a new kind of terror, a fresh complication in the already disordered system, a deeper fit of melancholy or more irritable condition of the mind which I had to restrain to prevent it from completely overwhelming me by keeping myself alert, usually after a completely sleepless night; and after withstanding patiently the tortures of the day, I had to prepare myself for the even worse torment of the night. A man cheerfully overcomes insurmountable difficulties and bravely faces overwhelming odds when he is confident of his mental and physical condition. I completely lost confidence in my own mind and body and lived like a haunted, terror-stricken stranger in my own flesh, constantly reminded of my precarious state. My consciousness was in such a state of unceasing flux that I was never certain how it would behave within the next few minutes. It rose and fell like a wave, raising me one moment out of the clutches of fear to dash me again the next into the depths of despair. It seemed as if the stream of vitality rising into my brain through the backbone connected mysteriously with the region near the base of the spine was playing strange tricks with my imagination. Also I was unable to stop it or to resist its effect on my thoughts. Was I losing my mind? Were these the first indications of mental disorder? This thought constantly drove me to desperation. It was not so much the extremely weird nature of my mental condition as the fear of incipient madness or some grave disorder of the nervous system which filled me with growing dismay.

I lost all feeling of love for my wife and children. I had loved them fondly from the depths of my being. The fountain of love in me seemed to have dried up completely. It appeared as if a scorching blast had raced through every pore in my body, wiping out every trace of affection. I looked at my children again and again, trying to evoke the deep feeling with which I had regarded them previously, but in vain. My love for them seemed to be dead beyond recall. They appeared to me no better than strangers. To reawaken the emotion of love in my heart I fondled and caressed them, talked to them in endearing terms, but never succeeded in experiencing that spontaneity and warmth which are characteristic of true attachment. I knew they were my flesh and blood and was conscious of the duty I owed to them. My

critical judgment was unimpaired, but love was dead. The recollection of my departed mother, whom I always remembered
with deep affection, brought with it no wave of the deep emotion
which I had invariably felt at the thought of her. I viewed this
unnatural disappearance of a deep-rooted feeling with despondency, finding myself a different man altogether and my un-
happiness increased at seeing myself robbed of that which gives
life its greatest charm.

I studied my mental condition constantly with fear at my heart.
When I compared my new conscious personality with what it had
been before, I could definitely see a radical change. There had been
an unmistakable extension. The vital energy which lighted the
flame of being was pouring visibly inside my brain; this had not
been the case before. The light, too, was impure and variable.
The flame was not burning with a pure, imperceptible and steady
lustre as in normal consciousness. It grew brighter and fainter by
turns. No doubt the illumination spread over a wider circle, but
it was not as clear and transparent as before. It seemed as if I were
looking at the world through a haze. When I glanced at the sky
I failed to notice the lovely azure I used to see before. My eyesight
had always been good and even now there was nothing obviously
wrong with it. I could easily read the smallest type and clearly
distinguish objects at a distance. Obviously my vision was unimpaired, but there was something wrong with the cognitive
faculty. The recording instrument was still in good order, but
something was amiss with the observer.

In the normal man, the flow of the stream of consciousness is so
nicely regulated that he can notice no variation in it from boyhood to death. He knows himself as a conscious entity, a non-
dimensional point of awareness located more particularly in the
head with a faint extension covering the trunk and limbs. When
he closes his eyes to study it attentively, he ends by observing a
conscious presence, himself in fact, round the region of the head.
As I could easily discern even in that condition of mental dis-
quietude, this field of consciousness in me had vastly increased. It
was akin to that which I had experienced in the vision, but
divested of every trace of happiness which had characterized my

first experience. On the contrary, it was gloomy and fear-ridden, depressed instead of cheerful, murky instead of clearly transparent. It seemed as if prolonged concentration had opened a yet partially developed centre in the brain which depended for its fuel on the stream of energy constantly rushing upward from the reproductive region. The enlarged conscious field was the creation of this hitherto closed chamber, which was now functioning imperfectly, first because it had been forced open prematurely, and secondly because I was utterly ignorant of the way to adjust myself to the new development.

For weeks I wrestled with the mental gloom caused by my abnormal condition, growing more despondent each day. My face became extremely pale and my body thin and weak. I felt a distaste for food and found fear clutching my heart the moment I swallowed anything. Often I left the plate untouched. Very soon my whole intake of food amounted to a cup or two of milk and a few oranges. Beyond that I could eat nothing. I knew I could not survive for long on such an insufficient diet, but I could not help it. I was burning inside but had no means to assuage the fire. While my intake of food was drastically reduced, the daily expenditure of energy increased tremendously. My restlessness had assumed such a state that I could not sit quietly for even half an hour. When I did so, my attention was drawn irresistibly towards the strange behaviour of my mind. Immediately the ever-present sense of fear was intensified, and my heart thumped violently. I had to divert my attention somehow to free myself from the horror of my condition.

In order to prevent my mind from dwelling again and again on itself, I took recourse to walking. On rising in the morning, as long as I possessed the strength to do so, I left immediately for a slow walk to counteract the effect of an oppressive sleepless night, when, forced to lie quiet in the darkness, I had no alternative but to be an awed spectator of the weird and fearsome display visible inside. On the way, I met scores of my acquaintances taking their morning constitutional, laughing and talking as they went. I could not share their enjoyment, and passed them in silence with merely a nod or gesture of salutation. I had no interest in any person or in any subject in the world. My own abnormality blotted out everything else from my mind. During the day I walked in my room or in the compound, diverting my attention from object to object without allowing it to rest on one particular thing for any length of time. I counted my steps or looked at the ceiling or at the wall, at the floor or at the surrounding objects one by one, at each for but a fleeting instant, thus with all the will-power at my command preventing my brain from attaining a state of fixity at any time. I was fighting desperately against my own unruly mind.

But how long could my resistance last? How long could I save myself from madness creeping upon me? My starving body was becoming weaker and weaker; my legs tottered under me while I walked, and yet walk I had to if I was to rid myself of the clutching terror which gripped my heart as soon as I allowed my mind to brood upon itself. My memory became weaker and I faltered in my talk, while the anxious expression on my face deepened. At the blackest moments, my eyebrows drew together into an anxious frown, the thickly wrinkled forehead and a wild look in my gleaming eyes giving my countenance a maniacal expression. Several times during the day I glanced at myself in the looking-glass or felt my pulse, and to my horror found myself deteriorating more and more. I do not know what sustained my will so that even in a state of extreme terror I could maintain control over my actions and gestures. No one could even suspect what was happening to me inside. I knew that but a thin line now separated me from lunacy, and yet I gave no indication of my condition to anyone. I suffered unbearable torture in silence, weeping internally at the sad turn of events, blaming myself bitterly again and again for having delved into the supernatural without first acquiring a fuller knowledge of the subject and providing against the dangers and risks of the path.

Even at the times of greatest dejection, and even when almost at the breaking point, something inside prevented me from consulting a physician. There was no psychiatrist at Jammu in those days, and even if there had been one, I am sure I should not have gone to see him. It was well that I did not do so. The little knowledge of diseases that I possessed was enough to tell me that my abnormality was unique, that it was neither purely psychic nor purely physical, but the outcome of an alteration in the nervous activity of my body, which no therapist on earth could correctly diagnose or cure. On the other hand, a single mistake in treatment in that highly dangerous condition, when the whole system was in a state of complete disorder and not amenable to control, might have proved fatal. Mistakes were inevitable in view of the entirely obscure and unidentifiable nature of the disease.

A skilled physician bases his observations on the symptoms present in an ailment, relying for the success of his treatment on the uniformity of pathological conditions in the normal human body. Physiological processes follow a certain specific rhythm which the body tries to maintain under all ordinary circumstances. In my case, since the basic element responsible for the rhythm and the uniformity was at the moment itself in a state of turmoil, the anarchy prevailing not only in the system but also in the sphere of thought, nay in the innermost recesses of my being, can be better imagined than described. I did not know then what I came to grasp later on—that an automatic mechanism, forced by the practice of meditation, had suddenly started to function with the object of reshaping my mind to make it fit for the expression of a more heightened and extended consciousness, by means of bio-logical processes as natural and as governed by inviolable laws as the evolution of species or the development and birth of a child. But to my great misfortune I did not know this at the time. To the best of my knowledge, this mighty secret of nature is not known on earth today, although there is ample evidence to show that certain methods to deal with the condition, when brought about suddenly by the practice of Hatha Yoga, were fully known to the ancient adepts.

I studied my condition thoroughly from day to day to assure myself that what I experienced was real and not imaginary. Just as a man finding himself in an unbelievable situation pinches him-self to make certain that he is not dreaming but awake, I invari-ably studied my bodily symptoms to find corroboration for my mental condition. It would be a fallacy to assume that I was the victim of a hallucination. Subsequent events and my present condition absolutely rule out that possibility. No, the crisis I was passing through was not a creation of my own imagination. It had a real physiological basis and was interwoven with the whole organic structure of my body. The entire machinery from the brain to the smallest organ was deeply involved, and there was no escape for me from the storm of nervous forces which blew through my system day and night, released unexpectedly by my own effort.

Chapter Four

DURING recent times there have hardly been any instances of individuals in whom the serpent fire burnt ceaselessly from the day of awakening of Kundalini to the last, bringing about mental transformations known to and hinted at by the ancient sages of India. But that there have been many cases of a sporadic type in which the shakti* was active intermittently admits of no doubt. The mystics and saints of all countries, who from an early age are prone to transcendental visions and pass occasionally into ecstatic trances, thereafter reverting to their normal consciousness, belong to the latter category. The psychics and mediums and all those possessing the power of clairvoyance, mind reading, prediction, and similar supernormal faculties owe their surprising gifts to the action of an awakened Kundalini, operating in a limited way in the head without reaching the highest centre, when it only overshadows the whole consciousness. The same is true of the men of genius in whom the energy feeds certain specific regions of the brain, stimulating them to extraordinary phases of intellectual, literary, or artistic activity.

In all the cases mentioned above, either the flow of the more potent vital current is so regulated and circumscribed that it does not create any disturbance in the system or, as in the case of mystics in whom the impact of the current on the brain is very

* Cf. p. 88.

powerful at times, the condition begins at birth so that the nervous system usually becomes accustomed to it from infancy, when one is not aware of the variations in consciousness nor able to place a meaning on the abnormal happenings in the body and feel the sense of fear. But even so, the latter have often to face many a crisis and to endure unusual suffering and torment before they acquire a stable and peaceful condition of the mind and are in a position to study and express comprehensively the experience which marks them as a class apart from the normal run of mortals. The individuals belonging to these categories, excepting mystics, do not perceive the luminosity and the movement of nervous currents, except in exceptional cases, as the flow of the vital energy is too restricted to create weird effects. Moreover, having been an integral part of the organism from birth, it becomes an inherent trait of their personalities.

The popular books on Yoga that I had read years before contained no hint of such an abnormal development and nerve-shattering experience. The learned authors confined themselves to the description of various postures and methods, all borrowed from the ancient writings on the subject. Few of them claimed to have had the experience but were eager to teach to others what they had never learned themselves. In some of the books there was a passing reference to Kundalini Yoga. A couple of pages or a small chapter was all that the authors thought sufficient for describing this most difficult and least known form of Yoga. It was stated that Kundalini represents the cosmic vital energy lying dormant in the human body which is coiled round the base of the spine, a little below the sexual organ, like a serpent, fast asleep and closing with her mouth the aperture of the *Sushumna*, the hair-like duct rising through the spinal cord to the conscious centre at the top of the head. When roused, Kundalini, they said, rises through the *Sushumna* like a streak of lightning carrying with her the vital energy of the body, which for the time being becomes cold and lifeless, with complete or partial cessation of vital functions, to join her divine spouse Shiva in the last or seventh centre in the brain. In the course of this process, the embodied self, freed from the bondage of flesh, passes into a condition of ecstasy known as

Samadhi, realizing itself as deathless, full of bliss, and one with the all-pervading supreme consciousness. In only one or two writings were there vague hints of dangers to be met on the path. The nature of the danger and the methods to prevent or overcome it were not explained by the authors.

From the vague ideas I had gathered from these works or picked up in the course of discussions or talks about Yoga, it was only natural for me to infer that the abnormal condition I had brought upon myself was the direct outcome of my meditation. The experience I was having corresponded in every respect with the descriptions given of the ecstatic state by those who had attained this condition themselves; there was therefore no reason for me to doubt the validity or the possibility of my vision. There could be no mistake about the sounds I had heard and the effulgence I had perceived. Above all, there certainly could be no mistake about the transformation of my own consciousness, the nearest and the most intimate part of me, that I had experienced more than once, and the memory of which was so strong that it could never be effaced or mistaken for any other condition. It could not be a mere figment of my fancy because during the vision I still possessed the capacity to make a comparison between the extended state of consciousness and the normal one, and when it began to fade, I could perceive the contraction that was taking place. It was undoubtedly a real experience, and has been described with all the power of expression at their command by mystics and saints all over the world. But in my case there was one particular and unmistakable deviation from the usual type of vision: the most extraordinary sensation at the base of the spine followed by the flow of a radiant current through the spinal column into the head. This part of the strange experience tallied with the phenomena associated with the awakening of Kundalini, and hence I could not be mistaken in supposing that I had unknowingly aroused the coiled serpent and that the serious disturbance in my nervous system as well as the extraordinary but most awful state I was in, was in some way occasioned by it.

I made no mention of my condition to anyone save my brother-in-law, who came to Jammu during those days on a short business visit. He was many years older than I and loved me like a son. I talked to him unreservedly, aware of his deep affection for me. He had himself practised meditation for many years under the guidance of a preceptor who claimed knowledge of Kundalini Yoga. Frank and noble by nature, he often narrated to me his own experiences in the simple manner of a child, seeking corroboration from me for the results he had achieved by his labours. Without the least pretension to knowledge, he gave me every bit of information he possessed, and thus in a way was instrumental in saving my life. My wife knew nothing of the life and death struggle in which I was engaged, but alarmed by my strange behaviour, lack of appetite, bodily disturbances, constant walks, and above all by the never-lifting cloud of anxiety and gloom on my face, she advised me again and again to consult a physician and constantly watched over me day and night, frantic with anxiety.

My brother-in-law could not grasp the significance of what I related to him, but said that his *guru* had once remarked that if by mistake Kundalini were aroused through any other *nadi* (nerve) except *Sushumna*, there was every danger of serious psychic and physical disturbances, ending in permanent disability, insanity, or death. This was particularly the case, the teacher had said, if the awakening occurred through *pingala* on the right side of the spine when the unfortunate man is literally burned to death due to excessive internal heat, which cannot be controlled by any external means. I was horrified by this statement and in desperation went to consult a learned ascetic from Kashmir who had come to spend the winter at Jammu. He heard me with patience and said that the experience I had undergone could not at all be due to the awakening of the serpent power, as that was always blissful and could not be associated with any agency liable to cause disease or disturbance. He made another gruesome suggestion, heard from his teacher or picked up from some ancient work, to the effect that my malady was probably due to the venom of malignant spirits that beset the path of Yogis, and prescribed a decoction, which I never took.

On the suggestion of someone I glanced through a couple of books on Kundalini Yoga, translations in English of ancient Sanskrit texts. I could not read even a page attentively, the attempt involving fixity of attention which I was incapable of maintaining for any length of time. The least effort instantly aggravated my condition by increasing the flow of the new born energy into the brain, which added to my terror and misery. I just glanced through the books, reading a line here and a paragraph there. The description of the symptoms that followed the awakening corroborated my own experience and firmly strengthened my conviction that I had roused the vital force dormant in me; but whether the agony of mind and body that I was passing through was an inevitable result of the awakening or whether I had drawn up the energy through a wrong nerve, I could not be sure. There was, however, one very briefly stated injunction—call it accident or divine guidance—I picked up from the huge mass of material in that very cursory glance. It was to the effect that during the course of the practice the student is not permitted to keep his stomach empty, but should take a light meal every three hours. This brief advice, flashing across my brain at a most critical moment when I hovered between life and death and had lost every hope of survival, saved my life and sanity and continues to do so to this day.

At the time I paid no attention to this significant hint which, based on the experience of countless men, many of whom had probably lost their lives in the attempt to arouse the serpent, had come down through the ages as guidance for the initiates. Even if I had tried my hardest to do so, I could not have acted upon the advice at that time, as food was so abhorrent to me that my stomach revolted at the mere thought of it. I was burning in every part of my body while my mind, like a floating balloon, bobbed up and down and swayed sideways erratically, unable to keep itself steady even for a moment.

Whenever my mind turned upon itself I always found myself staring with growing panic into the unearthly radiance that filled my head, swirling and eddying like a fearsome whirlpool; even found its reflection in the pitch darkness of my room during the slowly dragging hours of the night. Not infrequently it assumed horrible shapes and postures, as if satanic faces were grinning and inhuman forms gesticulating at me in the blackness. This hap-

pened night after night for months, weakening my will and
sapping my resistance until I felt unable to endure the fearful
ordeal any longer, certain that at any moment I might succumb
to the relentlessly pursuing horror and, bidding farewell to my
life and sanity, rush out of the room a raving maniac. But I
persisted, determined to hold on as long as I had a vestige of will
power, resolved at the first sign of breaking to surrender my life
rather than lose myself in the ghastly wilderness of insanity.

When it was day I longed for the night and during the night I
fervently prayed for the day. As the time wore on, my hope
dwindled and desperation seized me. There was no relaxation in
the tension or any abatement in the ceaselessly haunting fear or
any relief from the fiery stream that darted through my nerves
and poured into my agonized brain. On the other hand, as my
vitality ebbed as a result of fasts, and my resistance weakened, the
malady was aggravated to such a pitch that every moment I
expected the end.

It was in such a frame of mind that the holy festival of Shivratri
or the night of Shiva, came to pass towards the end of February.
As usual every year my wife had prepared painstakingly some
dainty dishes on the day and gently insisted that I, too, should
partake of the food. Not to disappoint her and cast a cloud of
gloom on her already anxiety-filled mind, I acquiesced and
forcibly swallowed a few morsels, then gave up and washed my
hands. Immediately I felt a sinking sensation at the pit of my
stomach, a fiery stream of energy shot into my head, and I felt
myself lifted up and up, expanding awfully with unbearable
terror clutching at me from every side. I felt a reeling sensation
while my hands and feet grew cold as ice, as if all the heat had
escaped from them to feed the fiery vapour in the head which had
risen through the cord like the ruddy blast from a furnace and
now, acting like a poison on the brain, struck me numb. I was
overpowered by faintness and giddiness.

I staggered to my feet and dragged myself heavily towards my
bed in the adjacent room. With trembling hands I lifted up the
cover and slipped in, trying to stretch myself into a position of
ease. But I was in a terrible condition, burning internally from

head to toes, outwardly cold as ice, and shivering as if stricken
with ague. I felt my pulse; it was racing madly and my heart was
thumping wildly below my ribs, its pounding distinctly audible
to me. But what horrified me was the intensity of the fiery currents that now darted through my body, penetrating into every
part and every organ. My brain worked desperately, unable to
give coherence to my frenzied thoughts. To call in a doctor for
consultation in such an unheard of disease would be a mere waste
of effort. His first thought on hearing of my symptoms would
turn to a lunatic asylum. It would be futile on my part to seek help
from any other quarter for such an affliction. What could I do
then to save myself from this torture? Could it be that in my
previous semi-starved condition, subsisting only on a few oranges
and a little milk, the fiery current could not attain such awful intensity as it had done now with the entry of solid food in my
stomach? How could I save myself? Where could I go to escape
from the furnace raging in my interior?

The heat grew every moment, causing such unbearable pain
that I writhed and twisted from side to side while streams of cold
perspiration poured down my face and limbs. But still the heat
increased and soon it seemed as if innumerable red-hot pins were
coursing through my body, scorching and blistering the organs
and tissues like flying sparks. Suffering the most excruciating
torture, I clenched my hands and bit my lips to stop myself from
leaping out of bed and crying at the top of my voice. The throbbing of my heart grew more and more terrific, acquiring such a
spasmodic violence that I thought it must either stop beating or
burst. Flesh and blood could not stand such strain without giving
way any moment. It was easy to see that the body was valiantly
trying to fight the virulent poison speeding across the nerves and
pouring into the brain. But the fight was so unequal and the fury
let loose in my system so lethal that there could be not the least
doubt about the outcome. There were dreadful disturbances in all
the organs, each so alarming and painful that I wonder how I
managed to retain my self-possession under the onslaught. The
whole delicate organism was burning, withering away completely under the fiery blast racing through its interior.

I knew I was dying and that my heart could not stand the tremendous strain for long. My throat was scorched and every part of my body flaming and burning, but I could do nothing to alleviate the dreadful suffering. If a well or river had been near I would have jumped into its cold depths, preferring death to what I was undergoing. But there was no well and the river was half a mile away. With a great effort I got up, trembling, with the idea of pouring a few buckets of cold water over my head to abate the dreadful heat. But at that moment my eyes fell on my small daughter, Ragina, lying in the next bed awake, watching my feverish movements with wide-open anxious eyes. With the remnant of sense still left in me I could understand that the least unusual movement on my part at that time would make her cry and that if I started to pour water over my body at such an un-earthly hour, both she and her mother, who was busy in the kitchen, would almost die with fright. The thought restrained me and I decided to bear the internal agony until the end, which could not be far off.

What had happened to me all of a sudden? What devilish power of the underworld held me in its relentless grasp? Was I doomed to die in this dreadful way, leaving a corpse with blackened face and limbs to make people wonder what unheard-of horror had overtaken me as a punishment for crimes committed in a previous birth? I racked my distracted brain for a way of escape, only to meet blank despair on every side. The effort exhausted me and I felt myself sinking, dully conscious of the scalding sea of pain in which I was drowning. I tried desperately to rouse myself, only to sink back again, deadened by a torment beyond my power to endure. After a while with a sudden, inexplicable revival of strength, marking the onset of delirium, I came back to life with a shred of sanity left, Almighty alone knows how, just sufficient to prevent me from giving way completely to acts of madness and self-violence.

Pulling the cover over my face, I stretched myself to my full length on the bed, burning in every fibre, lashed as it were by a fiery rain of red-hot needles piercing my skin. At this moment a fearful idea struck me. Could it be that I had aroused Kundalini through *pingala* or the solar nerve which regulates the flow of heat in the body and is located on the right side of *Sushumna*? If so, I was doomed, I thought desperately and as if by divine dispensation the idea flashed across my brain to make a last-minute attempt to rouse *Ida*, or the lunar nerve on the left side, to activity, thus neutralizing the dreadful burning effect of the devouring fire within. With my mind reeling and senses deadened with pain, but with all the will-power left at my command, I brought my attention to bear on the left side of the seat of Kundalini, and tried to force an imaginary cold current upward through the middle of the spinal cord. In that extraordinarily extended, agonized, and exhausted state of consciousness, I distinctly felt the location of the nerve and strained hard mentally to divert its flow into the central channel. Then, as if waiting for the destined moment, a miracle happened.

There was a sound like a nerve thread snapping and instantaneously a silvery streak passed zigzag through the spinal cord, exactly like the sinuous movement of a white serpent in rapid flight, pouring an effulgent, cascading shower of brilliant vital energy into my brain, filling my head with a blissful lustre in place of the flame that had been tormenting me for the last three hours. Completely taken by surprise at this sudden transformation of the fiery current, darting across the entire network of my nerves only a moment before, and overjoyed at the cessation of pain, I remained absolutely quiet and motionless for some time, tasting the bliss of relief with a mind flooded with emotion, unable to believe I was really free of the horror. Tortured and exhausted almost to the point of collapse by the agony I had suffered during the terrible interval. I immediately fell asleep, bathed in light and for the first time after weeks of anguish felt the sweet embrace of restful sleep.

As if rudely shaken out of my slumber I awoke after about an hour. The stream of lustre was still pouring in my head, my brain was clear, my heart and pulse had stopped racing, the burning sensations and the fear had almost vanished; but my throat was still dry, my mouth parched, and I found myself in a state of extreme exhaustion, as if every ounce of energy had been drained out of me. Exactly at that moment another idea occurred to me; as if suggested by an invisible intelligence, and with irresistible power came the direction that I should eat something immediately. I motioned to my wife, who as usual was lying awake in her bed anxiously watching my every movement, to fetch me a cup of milk and a little bread. Taken aback by this unusual and untimely request, she hesitated a moment, and then complied without a word. I ate the bread, swallowing it with difficulty with the help of the milk and immediately fell asleep again.

I woke up again after about two hours, considerably refreshed by the sleep. My head was still filled with the glowing radiance and, to my surprise, in this heightened and lustrous state of consciousness I could distinctly perceive a tongue of the golden flame searching my stomach for food and moving round along the nerves lining it. I took a few bites of bread and another cup of milk, and as soon as I had done so I found the halo in the head contracting and a larger tongue of flame licking my stomach, as if a part of the streaming energy pouring into my brain was being diverted to the gastric region to expedite the process of digestion. I lay awake, dumb with wonder, watching this living radiance moving from place to place through the whole digestive tract, caressing the intestines and the liver, while another stream poured into the kidneys and the heart. I pinched myself to make sure whether I was dreaming or asleep, absolutely dumbfounded by what I was witnessing in my own body, entirely powerless to regulate or to guide the current. Unlike the horror I had experienced before, I felt no discomfort now; all that I could feel was a gentle and soothing warmth moving through my body as the current travelled from point to point. I watched this wonderful play silently, my whole being filled with boundless gratitude to the Unseen for this timely deliverance from a dreadful fate; and a new assurance began to shape itself in my mind that the serpent fire was in reality now at work in my exhausted and agonized body; and that I was safe.

Commentary to Chapters Three and Four

We encounter here a term central to the theories which Gopi Krishna discusses more fully later. This term is *prana*. He defines it as a subtle life element and compares it to a fluid and to electricity. He further gives it a materialistic description: 'an extremely fine biochemical essence of a highly delicate and volatile nature, extracted by the nerves from the surrounding organic mass. After extraction, this vital essence resides in the brain and the nervous system . . . it circulates in the organism as motor impulse and sensation . . .'

It would take us far afield to discuss in an adequate way the comparable ideas in Western psychology. I have already given some attention to the history of the idea of *psychic energy* as a circulating flow within the organism in Chapter Six of my book *Emotion*.

Prana is both a super-intelligent cosmic life-energy and the subtle biological conductor in the body, that is, it is both a universal life-force and a physiological actuality. It is both immaterial and material, both independent of here-and-now yet inextricably interwoven with the life of the body. As an energy endowed with intelligence *prana* compares with our similar notion of spirit.

Western psychology used the same model of thought from the earliest of Greek ideas until the end of the 18th century. But we no longer use this model of thought in describing psychic energy. In the West energy is either material and therefore nervous energy which can be measured and is reducible to electrical or chemical descriptions, or it is an immaterial principle called the soul or mind or libido or '*élan vital*' which has no physical description. Freud in his early thinking tried to connect the two by deriving libido from sexual liquids; Reich tried to connect psychic energy both to sexual physiology and to a cosmic orgone energy in the universe. We are unable to conceive of a unified energy principle, since we suffer in the West from the Cartesian division of experience into material and mental.

Now, the value of Gopi Krishna's account of *prana* lies less in the traditional description of it, which one can find as he says in

Hindu thought and Yoga texts, than in his own experiences. His actual *experience of enlightenment* on the first day (the first page of this book) was of the flow into the head of a living liquid light. In other words, what was called in Greek, Arabic, and medieval thought the 'breath', 'the animal spirits' or 'spirits of the soul', and which corresponds in description with *prana*, and with the circulating light in Chinese yoga and alchemy (see Wilhelm and Jung, *The Secret of the Golden Flower*) was spontaneously experienced by our author as such: a living liquid light. It is important to note that he was astonished by what happened and that he attempted to fix his attention upon it, as one would observe carefully a spontaneous event occurring in a routine laboratory experiment. He did not make it happen, nor could he make it happen at will. The identification of his consciousness (the watching, attentive ego) with the light yielded a supra-personal experience (outside and above his body) which accords with the theory of *prana* as a universal energy unbounded by body.

We may gain a glimpse of how enlightenment can be accounted for psychologically. I do not mean explained, only 'given an account of'. Evidently, there is an archetypal experience of the circulation or flow of light which has been formulated in many cultures and times into various terms that we now call 'psychic energy'. The flow of this psychic energy in its totality is the entire psychological self, or the Self. When the partial system of the ego is released to, identifies with, or is overwhelmed by, the self, an experience of enlightenment ensues. This is what Gopi Krishna describes. The immersion of the ego in this stream of light is a common theme of religious mysticism, and also of psychopathological derangement.

Our author was at once confronted with this problem, and the major part of the book deals not with the experiences, but with their *integration*. The road to the enlightenment experience has been made much shorter with modern hallucinatory drugs and other techniques. The real issue is how to integrate these experiences, how to live with them, how to keep them from overwhelming the body and external reality, how to translate them into awareness and human service, how to ground them in the

world—in other words, the 'return', how to return with them to
the human condition.

The first sign of disorder in the flow of light was the turmoil of
'sinister light', 'particles of an ethereal luminous stuff', the
'shower' or 'waterfall spray' effect. Intuitively, Gopi Krishna
knew that it was not right. Comparable effects are noted in states
of psychological dissociation, in which consciousness appears to
break up into multiples of itself, disintegrating into sparks,
scintillae, fragments, or hosts of tiny insects. From the Hindu point
of view the turmoil could be attributed to a state of mind called
'*vrtta*' ('whirling motion'), that is, the self, or light *per se*, is not
disordered, but the state of mind of the attachedly observing ego
is still affected by hyper-activity. And this we have in the author's
statements that he was searching, questing, questioning, examining, reading, writing letters, worrying, etc. It is the *introspective
worry* itself which we might interpret as *vrtta* and which splits up
experience into an anthill of particles.

In addition to the fear of madness, the inner derangement of
mind, other events occurred which we call in the language of
psychopathology, 'depersonalization', 'disorientation', 'alienation'.
The sense of belonging to his own body here-and-now and the
feeling connection to his own family were among the first
attachments to go. These secondary symptoms, as well as those
of roaring or other sounds and visual distortions which our author
describes, belong too to the symptomatology of various psychopathological states called: paranoid, schizophrenic, epileptoid.
One might well imagine that had our author presented himself
with this syndrome at a usual Western psychiatric clinic he would
have been diagnosed in the way that he himself intuitively feared.
From the psychiatric view, was this experience not a psychotic
episode?

With this question we come to the heart of a Western problem.
We have no other than these diagnostic categories for conceiving
states of this kind. Alien and altered states of consciousness are the
province of the alienist. Fortunately, Gopi Krishna had another
set of concepts (Kundalini yoga) which could place within a non-
pathological context what was going on. In so far as the awaken-

ing of Kundalini is not limited to the Indian sub-continent only,
it is conceivable that some of the experiences described in Western
psychiatric interviews could also be viewed as the beginnings of
enlightenment rather than as the beginnings of insanity. (I think
in particular of epilepsy and of Dostoevsky.) The touchstone,
again, is the same: the way in which the personality handles the
experience, the integration of it.

It is to our author's credit that he avoided psychiatry, and even
medicine, when later he was to go through the feverish experience
of being burned alive from within. Again, however, from the
viewpoint of modern psychiatry such avoidance is typical of a
man undergoing paranoid delusions. How close the borderlines
are! How much depends upon the quality of the person and the
way he grapples with the integration of his experience. Sometimes therapeutic psychology lays stress upon its therapeutic task
at the expense of the psychological. Then we find that what a
person has, his diagnosis, has become more important than who a
person is. Psychology is obliged to put the who first, the psyche
of the person, his soul with its qualities and virtues, its uniqueness
as a moral being for whatever diagnosis it may accrue. Our
author was holding to this position. He did not want to be treated,
whereas to be 'cured' of what he had would have meant loss of
both who he was and why he was. As A. Bharati points out in his
The Tantric Tradition (London, 1965, p. 290), 'if an adept seems to
"act mad" it is just because people around him do not see what it
is all about, as they are lacking the adept's frame of reference'.
Tantric preceptors deny mental disease en route to *samadhi* and
warn the adept: 'Do not think the mind is sick when there is
samadhi.' Therefore, Gopi Krishna was following the tradition by
avoiding professional help, and by staying within the guidelines
of tradition he guaranteed his own sanity. Professional counsel,
whether medical or spiritual (guru or master) admits the views of
another—and superior—into one's momentarily abject helplessness. At that moment of seeking help the relationship is not
symmetrical: one is professional, the other at a loss. All the health
is on one side, sickness on the other. In this condition one too
easily hears the collective voice in oneself that does not understand

or believe, and so turns the matter and oneself over with suicidal relief to the professional. Gopi Krishna did not split the archetype of the healed one and the wounded one. He stayed right with his ambivalence, believing and doubting, feeling himself found and lost at the same time. This ambivalence was his balance. Had he been more sure, he might have been more deluded; had he been less sure, he might have turned himself in for professional treatment and had his doubts confirmed with a diagnosis.

Next occurs a passage which seems banal enough to skip over, but I believe it deserves a comment. I refer to the information that so reduced was our author in all activities that he took to *walking*. I have found in my own work with people that during periods of acute psychological pressure, walking was an activity to which they naturally turned; walking not just in idylls of the woods and mountains or by the sea, but simply around the city for hours in the early morning or at night. Prisoners circumambulate the yard, animals exercise in their cages, the anxious pace the floor. One goes for a walk. Man is *homo erectus*, he is in his element when vertical. More, the agitation of the whirling motion of the mind is placed into an organic rhythm by walking, and this organic rhythm takes on symbolic significance as one places one foot after the other, left/right, left/right, in a balanced harmony. Thus the wild spiritual adventure within takes on the deliberate movement of the pilgrimage, even if only around a confined space. So in dreams the symbolism of walking rather than driving or being driven in a vehicle, or even riding a bicycle or an animal, is an 'improvement'. It reflects man's contact with the earth directly, his freedom to wander up and down it, and his continually alternating standpoint of left/right, left/right.

I see no reason why we cannot accept our author's own view of the *heat episode*. Can our psychology provide a better explanation of it? It can be compared with some of the wrong turns in alchemy in which there is too much sulphur and the work is burnt black; or where the fire itself (the inner heat, or *tapas*) is not kept at a low slow temperature but rages up too quickly; or in the language of Christian mysticism the fires of Hell, the scorched *siccitas*. In psychological practice, comparable experiences are

sometimes referred to as unexplained psychosomatic fevers.
An interpretation of the shift from the right-sided pingala to
the left-sided ida can be made in this way: habitual consciousness
attempts to integrate a new experience in its manner. Despite the
shattering of the old vessels (mind, orientation, physical strength,
feeling connections, body image), the emotional basis of his
masculine consciousness remained intact. This habitual canaliza-
tion of his energies we might call pingala. We may make a comparison to the sulphur in alchemy as the principle of masculine
will which must be sublimated by connection to the unconscious
(mercury) and joined with its opposite, the feminine principle of
salt. The channel through which his will, his control, his ambition,
the structure of his energy itself had to be altered. The new wine
required a new bottle. The shift from the right to the left side
meant an abandonment of his former personality and his identification with what had held him up for the first thirty-five years.
No wonder he was laid low; no wonder it was a death experience!
The left side of ida is appropriately feminine, just as it is in
Western symbolism. It is the side of softness, where the heart is,
and it belongs to the moon. We would call this redemptive cooling grace of ida the first appearance in our text of the archetypal
effects of the anima.

Chapter Five

Here, while begging to be excused for a little digression from the main thread of my narrative, I wish to make it clear that I have no intention of inflicting the variegated story of my life upon the already overtaxed patience of the reader. But I am obliged to embark upon this course, as otherwise the extraordinary development that occurred in me when I was forty-six would not appear in its proper perspective and would lose the immense scientific value which, in my estimation, it possesses and which it is the object of this work to establish. It is with the purpose of aiding scientific inquiry in the much disputed realm of the supernatural that only such of the incidents of my life have been allowed to have a place in this introductory work as had a direct bearing upon the climax and without which scientific investigation of that unique culmination would not be possible.

I hesitated for nearly twenty years in making the experience public because in the first place, I wanted to make myself completely sure about my own condition, and secondly, I was entirely averse to exposing myself to the criticism of well-meaning friends and the ridicule of opponents. The story I had to relate was so out of the ordinary and so full of strange episodes that I was very doubtful about its being accepted as a truthful account of an experience which, extremely rare, has always remained wrapped in mystery from times immemorial. I thought there might be but few who would straight away believe what I had to narrate about the bizarre phenomenon, but the urge to make the hidden truth known prevailed at last. I know that with the publication of this work I am exposing myself to criticism from various quarters, especially from those who should be more interested in the subject. Men of science on the one hand and those of faith on the other, some of whom instead of snatching at the chance of reconciliation offered now are likely to treat it as an encroachment upon the preserves of their idolized opinions and views, forgetting for the moment the fact that truth is an entity that grows richer in adversity and stronger in opposition.

I know all this, but yielding to an irrepressible urge, which took shape in my mind soon after the appearance of the abnormal condition and which since then has never been wholly absent, demanding wide publicity for the experience as the first step towards organized research in all manifestations of the superconscious for which the time is now opportune, I have applied myself to the task of recapitulating the incidents in my life relevant to the subject with a view to giving coherence to the subsequent surprising development, which though existing in a certain class of men as a natural endowment, has so far eluded every effort directed to its investigation. I have, at the same time, tried to draw attention to the mental and physiological conditions that precede the manifestation of such abnormal developments in man, bearing a resemblance in essentials, though differing in detail, to other phenomena of the kind in the past. But for the fact that the manifestations attending the awakening of Kundalini are at present a sealed book to the world, barring perhaps a few exceptions, there is in actual fact nothing uncommon in my experience, as may be established by other similar occurrences in the future for which this work may create the necessary conditions.

Excepting the abnormal physiological reactions and the existence and extraordinary behaviour of the luminous vital currents in the body, which to uninitiated and unprepared subjects like me are sure to bring a host of terrors in their wake, there is nothing in my experience which even remotely approaches the uncanny and entirely abnormal phenomena witnessed by professional mediums and other psychic subjects. What made me hesitate in according publicity to it is the unique nature of the phenomenon; it neither falls in line with the known manifestations observed in mediums, nor does it seem similar in kind to the recorded experience of any known mystic or saint, Eastern or Western. Its peculiarity lies in the fact that in its entire character the phenomenon represents the attempt of a hitherto unrecognized vital force in the human body, releasable by voluntary efforts, to mould the available psycho-physiological apparatus of a man to such a condition as to make it responsive to states of consciousness not normally perceptible to that individual before. It is this particular aspect of my extraordinary experience which makes it remarkable and demands attention from quarters interested in the supernormal or in ascertaining the physiological basis of super-organic psychic phenomena.

It is an undeniable fact that the quest of the unknown was as unmistakable a feature of ancient civilizations as it is now. There was as persistent a search for the spiritual and the supernatural and as strong a thirst in countless people for the acquirement of supernormal powers and for tearing aside the veil that hides the beyond. But either because of the fact that time was not ripe for complete unravelling of the mystery or because the human mind revels in keeping the subject dealing exclusively with its own nature enshrouded in uncertainty, fear, and superstition, the discoveries made in this domain were kept the closely guarded secret of a select few. There is not a shadow of doubt that to the ancient adepts of India, China, or Egypt, the cult of Kundalini was better known than it is to the foremost thinkers of today. On the basis of my own experience I can assert unhesitatingly that the phenomenon of the effulgent current, its circulation through the nerves, the methods of awakening the Power, the regimen to be followed, precautions to be taken, and the part played by the reproductive organs were, as is apparent from the ancient writings or, in the absence of those, from the nature of the ceremonial followed by the initiated, to some extent known to the experts, who, because of the risky nature of the experiment, the hereditary

factors involved, and the required mental and physical qualifications, could be but few.

It must be said at once to avoid misunderstanding that the cult
of Kundalini was not the only path by which the ancients approached the difficult-to-reach domain of the supernatural; there
existed contemporaneously other creeds, schools, and systems
dealing with the mysterious and the supernatural. As happens
even during these days, the followers of the various sects must
have tried to tear each other down, belittling the methods of their
rivals and extolling their own. The existence of this unceasing
warfare, as is obvious, could not but be detrimental to the general
acceptance of the system relating to Kundalini, which in consequence was relegated to the background, especially because of the
rigid physical regimen, the magnitude of the risk and last but not
the least the rarity of a successful consummation, and in the course
of time was consigned to the lumber room of obsolete creeds. It
can also be said without any fear of contradiction that the rise of
all great religions of the world, in spite of the fact that each is
rooted inextricably in the soil prepared and watered by this prehistoric cult, contributed not a little to eclipse the creed of
Kundalini as an honoured and established system of mental and
physical discipline for gaining approach to the transcendental. It,
however, continues to exist in India in form only, divested of its
former importance and influence, though still retaining much of
the fascination that it once exerted on seekers trying to reach the
Unseen.

It is obvious that all religions, all creeds, and all sects, including
even the bloody cults of savages and the self-torturing or self-
mutilating creeds found up to recent times, owe their origin to the
existence of an urge, rooted deep in human nature, which finds
expression in countless ways, healthy and unhealthy, and has been
the constant companion of man all through his ascent from the
most primitive condition to the present state. The desire for re-
solving the riddle of existence, for supersensual experience, for
establishing contact with the hidden forces of nature or for gaining supernormal powers, present in many minds with over-
powering and compelling effect, is but a mode of expression of

this yet incompletely understood but potent impulse, which, rising from the depths of being, emerges as a part and parcel of one's personality, often discernible in thought and action from an early age.

All religious observances, all acts of worship, all methods of spiritual development, and all esoteric systems which in one way or another aim to provide a channel of communication with the supersensible, the divine or the occult, or offer an avenue for exploring the mystery of being, are all means, both effective and defective, to procure satisfaction for this deeply seated and universally present urge. The form taken may be of a heinous bloody sacrifice, a gaping self-inflicted wound, the self-caused blindness of the sun-gazer or constant torture to the body on a bed of nails, melodious chanting of hymns, recitation of prayers, prostration in devout worship, the discipline of Yoga, or any other spiritual exercise; the objective invariably is the occult, the mysterious, or the supersensible in divine, demoniac, spiritual or any other form.

From the very beginning the urge has expressed itself in an infinite variety of religious beliefs and creeds, superstitions and taboos traceable to the remotest epochs of man's existence. The impulse to invest the inanimate forces of nature with intelligence and to credit the spirits of the dead with continued existence beyond the grave, characteristic of the primitive mind and the civilized man's attempt to postulate an almighty Creator and to offer worship to Him, arose from the same source and owe their existence to the presence in the human organism of an extremely complicated and difficult to locate mechanism, which the ancient Indian *savants* called Kundalini.

Whether the aim be religious experience, communication with disincarnate spirits, the vision of reality, liberation of the soul, or the gift of clairvoyance and prediction, the power to influence people or success in worldly undertakings by supernatural means or any other mundane or super-mundane objective, connected with the occult or divine, the desire springs from the same psychosomatic source and is a twig or branch of the same deeply rooted tree. Kundalini is as natural and effective a device for the attainment of a higher state of consciousness and for transcendental experience as the reproductive system is an effective natural contrivance for the perpetuation of the race. The contiguity of the two is a purposely designed arrangement, as the evolutionary tendency and the stage of progress reached by the parent organism can only be transmitted and perpetuated through the seed.

Men have never been able to understand the surpassing efficiency which a man of genius brings to bear on his intellectual or manual creations, and still less are able to comprehend the mental condition of an ecstatic. The former completely engrossed in his problem or handiwork and the latter lost in the rapt contemplation of a beatific internal display or an external object of adoration, carried for the time being away from the world to a more alluring state of existence, present an enigma for the solution of which it is necessary to look again carefully inside the human frame in order to locate the hidden source from which the brain in these conditions of extreme absorption draws the nourishment required to maintain the highly developed activity for long periods. The completely isolated nature of individual consciousness, caused by the segregating effect of the ego, makes it impossible for any man to look into the locked compartment of another mind, even of one nearest and dearest to him. This utter lack of access of one mind to another has given rise to certain common misconceptions which it will take a long time to remove from human thought.

The average man, when studying a genius, a mystic, or a medium, is apt to presume, because of his inability to look into their minds as he does into his own, that they are conscious entities like himself, with the difference that one has more intelligence and more skill in wielding the pen or brush or chisel, with a greater power of sustained attention and application and a more observing eye. The other, he supposes, has more love and devotion for the deity, with a stronger control over passions and appetites and a greater power of sacrifice or an incomprehensible link with other minds or hidden forces of nature with the power to create a condition of the brain that allows disembodied intelligences to act through it at times. Without entering into a detailed discussion of the various hypotheses put forward to account for the existence of genius or of supernormal faculties in sensitives and psychics, it is sufficient for our purpose to say that whatever explanation is offered, it is invariably based on the supposition, tacit or expressed, that the individuals possessing these extraordinary gifts, in spite of the surprising intellect or uncanny powers and the immense distance between them and the normal mind, have the same nature of consciousness as the average man and woman. This is a most erroneous conception which has always stood in the way of a proper understanding and investigation of the phenomenon.

On their side, the gifted endowed by nature from birth, unable to peep into the minds of others, and often entirely in the dark about the real source of the remarkable variation in themselves, reciprocate the feelings of the common man about them, often attributing their own exceptional talents to the same causes to which they are traced by the latter, ignorant of the always overlooked fact that there exists a basic and fundamental difference in the nature of consciousness, in the very depths of the conscious personality, tenanting their bodies, and in the very nature of the vital essence which animates them. There exists at present a general ignorance about the demonstrable fact that the evolving human frame is tending to develop a higher personality endowed with the attributes which characterize men of genius and seers by the refining and development of the vital principle with corresponding adjustments in the brain and the nervous system, somewhat in the same manner as a more powerful electric current passing through a more properly adjusted filament in a bulb leads invariably to brighter illumination.

The point has been merely touched here in passing in order to lend clarity to what is to follow in the succeeding chapters. It will be discussed in more detail in another work. The urge for knowing the unknown, for supersensory knowledge and religious experience, existing deep in the human mind, is the expression of the embodied and incarcerated human consciousness to win nearer to its innate majestic form, overcoming in this process the disabilities imposed on it by the carnal frame. The evolution of man in actual fact signifies the evolution of his consciousness, of the vital principle inhabiting his body, by which alone the embodied self can become cognizant of its true immortal state. It does not signify merely the development of the intellect or reason, which are but instruments of the indwelling spirit, but of the whole personality, of both its conscious and subconscious parts, which involves an overhauling and reshaping of the organic machine to make it a fit abode for a higher intelligence, essentially superior in nature to that which resides in the normal human body. It is for this reason that the mode of conduct or intellectual activity normal to a prophet appears entirely beyond the capacity of the average man, whose mind, flooded with passion at the touch of the beloved or assailed by desire at the sight of a coveted object, has seldom been able to live up to the standard of morality prescribed by the former, whose brain, fed by a higher form of vital energy permeating the whole personality, belongs more to heaven than to earth.

Chapter Six

BEFORE that fateful morning in December, when I had my first glimpse into the superconscious state and saw fabulous Kundalini in action, if even the most truthful man on earth had narrated to me a similar episode, I should have unhesitatingly placed him in that class of intelligent but credulous men who, while most accurate and conscientious in all other matters, exhibit a streak of puerility in respect of the supernatural. As the sequel will show, I remained in uncertainty about my strange condition for a long time, utterly at a loss to put a meaning on the occurrence. It was only when after years of suspense the adventure culminated in the development of clearly marked psychic attributes, not in evidence before, that I decided to put the extraordinary episode on paper. This resolve was further fortified by the consideration that Kundalini is active in millions of intelligent men of all civilized nations, though in a lesser degree and imperceptibly, creating in the majority psychic and physical disturbances which modern therapy is incapable of preventing or curing because of absolute ignorance about the cause.

Considering the colossal nature of the physical and mental metamorphosis that has to be effected as a prelude to spiritual unfoldment, I do not wonder at the accompanying trials and tribulations, since the mystic state represents the last and most arduous lap of the journey which began with man's ascent from dust; it terminates with his tasting, after suffering and travail, the incomparable bliss of unembodied existence, not after death, but within his span of life on earth. The path in front of him now is so difficult and of such bewildering alignment that it will need all his will-power and all the resources of his intellect to negotiate it safely step by step until the goal comes clearly in sight.

When I awoke the following morning, I found myself too weak to rise from bed without assistance, and I remained lying down, revolving in my mind the fearful incidents of the night, while profuse tears of thankfulness streamed down my face at what I thought was divine intervention at a most critical time to save me from a dreadful fate. The more I thought about it, the more convinced I became that a superhuman agency acting through my mind had conveyed the hint, which in that terribly agitated state I could never have thought of myself, by which I was able to extricate myself from an entirely hopeless situation absolutely beyond the reach of mortal aid. No power on earth could have saved me from death or insanity, nor could any medicine have alleviated my suffering. As if planted in my mind from the very start to save me from submitting my body for experimentation by healers not competent to deal with my condition and to protect me from the deleterious effects of common drugs that would have acted as veritable poisons in that extremely sensitive and delicate state of my nerves, I felt from the first day of my affliction a deeply rooted aversion to take medical men into my confidence about this extraordinary ailment; not that I had no respect for the profession, but because I had a feeling that my malady was beyond the grasp and power of the highest medical authority.

With a feeling of relief I at last rose weakly from bed like a man in whom an invisible but intense internal fire has burnt for hours and who finds that not only has the fire been extinguished but even the excruciating pain of the burns has disappeared miraculously overnight. I looked at myself in a mirror and found my face pale and haggard, but the maniacal expression had nearly vanished and the gleam of madness was almost gone from my eyes. I was looking at a sane but terribly weak and anguished countenance that had borne, as it were, the torture of hell for days and days. My tongue was still coated and my pulse weak and irregular, but all other signs and symptoms regarding the condition of my organs were so reassuring that my heart leapt with joy and hope. There was no diminution in the vital radiation which, emanating from the seat of Kundalini, sped across my nerves to every part of the body, filling my ears with strange sounds and my head with strange lights; but the current was now warm and pleasing instead of hot and burning, and it soothed and refreshed the tortured cells and tissues in a truly miraculous manner.

During the next day and the days following, I paid scrupulous attention to my diet, taking only a few slices of bread or a little boiled rice with a cup of milk every three hours from morning until about ten o'clock at night. The amount of food taken each time was extremely small, a few morsels and no more. After the last meal, when I laid myself down to sleep, I found to my great joy a gentle drowsiness stealing upon me in spite of the shining halo surrounding my head, and I fell asleep enveloped in a radiating and soothing mantle of light. I awoke next morning greatly refreshed in mind, but still extremely weak in body. I had no strength to walk and reeled when I stood up. But my head was clear and the fear that had pursued me had decreased considerably. I was able, for the first time after weeks of anguish, to collect my thoughts and to think clearly. It took me about a week to gain sufficient strength to walk from one room to another and to remain standing for any length of time. I do not know what reserve store of energy sustained me during the terrible ordeal before the last miraculous episode, as I had had practically no food for more than two months. I did not feel as weak then as I now felt, probably because in the poisoned state of my nerves I was wholly incapable of assessing correctly the condition of my body.

Days and weeks passed, adding to my strength and to the assurance that I was in no imminent mental or physical danger. But my condition was abnormal, and the more I studied it with growing clarity of mind, the more I wondered and the more uncertain I became about the outcome. I was in an extraordinary state: a lustrous medium intensely alive and acutely sentient, shining day and night, permeated my whole system, racing through every part of my body, perfectly at home and absolutely sure of its path. I often watched the marvellous play of this radiant force in utter bewilderment. I had no doubt that Kundalini was now fully awake in me, but there was absolutely no sign of miraculous psychic and mental powers associated with it by the ancients. I could not detect any change in me for the better; on the contrary, my physical condition had considerably deteriorated and my head was yet far from steady. I could not read attentively or devote myself with undivided mind to any task. Any sustained effort at concentration invariably resulted in an intensification of the abnormal condition. The halo in my head increased enormously in size after every spell of prolonged attention, creating a further heightening of my consciousness with a corresponding increase in the sense of fear now present only occasionally, and that, too, in a very mild form.

Perceiving no sign of spiritual florescence and always confronted by the erratic behaviour of an altered mind, I could not but be assailed by grave misgivings about myself after watching my condition for a few weeks. Was this all that one could achieve after rousing the serpent fire? I asked myself this question over and over again. Was this all, for which countless men had risked their lives, discarded their homes and families, braved the terrors of trackless forests, suffered hunger and privations, and sat at the feet of teachers for years to know? Was this all that yogis, saints, and mystics experienced in ecstatic trances, this extension of consciousness accompanied by unearthly lights and sounds, carrying a man momentarily into an abnormal mental state and then dashing him again to earth, without creating any extraordinary talent or quality to distinguish him from the average run of mortals? Was this ebb and flow of a subtle radiant essence and the resultant widening and narrowing of consciousness which I witnessed day and night the ultimate goal to which the occult doctrines of the world pointed with confidence? If this were all one could achieve, then surely it was far better not to delve into the supernatural, but to devote oneself with undivided attention to worldly pursuits and to follow the common path, to pass an undisturbed, happy existence free from the uncertainty and fear which had now become an inseparable part of my life.

I continued to pay careful attention to my diet, as experience had now made me fully alive to the fact that my life and sanity depended on it. I did not eat in excess of the quantity I deemed proper for myself, fixing the amount according to the reaction of my digestive parts, nor did I allow any delicacy to tempt me to depart from my self-imposed regimen. There was reason enough to make me extremely cautious on this score, as the slightest indiscretion in respect to the quantity or quality of the food consumed and any disregard of time created results and reactions so disagreeable and distressing as to make me upbraid myself severely for having committed the mistake. This happened time after time as if to impress indelibly upon my mind the fact that from now onwards I had not to eat for pleasure or the mechanical satisfaction of hunger, but to regulate the intake of food with such precision as not to cause the least strain on my oversensitive and over-stimulated nervous system. There was no escape from this forced regimentation, and during the first few weeks, even the slightest error was instantaneously punished with an intensification of fear and a warning disturbance at the heart and digestive centres. Usually, on such occasions my mind lost its flexibility and I felt powerless to shake myself free of the gloom that unaccountably settled upon me all of a sudden after eating the offending morsel. In my anxiety to avoid those unpleasant visitations, I was meticulous not to commit the least error; but try as I might, mistakes did occur now and then, almost always followed by suffering and penitence on my part.

For the proper understanding of my condition after the memorable night of my release, it is necessary to say a few words about my mental state as well as about the radiating vital current, darting up and down my spine, which was now a part of my being. My mind did not function as before. There had occurred a definite and unmistakable change. At that time my thought images came and went against a sombre background possessing vaguely the same combination of light, shade, and colour as characterized the original objects which they represented; but now the images were vivid and bright as if carved out of living flame, and they floated against a luminous background as if the process of thought was now done with another kind of lustrous mental stuff, not only bright itself but also capable of perceiving its own brilliance. Whenever I turned my mental eye upon myself I invariably perceived a luminous glow within and outside my head in a state of constant vibration, as if a jet of an extremely subtle and brilliant substance rising through the spine spread itself out in the cranium, filling and surrounding it with an indescribable radiance. This shining halo never remained constant in dimension or in the intensity of its brightness. It waxed and waned, brightened and grew dim, or changed its colour from silver to gold and vice versa. When it increased in size or brilliance, the strange noise in my ears, now never absent, grew louder and more insistent, as if drawing my attention to something I could not understand. The halo was never stationary but in a state of perpetual motion, dancing and leaping, eddying and swirling, as if composed of innumerable, extremely subtle, brilliant particles of some immaterial substance, shooting up and down, this way and that, combining to present an appearance of a circling, shimmering pool of light.

The constant presence of the luminous glow in my head and its close association with my thought processes was not a matter for such bewilderment as its ceaseless interference with the normal working of my vital organs. I could distinctly feel and perceive its passage across the spine and other nerves into the heart or liver or stomach or other organs in the body, whose activity it seemed to regulate in a mysterious manner. When it penetrated the heart, my pulse became fuller and stronger, showing unmistakably that some kind of tonic radiation was being poured into it through the connecting nerves. From this I concluded that its penetration into the other organs had the same vivifying and invigorating effect and that its purpose in darting through the nerves to reach them was to pour its tonic substance into their tissues and cells through the slender nerve filaments, stimulating or modifying their action. The penetration was occasionally

followed by pain, either in the organ itself or at the point where
the linking nerve entered it, or at the point of contact with the
spinal cord, or both, and was often accompanied by feelings of
fear. It appeared on such occasions that the stream of radiant
energy rising into the brain was sending offshoots into the other
vital organs to regulate and improve their functions in harmony
with the new development in my head. I searched my brain for
an explanation and revolved every possibility in my mind to
account for the surprising development as I watched attentively
the incredible movement of this intelligent radiation from hour
to hour and day to day. At times I was amazed at the uncanny
knowledge it displayed of the complicated nervous mechanism
and the masterly way in which it darted here and there as if aware
of every twist and turn in the body. Most probably it was because
of its almost unlimited dominance over the whole vital mechanism that the ancient writers named Kundalini as the queen of the
nervous system, controlling all the thousands of 'nadis' or nerves
in the body, and for the same reason have designated her as
'Adhar Shakti',* on which depends the existence of the body and
the universe, the microcosm and the macrocosm.

But I could detect no change in my mental capacity; I thought
the same thoughts and both inside and out was the same mediocre
type of man like millions of others who are born and die every
year without creating the least stir on the surface of the ever-
flowing stream of humanity. There was no doubt an extraordinary change in my nervous equipment, and a new type of
force was now racing through my system connected unmistakably
with the sexual parts, which also seemed to have developed a new
kind of activity not perceptible before. The nerves lining the parts
and the surrounding region were all in a state of intense ferment,
as if forced by an invisible mechanism to produce the vital seed in
abnormal abundance to be sucked up by the network of nerves
at the base of the spine for transmission into the brain through the
spinal cord. The sublimated seed formed an integral part of the
radiant energy which was causing me such bewilderment and
about which I was as yet unable to speculate with any degree of

* Basic shakti.

assurance. I could readily perceive the transmutation of the vital seed into radiation and the unusual activity of the reproductive organs for supplying the raw material for transformation in the mysterious laboratory at the lowest plexus, or *muladhara chakra*, as the yogis name it, into that extremely subtle and ordinarily imperceptible stuff we call nervous energy, on which the entire mechanism of the body depends, with the difference that the energy now generated possessed luminosity and was of a quality allowing detection of its rapid passage through the nerves and tissues, not only by its radiance but also by the sensations it caused with its movement.

For a long time I could not understand what hidden purpose was being served by the unremitting flow of the new-born nervous radiation and what changes were being wrought in the organs and nerves and in the structure of the brain by this unceasing shower of the powerful vital essence drawn from the most precious and most potent secretion in the body. Immediately after the crisis, however, I noticed a marked change in my digestive and eliminatory functions, a change so remarkable that it could not be assigned to accident or to any other factor save the serpent fire and its effect on the organism. It appeared as if I were undergoing a process of purgation, of internal purification of the organs and nerves, and that my digestive apparatus was being toned to a higher pitch of efficiency to ensure a cleaner and healthier state of the nerves and other tissues. I encountered no constipation or indigestion, provided I refrained from overloading the stomach and followed strictly the regimen of eating which experience was forcing on me. My most important and essential duty now was to feed the sacred flame with healthy food, at proper intervals, with due regard to the fact that the diet was nourishing, containing all the ingredients and vitamins needed for the maintenance of a robust and healthy body.

I was now a spectator of a weird drama enacted in my own body in which an immensely active and powerful vital force, released all of a sudden by the power of meditation, was incessantly at work, and after having taken control of all the organs and the brain, was hammering and pounding them into a certain shape. I merely observed the weird performance, the lightning-like movements of the lustrous intelligent power commanding absolute knowledge of and dominance over the body. I did not know at the time that I was witnessing in my own body the immensely accelerated activity of an energy not yet known to science, which is carrying all mankind towards the heights of superconsciousness, provided that by its thought and deed it allows this evolutionary force full opportunity to perform unhindered the work of transformation. I little knew that the chaste sacrificial fire, to which so much sanctity and importance has been attached by all the ancient scriptures of India, fed after being lighted with the oblation of clarified butter, dry fruits of the choicest kind, sugary substances, and cereals, all nourishing and purifying articles of food, is but a symbolic representation of the transforming fire lit in the body by Kundalini, requiring when lighted the offering of easily digestible and nutritive food and complete chastity of thought and deed to enable it to perform its godly task, which normally takes epochs, within the span of a man's life.

After only a few days I found that the luminous current was acting with full knowledge of the task it had to perform and functioned in complete harmony with the bodily organs, knowing their strength and weakness, obeying its own laws and acting with a superior intelligence beyond my comprehension. The living fire, invisible to everyone else, darted here and there as if guided unerringly by a master-mind which knew the position of each vein and artery and each nerve fibre, and decided instantaneously what it had to do at the least sign of a hitch or disturbance in any organ. With marvellous agility it raced from one spot to another, exciting this organ to greater activity, slowing down another, causing a greater or lesser flow of this secretion or that, stimulating the heart and liver, bringing about countless functional and organic changes in the innumerable cells, blood vessels, nerve fibres, and other tissues. I watched the phenomenon in amazement. With the aid of the luminous stuff now filling my nerves, I could, by diverting my attention towards my interior, discern clearly the outlines of the vital organs and the network of nerves spread all over my body, as if the centre of consciousness in the brain, now always ablaze with light, had acquired a more penetrating inner sight by which it could look inside and perceive dimly the interior of the body as it could see its exterior in a hazy, uncertain light. At times, turning my attention upon myself, I distinctly saw my body as a column of living fire from the tips of my toes to the head in which innumerable currents circled and eddied, causing at places whirlpools and vortices, all forming part of a vast heaving sea of light, perpetually in motion. It was not a hallucination, as the experience was repeated innumerable times. The only explanation to account for it that occurred to me was that on such occasions my undeniably extended consciousness was in contact with the world of 'prana', or cosmic vital energy, which is not normally perceptible to the common man, but is the first subtle, immaterial substance to come within the range of superconscious vision.

Like a man suddenly transported to a distant planet, where he finds himself utterly confused by the weird and fantastic nature of the surroundings which he could not even conceive of on earth, filling him with awe and amazement, I was completely bewildered and unnerved by this sudden plunge into the occult. From the very first day I felt myself walking on a ground that was not only unfamiliar but presented such queer formations that, losing my bearings and self-confidence, I trod hesitatingly with utmost caution, fearing a pitfall at every step. I looked around desperately for guidance, only to face disappointment on all sides.

Without mentioning my condition, I talked to several scholars and Sadhus well versed in Tantric lore, with the object of gleaning some useful hints for myself, but found to my sorrow that beyond a parrot-like repetition of information gathered from books, they could not give me any advice or authoritative guidance based on experience. On the other hand, not infrequently they admitted frankly that it was not easy to grasp the meaning of the texts dealing with Kundalini yoga, and that they themselves had encountered difficulties at many a place. What was I to do then to set my doubts at rest and to find some sort of an explanation for and, if possible, some effective method to deal with my abnormal condition?

I made a mental survey of all possible sources in India of which I had any knowledge to decide which of them I could approach. There were the dignified heads of various orders with hundreds of devoted followers. There were the princely divines residing in cities, counting titled aristocrats, rajahs, and magnates among their disciples, and there were the silent ascetics living by themselves in out-of-the-way spots whose fame brought large crowds from distant corners to pay homage to them. Then there were the ordinary Sadhus gathered in colonies or living alone or roaming about from place to place, diversely garbed or almost unclad, belonging to various sects with striking peculiarities and quaint accoutrements and carrying with them an atmosphere of weirdness and mystery wherever they went. I had seen and talked to many of them from my boyhood, the most accomplished as well as the least sophisticated, and the impressions I had gathered provided no room for hope that there would be even one among them capable of advising me correctly about my condition. At least I did not know of any, and therefore the only alternative open to me was to make a widespread search for one. But I had neither the means nor the physical capacity to travel from place to place looking for a Yogi in the whole of the vast subcontinent of India, with all its endless variety of monastic orders and spiritual cults, its religious mendicants, Sadhus and saints, who could correctly diagnose my trouble and heal it with his own spiritual powers.

At last mustering my courage, I wrote to one of the best-known modern saints of India the author of many widely read books in English on Yoga, giving him full details of my extraordinary state and sought for guidance. I waited for his reply in trepidation, and when it failed to come for some days, I sent a telegram also. I was passing a very anxious time when the answer came. It said that there was no doubt that I had aroused Kundalini in the Tantric manner and that the only way for me to seek guidance was to find a Yogi who had himself conducted the Shakti successfully to the Seventh Centre in the head. I was thankful for the reply which fully confirmed my own opinion, thereby raising my hopes and self-confidence. It was obvious that the symptoms mentioned by me had been recognized as those characterizing the awakening, thereby giving to my weird experience a certain appearance of normality. If I were passing through an abnormal condition, it was not an isolated instance nor was the abnormality peculiar to me alone, but must be a necessary corollary to the awakening of Kundalini, and with modifications suited to different temperaments must have occurred in almost all those in whom awakening had taken place. But where was I to find a Yogi who had raised the Shakti to the Seventh Centre?

After some time I met another Sadhu, a native of Bengal, at Jammu and described my condition to him. He studied my symptoms for a while and then gave me the address of an Ashram in East Bengal, the head of which was supposed to be a Yogi of the highest order, who had himself practised Kundalini yoga. I wrote to the address given, receiving a reply that I had undoubtedly aroused the Shakti but the man who could guide me had left on a pilgrimage. I consulted other holy men and sought for guidance from many reputed quarters without coming across a single individual who could boldly assert that he actually possessed intimate personal knowledge of the condition and could confidently answer my questions. Those who talked with dignified reserve, looking very wise and deep, ultimately turned out to be as wanting in accurate information about the mysterious power rampant in me as those of a more unassuming nature who unbosomed themselves completely on the very first occasion without in the least pretending to know any more than they really did. And thus in the great country which had given birth to the lofty science of Kundalini thousands of years ago and whose very soil is permeated with its fragrance and whose rich religious lore is full of references to it from cover to cover, I found no one able to help me.

The only thing I was sure of was that a new kind of activity had developed in my nervous system, but I could not determine which particular nerve or nerves were involved, though I could clearly mark the location at the extremity of the spinal cord and round the lower orifice. There undeniably was the abode of Kundalini, as described by Yogis, the place where she lies asleep in the normal man, coiled three and a half times round the lowest triangular end of the spine, awakened to activity with proper exercises of which concentration is the main adjunct.

Had I been under the guidance of a master my doubts might have been resolved on the very first day or at least on the day when I passed the crisis, but having neither the practical experience of a teacher to draw upon nor enough theoretical knowledge of the subject to enable me to form a conclusive opinion independently, I remained vacillating in my ideas about the condition. This wavering state of mind was further enhanced by the variations in and the waxing and waning of my consciousness. Perhaps it was destined that it should be so and that I should be guideless and without adequate knowledge to allow me to form an independent judgment about the phenomenon, without prejudice or prepossession. Perhaps it was destined also that I should suffer acutely for years because of lack of guidance and my ignorance, to enable me by suffering to make smooth the path of those in whom the sacred fire will burn in the days to come.

Commentary to Chapters Five and Six

We meet in Chapter Five the *ideational context* of our author's experience. This cannot be overestimated. Our author did well to place it at this point, because it is the supporting frame which kept his experience from going wrong. He had developed subjective anchors during the first part of his life. He had practised yoga, but the practise itself was not enough. For a Westerner even more the practise of yoga is not enough. Yoga is based on a philosophical system of ideas, a *weltanschauung*, a way of viewing self and world, and this must be operative in a critical time as that context of meaning on to which one can fall. This context of meaning made it possible for Gopi Krishna to comprehend and thus to further and to integrate what was happening to him.

Again, to our loss in the West, we are so lacking in an adequate context that we do indeed go to pieces at the eruption of the unconscious, thereby justifying the psychiatric view. Fortunately, Jaung's analytical psychology gives in its account of the process of individuation a context within which these events can be meaningfully comprehended. Fortunately, too, Jung studied as a psychologist this branch of yoga. He called the Kundalini an example of the instinct of individuation. Therefore, comparisons between its manifestations and other examples of the individuation process (e.g. alchemy) provide a psychologically objective knowledge without which there would be no way of taking hold (comprehending, *begreifen*) what is going on. Very often, therefore, it is of utmost value during a period of critical psychological pressure in which the unconscious boils over, to provide the sufferer with psychological knowledge. His experience needs to be confirmed with objective material much as the yoga disciplines provide, showing that what he is going through is appropriate and belongs to the process. The analyst is called on to confirm the other's experiences through his own, and what he has gained from working with others; as well, he has at his disposal knowledge of the process in general as described in mysticism, rituals of primitives, mythologies, spiritual disciplines, and works such as this by Gopi Krishna.

Our author stresses the *evolutionary importance of the events*, and indeed calls his book 'The Evolutionary Energy in Man'. I do not wish to contend this point. It is a favourite idea of many, including Teilhard de Chardin. This much, however, can be said: there is evidently an archetypal connection between profound mystical experiences of this sort in which one's own consciousness has evolved and personality developed, and the idea that the same experience is fundamentally possible for all men and therefore meant for all men.

Religious experience of this sort brings with it the gift or curse of messianism and prophecy. Psychologically, it was evidently valuable for our author to feel that what he was going through was not only personally meaningful but that it had as well a universal meaning. Experiences of the Self have this universality.

We often then speak of inflation when the ego does not integrate the cosmic idea but takes it at face value. And perhaps it is meant to be taken at face value. How is one to know? Enough for our purpose to recognize the appearance of a sense of transcendent purposefulness as the events unfolded, and that this transcendent purposefulness was interpreted by our author in the traditional manner as a call.

There are many references to *diet* in the text. Of course, they can be said to represent the obsessive concern of the highly intuitive person with the sensation details of life, especially life of the body. I recall a paranoid man in hospital, the subject of whose conversations with me was on the one hand abstract mathematical theories and visionary poetry and on the other the system of his food intake—how many slices of bread to eat at lunch, the nutritive value of tomatoes, etc. But diet cult cannot be reduced to compensation alone. The popular press gives accounts to fascinated readers exactly how, what, and when the great men eat. The great are often obsessed with diet. Food after all quite simply means world, and one's eating habits represent one's habitual way of taking in the world. Gopi Krishna clearly had to stop feeding himself in his former way. This shift of attitude towards food reflects a shift from the outer to the inner aspect of life-in-the-world, called in Hindu terminology a shift from the *sthula* to the *sukshma* aspect.

He writes: 'This happened time after time as if to impress indelibly upon my mind the fact that from now onwards I had not to eat for pleasure or the mechanical satisfaction of hunger, but to regulate the intake of food with such precision so as not to cause the least strain on my over-sensitive . . . nervous system.' In other words, genetically a most fundamental instinct, a primary level of psychological life (the oral stage) was also now in service of the ongoing process.

He approaches his diet with 'precision'. The mention of that word in this context indicates to me the differences between a wrong and right kind of compulsiveness. Precision about psychic life—whether in exercises and diet of the body, in details of dreams and fantasies, in the elaboration of imagination into art—

points to the way in which the drivenness of obsessive compulsion can be overcome from within by its own principle. Like cures like. The psyche has an affinity for precision; witness the details in children's stories, primitive rituals and primitive languages, and the exactitude with which we go about anything that is important. Precision is not a preserve of natural science nor is the precise method to be identified with measurements only. Our author realizes that to change his style he must be precise about every detail. He will now approach his diet with refined detailed attention, with the repetitive and ritualistic concern of a violinist who would change his fingering or a boxer aiming to speed his counter-punching. He shows us another way of transforming obsessive compulsion, not by letting go and taking it easy, but through the positive virtue that lies within the compulsiveness. Compulsion can be seen as precision miscarried, a ritualistic behaviour gone astray which asks to be set precisely right.

The changes taking place during this initial period of recovery affected principally the *body*. So, too, during an analysis we find all sorts of symptoms cropping up, sometimes symptoms of the most serious sort, synchronistic with dynamic changes in the analytical process. Alteration of consciousness does not leave the body out. How much more helpful it would be if we could understand these body changes in the way in which Gopi Krishna did, as necessary preparations for enlarged consciousness. If the body is the carrier of consciousness, it too must be altered. Yet, though Gopi Krishna understood this, each alteration he sensed brought *fear*. It seems as if there is a deep animal fear, a kind of biological resistance, to these changes, as if the body would rather not leave the paths of its instinctual ancestry. The animal in us shies and panics.

Perhaps this tells us something about symptoms. Perhaps they have to do with the fear of change and thus represent the conflicts caused by the new man coming into the old vessel of the body. By this I do not mean that with 're-birth' all symptoms disappear. But I do mean that the symptoms occurring concomitant with psychic change are protective as pain is protective. They hold us down and within our slow evolutionary patterns of the

body without whose fear and symptoms we might go up and out
of the body altogether in some foolish liberation above all symptoms that would actually be suicide.

A major change in body concerns *sexuality*. A reorganization
of the sexual impulse would seem required for every transition in
planes of consciousness. Initiation rites at puberty, and marriage
rites, as well as the vow of chastity for those entering religious
orders, all point to the importance of sexual changes in connection
with changes in states of being. The Kundalini serpent power is
supposed to lie curled asleep at the base of the spine in the region
of coccyx, anus, and prostate; opinions differ as to its exact locus.
It is intimately connected with sexuality, so that the transformation of sexuality through internalization becomes a necessary
activity, even the major opus in the discipline. The transformation
of sexuality through ritualization is an idea that can be found in
gnostic, alchemical and shamanistic practices, as well as in yoga.
It is also fundamental to Taoist sexual theories. (see R. van Gulik,
Sexual Life in Ancient China; M. Eliade, *Yoga—Immortality and
Freedom* and his *Shamanism*; my 'Towards an Archetypal Model
for the Masturbation Inhibition', *J. Analyt. Psychol.* 1966; all these
works have bibliographies). Freudian analysis too can be seen as a
ritualization of sexual life for the sake of its transformation,
especially since in its orthodox form 'acting-out' is discouraged
during an analysis. The principal idea is simple: semen is that
fluid in the body most highly charged with *prana*. Occult ana-
tomy envisages a direct connection between the genitals and the
nervous system, either via brain and spine or via the blood. Loss
of seed means loss of that vital essence which is the source of the
living liquid light. Semen must therefore be discerned and discharged upwards rather than outwards, thereby adding to the
internal circulation of *prana*. Bharati (*op. cit.*) speaks of the difference between Buddhist and Hindu attitudes. The former, as the
Taoists, retain the semen; the latter discharge it (left-hand path of
Tantrism) as sacrifice. In each of these varied traditions one idea
stands out: the transformation of consciousness requires the
transformation of sexuality which takes place through ritual.

Our text refers to unusual ferment in the genital parts and to the production of an increased abundance of semen. This runs contrary to the usual notions that yoga is an ascetic discipline through which the sexual impulse is depotentiated. Just not! And we can understand why chastity and continence and other sexual mystitiques (including the orgy and black mass) belong archetypally to the discipline of the 'holy man'. It is not that he has less sexuality than others, but more. (For example, an early sign of the call to shamanism among the American Mohave Indians is frequent childhood masturbation.) The 'holy man' as 'greater personality' implies the endowment of greater sexuality; therefore, the transformation of it raises all sorts of problems, answers to which have been formulated in various esoteric techniques and disciplines, West and East, of which chastity and *the ritual copulation of Tantric maithuna* would be opposite poles of the same archetypal formulation.

It is not infrequent in analytical practice that phases of obsessive sexuality (sexual dreams, fixations on the genitals, sado-masochism, masturbation, nocturnal emissions) occupy the centre of the stage for a time. Reduction of these events to œdipal conflicts is not alone sufficient. If a process of transformation is truly going on, then it will affect a person's sexual life, drawing his attention to his sexuality, and sexuality as such (which then takes on the numinous power of a God, formulated long ago in other cultures as the Lingam, or as Priapus). The ground of possibility for any transformation of sexuality is the recognition of it as an impersonal power. The *maithuna* aspect of tantric yoga makes this clear. It is not *my* sex and *my* pleasure and *my* orgasm; it is a force that flows through me, a force of play, joy, and creation. By separating the personal out of it, one can listen to it, obey or deny it, note its fluctuations and intentions—all of which means relating to it objectively. Once this step has been taken, the transformation at which our author hints, including seed retention, ejaculation control, and other practices described by van Gulik and Maspero become less a matter of personal suppression, an adolescent battle between good and evil, than a detached game, at once religiously sacrificial and erotically educative.

In several places, we note our author's difficulty with *reading*.

Not only could he not find the right material to study; he also could not concentrate. One of the first things that had to go was intellectual concentration. We call this in analytical work the *'sacrificium intellectus'*. It refers to the state when one is forced to abandon oneself to the on-going process, as to a river, without knowing where it will lead, without having a chart of the course, without knowledge aforehand. The intellect can easily take over experiences and deprive them of their livingness. So in Freudian analysis the patient is generally not supposed to read psychology. In Jungian analysis there is no such rule, for when and what to read depends entirely on the actual situation. And it was a long time before the ability to read again returned to Gopi Krishna, indicating how strong the hold of the intellect can be, and in his case, what a danger it was. We must remember that he originally set out for an intellectual life from which he was saved by the examination failure. This points to a psychological truth: the greatest danger to our true calling, whatever it may be, is the one closest to it, the one which is the shadow of the substance. One is less likely to mistake green or white for true red, than rose, pink, or burgundy. Each contact with reading and intellectual formulation led him astray by endangering the process as an experience in the body. This body was his true teacher. He had to go it alone, but his body, like the dumb ass of St. Francis or the ass of Jesus in whose stable He was born and on which He rode to his last week and body's crucifixion, was His constant companion. Is that not the point of all this body obsession? Does it not say: we are animals with animal hair and teeth and gut. And this animal is a god as so many religious images the world over insist. The animals belong to divinities, who come in the shape of animals, who *are* animals, saying perhaps that it is the animal in us that is holy. Even the Kundalini itself is a snake. The animal that is divine is the wisdom of nature, or the wisdom of the body, that knows from primeval times with a knowledge which we cannot hope to emulate no matter what we read. Noah saved what was holy in the creation: life, the animals; the Torah came later. It is the animal in us who cannot read. The 'serpent power' itself seemed to be demanding his obedience by preventing him from seeking another master with another kind of knowledge. He had no master, and was psychologically unable to read. Therefore, the letter of confirmation from the eminent master saying that what he was going through was authentic cannot be overvalued. The task of the Western analyst is often just that: to give an affirmation to the experiences which the other person is going through, to take them earnestly, to believe in his inner world and give credit to it. Above all, he mustn't be threatened by it or call it sick. This eminent master said that Gopi Krishna could be helped only by one who had already been there ('conducted the Shakti successfully to the Seventh Centre'). In Jungian analysis, we often say 'you can only take someone else as far as you have gone yourself'. This is a limiting statement and, if taken to heart, is quite depressing both for the student and the analyst. It also shows how all of us depend upon the very few real masters who have had to go so much of the way alone. It also makes us value what Gopi Krishna did on his own, and gives our text even further significance as a document which may be of use to others.

At the end of Chapter Six, our author raises in passing a question about his own *sufferings*. When one reads the texts of mystics and holy men, as he did, one is struck by all the references to bliss and beauty. And it was the absence of bliss and beauty which made Gopi Krishna vacillate and doubt his own experiences. Again, we can be grateful to him for his honesty in recording the bitterness and burning of his own experience, and we can admire him for his absence of resentment. Suffering belongs. The visions in the desert of the Christian Saints, the dark night of the soul of St. John of the Cross, the terrible suffering of the Old Testament prophets, point to the necessity of suffering. To believe that it could be otherwise is—as we know from analytical practice— a remnant of childish idealism. In regard to the archetypal suffering involved in personality transformation, Western mysticism, patterned after the images of the Bible and Jesus and the Saints, might here have been of more value to our author than his own tradition. In this sense, his work speaks to today and is an excellent bridge to Western experiences in which the expanded or intensified consciousness coming through analysis does not rise as a lotus from a quiet lake, but is riven and torn by neurosis before any light dawns. Suffering ushers birth; the new child is born in pain; and in defeat and rage one does not know where one is.

Chapter Seven

BEFORE proceeding to narrate the incidents that followed, it is necessary to say a few words about the long known but rarely found reservoir of life energy in man known as Kundalini. Many informed students of Yoga hear or read about it one time or another, but the accounts given in modern writings are too meagre and vague to serve as helpful sources of authentic information. The ancient treatises exclusively dealing with the subject of Kundalini Yoga abound in cryptic passages and contain details of fantastic, sometimes even obscene ritual allusions to innumerable deities, extremely difficult and often dangerous mental and physical exercises, incantations and formulas technically known as mantras; bodily postures called asanas, and detailed instructions for the control and regulation of breath, all couched in a language difficult to understand, with a mass of mythical verbiage which instead of attracting is likely to repel the modern student. Truly speaking, no illustrative material is available either in the modern or ancient expositions to convey lucidly what the objective reality of the methods advocated is and what mental and organic changes one may expect at the end.

The result is that instead of becoming illuminative and pragmatic, this strictly empirical science is falling into abuse and disrepute. Some of its practices, forming integral parts of a combined whole and serving as a means to a definite end, such as the asanas and breathing exercises, are now being regarded as laudable ulterior ends in themselves to the neglect of the ultimate object for which the exercises were devised. The real object of this system of Yoga is to develop a type of consciousness which crosses over the boundaries confining the sense-bound mind, carrying the embodied consciousness to supersensory regions. Distracted by the tyrannical demands of modern civilization and discouraged by the generally incredulous attitude towards the possibility of such a development in man, the present-day aspirants often content themselves with a few postures and breathing exercises in the fond belief that they are practising Yoga for spiritual uplift.

The descriptions of *Chakras* and lotuses, of supernatural signs and omens accompanying success in the practice, of the miraculous powers attainable, the genesis of the system and the origin of the various methods are so overdone and full of exaggeration that to the uninitiated the whole conception embodied in the ancient literature on the subject appears incredible if not preposterous. From such material it is extremely difficult for the modern seeker to gain plain knowledge of the subject divested of supernatural and mythological lore or to find clarification for his doubts and difficulties. Judged from the fantastic accounts contained in the writings not only in the original ancient treatises but also in some of the modern books, Kundalini for an intelligent, matter-of-fact man can be no more than a myth, a chimera born of the innate desire in men to find an easy way of escape from the rigours imposed by a rigidly governed world of cause and effect, like the philosopher's stone invented to satisfy the same desire in a different form by providing a short cut for the acquirement of wealth needed to achieve the same end. In India no other topic has such a mass of literature woven around it as Yoga and the supernatural, and yet in no book on the subject is a penetrating light thrown on Kundalini, nor has any expert provided more information than is furnished in the ancient works. The result is that except for perhaps a few almost inaccessible masters, as scarce now as the alchemists of yore, there is no one in the whole of India, the home of the science, to whom one can look for authoritative knowledge of the subject.

The system of complicated mental and physical exercises relating particularly to Kundalini is technically known as Hatha
Yoga, in contradistinction to other forms of Yoga in vogue in
India from very ancient times. Hatha in Sanskrit is a compound
of two words, *ha* and *tha*, meaning the sun and moon, and consequently the name Hatha Yoga is intended to indicate that form
of Yoga which results from the confluence of these two orbs.
Briefly stated, the moon and the sun as used here are meant to
designate the two nerve currents flowing on the left and right
sides of the spinal cord through the two *nadis*, or nerves, named
Ida, and *Pingala*. The former, being cool, is said to resemble the
pale lustre of the moon; the latter, being hot, is likened to the
radiance of the sun. All systems of Yoga are based on the supposition that living bodies owe their existence to the agency of an
extremely subtle immaterial substance, pervading the universe
and designated as Prana, which is the cause of all organic phenomena, controlling the organisms by means of the nervous system
and the brain, manifesting itself as the vital energy. The Prana, in
modern terminology 'vital energy', assumes different aspects to
discharge different functions in the body and circulates in the
system in two separate streams, one with fervid and the other
with frigid effect, clearly perceptible to Yogis in the awakened
condition. From my own experience I can also unhesitatingly
affirm that there are certainly two main types of vital currents in
the body, which have a cooling or heating effect on the system.
Prana and Apana exist side by side in the system in every tissue
and every cell, the two flowing through the higher nerves and
their tiny ramifications as two distinct currents though their
passage is never felt in the normal state of consciousness, the nerves
being accustomed to the flow from the very commencement of
life.

Because of its extremely subtle nature, vital energy has been
likened to breath by the ancient authorities on Yoga, and it is
maintained that the air we breathe is permeated with both Prana
and Apana and that the vital currents flow alternately through the
two nostrils along with the air at the time of inhalation and ex-
halation. As is well known, the air we breathe is composed mainly

of two gases, oxygen and nitrogen. Oxygen is the chief agent in combustion, burning up the impurities in the blood by its action through the lungs, while nitrogen exerts a moderating effect on its fervour. In view of the fact that the old writers on Kundalini Yoga sometimes use the same term for Prana or Apana, viz. Vayu, which is used for the air we breathe, there is a possibility of confusion being caused that breath and Prana are identical. This is absolutely not the case. Life as we know it on earth is not possible without oxygen, and it is noteworthy that this element is an ingredient of both air and water, the two essential requirements of earthly life. This is a clear indication of the fact that on the terrestrial globe the cosmic vital energy, or Prana Shakti, utilizes oxygen as the main vehicle for its activity. It is possible that biochemistry in the course of its investigations may have to accept at a future date the instrumentality of oxygen in all organic phenomena as the main channel for the play of the intelligent vital force Prana.

The earth has its own supply of Prana, pervading every atom and every molecule of all the elements and compounds constituting its flaming core, the fiery molten regions below the crust, the hard surface layer with its mountains and seas, and the atmosphere to its outermost fringe. The sun, a vast reservoir of vital energy, is constantly pouring an enormous supply of pranic radiation on earth as a part of its effulgence. The superstitions connected with eclipses may thus have an element of truth, as on all such occasions the pranic emanations from the sun or moon are partially or totally cut off for a time. The changes in the weather and in the vapour and dust content of the atmosphere, which have a marked effect on certain sensitive temperaments, might also be found to cause alterations in the flow of pranic currents. The moon is another big supply centre of Prana for earth. The planets and stars both near and far are all inexhaustible stores of Prana, vitalizing the earth with streams of energy conveyed by their lustre. The pranic emanations from the sun and moon, planets and stars, are not all alike, but each has a peculiar characteristic of its own in the same way as the light of heavenly bodies, when analysed on earth after travelling through enormous distances, shows variations in the spectrum peculiar to each one. It is impossible for the imagination of man to visualize even dimly the interactions of numberless streams of light emitted by billions upon billions of stars crossing and recrossing each other at countless points, filling the stupendous stretch of space at every spot from end to end. Similarly it is utterly impossible to picture or to depict even hazily the colossal world of Prana, or life energy, as described by seers, its unbounded extent traversed by streams and cross-streams, currents and cross-currents, radiating from innumerable stars and planets with motionless spots and storm centres, vortexes and eddies, all throbbing with activity everywhere, the animate worlds rising out of this marvellously intelligent but subtle ocean of vital activity as foam appears on the surface of the perennially moving oceanic currents.

In order to explain the phenomenon of terrestrial life there is no alternative but to accept the existence of an intelligent vital medium which, using the elements and compounds of the material world as bricks and mortar, acts as the architect of organic structures. All show evidence of extraordinary intelligence and purpose, built with such amazing skill and produced in such profusion and in so many diverse forms as to falsify any idea of spontaneous generation or chance. The existence of this medium cannot be proved empirically; human ingenuity and skill have not yet attained the perfection where one can experiment with media of such subtlety.

Immense significance has been attached to the pranic radiations coming to earth from the sun and moon. In fact, some ancient authorities trace the origin of the human mind to the moon. The whole structure of Yoga is based on the validity of Prana as a cognizable superphysical stuff. For thousands of years successive generations of Yogis have verified the assertions of their precursors. The reality of Prana as the chief agent leading to the superconscious condition known as Samadhi has never been questioned by any school of Yoga. Those who believe in Yoga must first believe in Prana. Considering the fact that to attain success in Yoga one must not only possess unusual mental and physical endowments, but must also have all the attributes of saintly character, honesty, chastity, and rectitude, it would be nothing short of obstinacy to discredit the testimony of numerous renowned seers, who in unequivocal terms have testified to their own experience of the superconscious conditions resulting from systematic manipulation of Prana as learnt by them from their own preceptors.

According to the religious beliefs in India, dating back to prehistoric times, the existence of Prana as a medium for the activity of thought and transference of sensations and impulses in living organisms and as a normally imperceptible cosmic substance present in every formation of matter in terms of the classifications made by Hindu cosmologists in earth, water, air, fire and ether, is an established fact, verifiable by the practice of Yoga when undertaken by the right type of man on proper lines. According to these beliefs, Prana is not matter, nor is it mind or intelligence or consciousness, but rather an inseparable part of the cosmic energy or Shakti which resides in all of them and is the driving force behind all cosmic phenomena, as force in matter and vitality in living organisms; in short, it is the medium by which the cosmic intelligence conducts the unimaginably vast activity of this stupendous world, by which it creates, maintains, and destroys the gigantic globular formations burning ceaselessly in space as well as the tiny microbes, both malignant and beneficent, filling every part of the earth. In other words, Shakti, when applied to inorganic matter, is force and when to the organic plane, life, the two being different aspects of the creative cosmic energy operating in both the inorganic and organic planes. For the sake of convenience and to avoid confusion, the term Prana or Prana-Shakti is generally applied to that aspect of the cosmic energy which operates in the organic sphere, as nervous impulse and vitality, while the generic name Shakti is applied to every form of energy, animate and inanimate; in brief, to the creative and active aspect of the Reality.

In dealing with Kundalini we are concerned only with Prana or Prana-Shakti, sometimes referred to as Shakti for the sake of brevity, though, strictly speaking, the designation Shakti is applied to cosmic energy, the creatrix of the universe. Present-day science is being irresistibly led to the conclusion that energy is the basic substance of the physical world. The doubt about the existence of life as a deathless vital medium apart from the corporeal appendages, is as old as civilization, and is occasioned mainly by the inexorable nature of physical laws operating on the body, the inevitability of decay and death, the extremely elusive nature of vital principle, the utter impossibility of perceiving it apart from the organic frame, the finality of death as the end of the organism, and above all the utter absence of any demonstrable or incontrovertible proof of survival after bodily death. According to the Yogis, however, the existence of the life energy as a deathless entity becomes subjectively apparent in the superconscious state of Samadhi, and its flow through the nerves can be experienced even before that as soon as certain measures of success are attained in meditation. When that happens, a greater demand for it is felt in the concentrated condition of the brain, and to meet this, vital energy or prana, residing in other parts of the body, flows to the head, sometimes to such an extent that even vital organs like the heart, lungs, and the digestive system almost cease to function, the pulse and the breathing become imperceptible, and the whole body appears cold and lifeless. With the additional fuel supplied by the enhanced flow of vital energy, the brain becomes more intensely alive; the surface consciousness rises above bodily sensations and its perceptive faculty is vastly enlarged, rendering it cognizant of superphysical existences. In this condition the first object of perception is Prana, experienced as a lustrous, immaterial stuff, sentient and in a state of rapid vibration both within and outside the body, extending boundlessly on every side.

In Yoga parlance Prana is life and life is Prana. Life and vitality, in the sense used here, do not mean soul or the spark of the divine in man. Prana is merely the life energy by which divinity brings into existence the organic kingdoms and acts on the organic structures, as it creates and acts on the universe by means of physical energy. It is not the reality as sunshine is not the sun, and yet is essentially a part of it, assuming different shapes and appearances, entering into countless types of formations, building persistently the units or bricks to create the complicated organic structures in the same way that physical energy starts with electrons, protons, and atoms to raise the mighty edifice of the universe, all its activity governed by eternal laws as rigid and universal as the laws which rule the physical world. After creating the atoms, physical energy is transformed into countless kinds of molecules, resulting in the existence of innumerable compounds diverse in form, colour, and taste, which again by combination and mixture, differences in temperature and pressure, create the amazingly diversified appearance of the physical world. Prana, starting with protoplasm and unicellular organisms, brings into existence the marvellous domain of life, endless in variety, exceedingly rich in shape and colour, creating classes, genera, species, subspecies, and groups, using the materials furnished by the physical world and the environment to create diversity, acting intelligently and purposefully with full knowledge of the laws and properties of matter as well as of the multitudinous organic creations it has to bring into being. While remaining constant and unaltered fundamentally, it enters into countless combinations, acting both as the architect and the object produced. It exists as a mighty universe vaster and more wonderful than the cosmos perceived by our senses, with its own spheres and planes corresponding to the suns and earths of the latter, its own materials and bricks, its own movement and inertia, its own light and shadow, laws and properties, existing side by side with the universe we see, interwoven with our thoughts and actions, interpenetrating the atoms and molecules of matter, radiating with light, moving with wind and tide, marvellously subtle and agile, the stuff of our fancies and dreams, the life principle of creation, which is woven inextricably with the very texture of our being.

We do not realise what mysterious stuff animates the cells and organs of living bodies, causing marvellous physical and chemical reactions while the owners of the bodies, even the most intelligent and keen, know nothing of what is happening in them, know nothing of the intelligence which regulates the body machine, which builds it in the womb, preserves it in illness, sustains it in danger, heals it when injured, cares for it when asleep or delirious or unconscious, creates urges and tendencies which move and sway them as wind does a reed. What is more astounding after doing each and everything, even to the extent of drawing the breath and inducing the thoughts, because of its own marvellous and, for the human intelligence, absolutely incomprehensible nature, it keeps itself always behind the scenes, allowing the surface consciousness, which it maintains as oil does a flame, to think and act as the master, utterly unconscious of the invisible but amazing activity of the real mistress of the abode, the superphysical medium, Prana Shakti, the life aspect of the cosmic energy.

The founders of Kundalini Yoga, accepting the existence of *prana* as a concrete reality both in its individual and cosmic aspects, no doubt, after experimentation carried out by many generations of savants, were led to the momentous discovery that it is possible to gain voluntary control over the nervous system to the extent of diverting a greater flow of Prana into the brain, resulting naturally in an intensification of its activity, and hence devised all their methods of body control and mental discipline to achieve this end. They succeeded admirably as the main exercise, concentration, which is the corner-stone of every system of Yoga, fits in with the methods prescribed by nature also for expediting human evolution. They found that on acquiring a certain degree of proficiency in mind control and concentration, they could, in favourable cases, draw up through the hollow backbone a vividly bright, fast-moving, powerful radiance into the brain for short periods of time in the beginning, extending the duration with practice, which had a most amazing effect on the mind, enabling it to soar to regions of surpassing glory, beyond anything experienced in the crude material world.

They named the channel Sushumna, and as the streaming radiance was distinctly felt mounting up from its base, they treated the spot as the seat of the goddess, representing her as lying asleep there in the guise of a serpent, closing with her mouth the aperture leading to the spinal canal. The systems of nerves on the left and right of the Sushumna, which contributed to the formation of the flaming radiance by yielding a part of the vital energy moving through them, were named Ida and Pingala. Though lacking in the knowledge made available by modern science, it did not take them long in their heightened state of consciousness to postulate the existence of the subtle world of life, interpenetrating and existing side by side with the material cosmos. Consequently the ancient writings on Hatha Yoga abound in cryptic references to Prana Shakti or vital energy and its conducting network systems in the body which are not infrequently a source of confusion for beginners.

Chapter Eight

I QUITE realize that it is impossible for me to convey accurately or for the average reader to understand clearly what I mean by the expression widening and contraction of consciousness, which I use frequently to denote the fluctuations in my mental condition. However, it is only by employing this phrase that I can describe even vaguely a purely subjective experience, which seldom falls to the lot of the average man. To the best of my knowledge the weird phenomena following the awakening of Kundalini have so far never been revealed in detail or made the subject of analytical study. The subject has remained shrouded in mystery not only because of the extreme rarity and astounding nature of the manifestation but also because certain essential features of the development are closely bound up with the intimate life and private parts of the individual who has the experiences. The disclosures made in this work are likely to appear startling, even incredible, because the subject has been discussed openly for the first time after centuries of a veiled existence.

We can more or less follow the meaning of words, however difficult they may be, which describe mental states common to us all or discuss intellectual problems and abstract propositions based on common experience and knowledge. But the phenomenon which I have tried to explain in these pages is so uncommon and so removed from ordinary affairs that in all probability only a few of those who happen to read this account will have even heard of anything so extraordinary. Accomplished masters of Kundalini Yoga, always extremely rare, are almost non-existent now, and the cases of a spontaneous type, where the awakening occurs suddenly at some period in life, more often than not end in mental disorder, which makes a coherent narration of the experience impossible. Under the circumstances it is no wonder that a detailed account of this strange experience is not available anywhere.

I may add, however, that in spite of all this the experience is not as singular or as unauthenticated as might at first appear. There is enough evidence available to suggest that from times immemorial, probably from the very birth of civilization and even before that, there have been cases, extremely rare indeed, of the awakening of Kundalini, spontaneously or by means of suitable exercises. In the few cases of the former type where the awakening proceeds towards a healthy culmination, the symptoms being usually mild and the development gradual, as in born mystics, the essential characteristics of the rebirth, which were startlingly apparent in my case, might conceivably escape notice or when noticed may be attributed to other causes due to ignorance about the real one. In the large proportion of cases of the same class where the awakening is morbid, the frenzied expressions of the stricken even when correct would be utterly disregarded as the senseless rubbish of a delirious brain. In the case of awakening brought about by voluntary effort, as the manifestations must generally have occurred behind the walls of inaccessible monasteries or in solitary hermitages or secluded yoga centres in the depths of forests, the extraordinary phenomena attending it were either not open to critical observation or, where observed, were treated as a necessary preternatural accompaniment to the adventure and hence not regarded seriously as something important to record and communicate or, considered too sacred to be divulged, were kept a closely guarded secret accessible to none save the initiates.

Accordingly labouring under the difficulty of describing in this critical age of science a bizarre mental phenomenon never des-

cribed in detail before, I am compelled for reasons of prudence
to keep back much that should have found a place in this work and
which, I am sure, will fall within the experience of many of those
who, like me, chance to kindle the serpent fire accidentally without
a preparatory period of training in the days to come. Acting on
this plan it is sufficient for me to say, without narrating many of
the almost uncanny happenings which I witnessed within myself,
that during the following months my mental condition continued
to be the same as already described, but there was a perceptible
improvement in my bodily health, and I found my former
strength and vigour gradually returning.

The Government Offices moved from Jammu to Srinagar, the
summer capital of the State, usually in the month of May, but
being on leave and finding myself unable to withstand the
deleterious effects of heat in the weakened state of my nerves, I
left for Kashmir in early April. The change did me good. The
valley was thick with blossoms and the crisp spring air filled with
fragrance had an invigorating effect upon me. There was absolutely no change in the constant movements of the radiant
current or in the intensified behaviour of the glow in my head.
On the other hand, their activity was more intensified. But my
mental strength, poise, and power of endurance, which seemed
to have been completely depleted, came back to me in part, and I
found myself able to take a lively interest in conversations. What
was more precious to me, the deep feelings of love for my family,
which had appeared to be dead, stirred in my heart again. Within
a few weeks after arriving, I found myself able to take long walks
and to attend to ordinary affairs not requiring too much exertion;
but still I could not read attentively for long and continued to
have a fear of the supernatural. I persistently avoided thinking of
or talking about the subject.

My former appetite returned and I could eat everything I used
to previously without any fear of a few morsels more or less
creating a storm in my interior. I could even prolong the interval
between meals, but not too long without discomfort. By the
time my office opened at Srinagar I had gained enough strength
and endurance to have the assurance that I could again take up my

official duties without the risk of aggravating my mental condition or making myself ridiculous by exhibiting a lack of efficiency in my work or any sign of abnormality in my behaviour. When I went through the papers on my desk, I noticed that my memory was unimpaired and the awful experience I had undergone had in no way adversely affected my ability.

I was easily fatigued, however, and became restless after only a few hours of attentive application. After a prolonged spell of mental work, I invariably found after closing my eyes and listening internally that the luminous circle was more extended and the buzzing in the ears louder than usual. This served as an indication that I was still not capable of maintaining a sustained state of attention for lengthy periods and that I should proceed with caution to avoid a recrudescence of the previous symptoms. Accordingly, I decided to alternate spells of work with intervals of relaxation by chatting with my colleagues, by looking out of the window, or by moving from the office into the busy street outside which offered a large variety of objects to divert my attention.

I do not know how it happened that even in that extremely abnormal state of my mind, needing constantly the application of new measures to adapt it to changing circumstances, I often hit upon the right procedure to deal with unexpected and difficult situations arising in my day-to-day contacts. If I had done so much as even breathed to others a word about my abnormality and the bizarre manifestations which were now a regular feature of my life, I might have been labelled as a lunatic and treated accordingly, meeting ridicule instead of compassion. If I had tried to make capital out of the mysterious occurrence and pretended a knowledge of the occult, which I did not in reality possess, I might have been hailed as a saint and pestered day and night by people seeking a miraculous way of escape out of their difficulties. Beyond a few hints which I let drop to some of my relatives in the very beginning when I was taken completely aback by the strange malady, and beyond revealing my condition as well as I could to a few Yoga experts for guidance, I maintained a strict reserve about my abnormal state and never referred to it in my conversation with intimate friends, although even in my most sanguine moments the fear of impending madness never left me completely.

The magnitude of the risk that one has to run in the event of a powerful awakening all of a sudden, can be gauged from the fact that simultaneously with the release of the new energy, profound functional and structural changes begin to occur in the delicate fabric of the nervous system with such rapidity and violence as to be sufficient to cause unhinging of the brain instantaneously if the organism as a whole does not possess enough power of adjustment to bear the tremendous strain, as actually happens in a large percentage of cases. Among the inmates of mental hospitals there are often some who owe their malady to a prematurely active or morbidly functioning Kundalini.

With the restoration of my faculties and the growing clarity of mind I began to speculate about my condition. I read all that came my way pertaining to Kundalini and Yoga, but did not come across any account of a similar phenomenon. The darting warm and cold currents, the effulgence in the head, the unearthly sounds in the ears, and the gripping fear were all mentioned, but there was no sign in me of clairvoyance or of ecstasy or of communication with disembodied spirits or of any other extraordinary psychic gift, all considered to be the distinctive characteristics of an awakened Kundalini from the earliest times.

Often in the silence and darkness of my room at night I found myself looking with dread at horribly disfigured faces and distorted forms bending and twisting into shapes, appearing and disappearing rapidly in the shining medium, eddying and swirling in and around me. They left me trembling with fear, unable to account for their presence. At times, though such occurrences were rare, I could perceive within the luminous mist a brighter radiance emanating from a luciferous, ethereal shape, with a hardly distinguishable face and figure, but nevertheless a presence, emitting a lustre so soft, enchanting, and soothing that on such occasions my mind overflowed with happiness and an indescribable divine peace filled every fibre of my being. Strangely enough, on every such occasion the memory of the primary vision, which

occurred on the first day of the awakening, came vividly to me
as if to hearten me in the midst of despondency with a fleeting
glimpse of a supercondition towards which I was being painfully
and inexorably drawn.

I was not sure at that time whether the visions afforded actual
glimpses of supermundane existence or were mere figments of my
now highly excited and virtually glowing imagination. I did not
know what was making me perennially conscious of luminosity
as if my own intangible mental stuff had been metamorphosed
into a radiant substance and this metamorphosis of the mind
substance was responsible for radiancy in the thought images.

I continued to attend to my household and official duties, gaining more and more strength every day. After a few more weeks
I was able to work attentively for hours with my now transformed mental equipment without feeling any distressing symptoms. But there was no perceptible change in my general outlook
or efficiency, and barring the introduction of this mysterious and
incomprehensible factor into my life, I was the same as before.
Gradually, as my power of endurance developed and moments of
fear grew rarer, I became more reconciled to my apparent abnormality which ceased to engage my attention throughout the day,
and I was left free to occupy myself as I pleased. I was not now
as acutely conscious of the movements of the newly generated
vital current in my spinal cord and other nerve tracks as I had been
before.

In the course of time the passage of the current through the
scattered nervous threads became less perceptible and often I did
not notice it at all. I could now devote myself attentively to any
work for hours. Comparing my later stable mental condition
with what it had been in the initial stages, after the crisis, the
realization came to me that I had escaped from the clutches of
insanity by the narrowest margin and that I owed my deliverance
not to any effort of mine but to the benign disposition of the
energy itself. In the primary stages, particularly before the crisis,
for certain very cogent reasons the vital current appeared to be
acting erratically and blindly like the swollen water of a flooded
stream which, pouring out through a breach in the embankment,

rushes madly here and there trying to scour out a new channel for its passage. Years later I had an inkling of what had actually happened and could guess at the marvel lying hidden in the human body, unsuspected, waiting for the needed invocation from the owner and a favourable opportunity to leap to action, when, ploughing its way through the flesh like the diverted stream in flood, it creates new channels in the nervous system and the brain to endow the fortunate individual with unbelievable mental and spiritual powers.

The six months of that summer spent in Kashmir passed without any remarkable event or noteworthy change in me. The stir caused by my strange indisposition died down gradually. Most of the men who had any knowledge of it attributed my sudden breakdown to mental causes. But as a whisper had gone round in some quarters that my strange distemper was the outcome of yoga practices, intimately connected with Kundalini, the curious came to see me on one pretext or another, trying to elicit further information to assure themselves by the exhibition of some supernatural feat on my part that I had really crossed the boundary which separates the human from the divine. For many of them, the mere awakening of the serpent power meant a precipitate plunge into the supernatural. They were not blameworthy. Most men seem to have the notion that it is but a step from human to cosmic consciousness, a step which one can take all at once with assistance from a teacher or with the aid of spiritual exercises as easily and safely as one crosses a threshold leading from a smaller into a larger room.

This fallacious idea is often bolstered by incompetent guides, trading on the credulity of mankind, who claim knowledge of yoga and ability to bring about positive results in their disciples, themselves utterly unaware of the fact that yoga as a progressive science has been dead for the last hundreds of years and that beyond a few parrot-like recitations from the works of ancient masters they know no more about it than the uninformed whom they profess to teach. In olden days the serious and difficult nature of the task was fully recognized and the aspirants who set about it took full care to divest themselves of all worldly responsibilities and to develop a stoical attitude of mind, prepared to meet all eventualities without flinching or yielding under stress.

To the inquiries directed to gathering more information about my experience for frivolous reasons, I usually turned a deaf ear, maintaining a reserve which has continued to this day. Failing to gain satisfaction for their curiosity and finding no remarkable change in me, the story of my spiritual adventure was treated as a myth, and to some I even became an object of ridicule for having mistaken a physical ailment for a divine dispensation.

At the end of summer I was almost as strong as before. Barring the luminous currents and the radiance in my head, I marked no other change in myself and felt none the worse for my awful adventure save that at certain times, usually in the afternoon, the passage of the current became disturbingly perceptible, accompanied by a slight uneasiness in the head. At such times I usually experienced a difficulty in applying myself attentively to any task and often spent the interval in talking or strolling in the open. Sometimes on such occasions I noticed a greater pressure on the nerve centres in the cardiac and hepatic regions, especially the latter, as if a greater flow of the radiation were being forced into the organ to increase its activity. There was no other indication of anything remarkable or unusual in me. I slept well, ate heartily, and in order to overcome the effects on my body of several months of forced inactivity, took a little exercise to which I had been accustomed since boyhood, avoiding undue strain and exhaustion. But after the hours spent in the office, I felt no inclination to read in the evening, as had been my habit in the past, or to do any mental work. Treating this as a hint from within not to tax the brain any further, I retired usually to my room for relaxation and rest soon after dinner.

Towards the end of October 1939, I made preparations for my departure to Jammu with the office. I felt myself so thoroughly fit for the journey and subsequent sojourn there for six months all by myself that for reasons of her health I left my wife, my one unfailing partner in all my vicissitudes, in Kashmir, confident of my own ability to look after myself. I did not realize at that time that I was taking a grave risk in not having her with me when away from home, that without my knowledge the stormy force released in my body was still as actively at work, and that though I was not acutely cognizant of its movements, the strain on my vital organs was no less heavy than it had been before. The thought that I was in an abnormal state internally was, however, never entirely absent from my mind, for I was reminded of it constantly by the luminosity within. But as time wore on and the condition remained constant it lost for me much of its strangeness and unnaturalness, becoming, as it were, a part of my being, my usual and normal state.

Chapter Nine

In view of the immense significance of the regenerative and transformative processes at work in my body, especially during sleep, which ultimately resulted in the development of psychic gifts, never possessed by me until the age of over forty-six, it is necessary to dwell on this most important phase of my singular experience. Not only the ancient treatises on Yoga but numerous other spiritual texts of India contain references to the miraculous power of Shakti, or feminine cosmic energy, to bring about transformations in her devotees. The famous Gayatri Mantra, which every Brahmin must recite daily after his morning ablutions, is an invocation to Kundalini to grant transcendence. The sacred thread worn by the Hindus, consisting generally of three or six separate threads held together by a knot, is symbolic of the three well-known channels of vital energy, Ida, Pingala and Sushumna, passing through the centre and on either side of the spinal cord. The tuft of hair on the top of the head usually worn by men indicates the location of the inoperative conscious centre in the brain which opens like a lotus in bloom when watered by the ambrosial current rising through Sushumna and functions as the seat of supersensible perception, the sixth sense or the third eye in those divinely favoured by Kundalini.

The obviously unambiguous references to her creative and transformative prowess, contained in the hymns composed in praise of the goddess by renowned sages and great spiritual teachers, venerated almost like gods and in most cases, if their own avowals are to be believed, themselves the beneficiaries of her grace, cannot be dismissed lightly as mere poetic effusions devoid of any material foundation. Considering also the fact that the results attained by the masters formed subjects for experiment and verification by their disciples, who had, therefore, necessarily to gauge their correctness, the assertions cannot be treated either as mere metaphors, intended to convey some other meaning, or as crude exaggerations of trivial achievements. In any case it is on the universal acceptance of the truth of these ancient beliefs in India that all the systems of Yoga and the massive structure of Vedic religion have been built, with a foundation so deeply laid that they have come to be an integral part of every religious act and ceremony of a Hindu. Consequently the average worshipper of Kali, Durga, Shiva or Vishnu, when prostrate before the image of his deity with tearful eyes and lips quivering with emotion, implores the boon of not only worldly favours but also of super-physical attributes to enable him to look behind the veil of illusory appearances.

If the historic record extending to more than thirty centuries as embodied in the Vedas and other spiritual texts is to be relied upon and credence lent to the unquestionable testimony of scores of clever investigators and shrewd observers, the ancient society of Indo-Aryans abounded with numerous genuine instances of transfiguration by means of spiritual strivings and Yoga, resulting in the complete metamorphosis of personality as a result of which individuals of a common calibre were transformed into visionaries of extraordinary attainments by the touch of an invisible power which they recognized and worshipped with appropriate ceremony. In fact one of the basic tenets of Hindu religion and the archstone of the science of yoga is the belief, emphatically upheld by almost every scripture, that by properly directed effort it is possible for a man to complete the evolutionary cycle of human existence in one life and blossom into a transfigured adept in tune with the infinite Reality beyond the phenomenal world, forever released from the otherwise endless chain of births and deaths.

In addition to cases of spontaneous transformation brought about suddenly or by slow degrees in mystics and saints, ancient or modern, both in the East and West, and supported by unimpeachable evidence which confronts modern science with an enigma as insoluble now as it was in mediæval times, there are also authentic instances where a definite alteration of personality has occurred as a result of yoga or other form of spiritual effort, undertaken deliberately and continued for some time, resulting ultimately in the sudden or slow development of abnormal psychic faculties and extraordinary mental attributes not visible before. What is the mystery behind this oft-repeated and generally accepted phenomenon? What force, spiritual, psychical or physical, is set into motion automatically or by voluntary striving, which, working mysteriously according to its own inscrutable laws, brings about a radical change in the organism, moulding it into a distinct type with certain common characteristics that have distinguished mystics and seers of all ages and climes?

Not only in India but in almost all the countries professing a revealed faith, the belief in the efficacy of worship, prayer, and other religious practices to induce a mental condition favourable to the dispensation of divine grace has been current from time immemorial, and the transformation occurring in consequence of such practices is, therefore, naturally attributed to divine favour. It must be remembered however, that a hasty recourse to supernatural agencies to account for any obscure phenomenon not explicable by the intellect has been a marked feature of man's existence from the earliest stage of his development as a rational being, and is almost as common now in the lower strata of any society as it was in pre-historic times. The habit is still there in the majority of mankind, though its operation has been somewhat restricted owing to the explanations furnished by science for many previously obscure phenomena of nature.

To bring in divinity for the explanation of isolated phenomena, when its perpetual suzerainty over the whole universe and its position as the primordial cause of all existence is recognized, is an inconsistency of which seasoned intellects should not be guilty. When viewed in the light of such recognition, neither a leaf can stir nor an atom move nor a raindrop descend nor any creature breathe without divine providence; the inconsistency lies in furnishing rational explanations for some of the problems and invoking a supermundane agency for the rest. To the great sorrow of mankind this has always been done in respect of matters temporal on the one hand and spiritual on the other. It has to be admitted that matter and spirit are radically different, perhaps diametrically opposite propositions, and that, therefore, what is true of one may not be true of the other; but that can only serve as a sound reason for employing different methods of approach to the problems presented by each, and not for denying to one what we concede to the other when the two owe their origin to the same eternal cause. The existence of extraordinary intellectual talent in some and less in others or of spiritual and psychic gifts in a few and none in the rest should not, therefore, be attributed to divine intervention; there can be no pampered favourites in the just hierarchy of heaven. But as in the case of material phenomena, the variations from the rule, repeatedly observed, should act as a spur to goad the intellect to the investigation of the problems presented by the extraordinary achievements of men of genius on the one hand and the amazing performances of men of vision on the other.

Working from this angle the first effort of any investigator should be directed towards ascertaining the degree of relationship between the body and the mind to determine whether the conditions and actions of the former invariably affect the latter and vice versa, or if each functions completely or partially as an independent unit. Only a moment's thought is enough to convince even the least intelligent that the body and mind are indissolubly bound to each other from birth to death, each exerting a tremendous influence over the other at every moment of their joint existence to such an extent that many keen observers are sharply divided on the issue as to whether mind is the product of the biochemical reactions of the body or the latter is the result of the ideative processes of the mind. One is astounded at the depth of knowledge and the keenness of intellect displayed on either side but neither group has been able to win the other completely to its view. For the purpose of our point it is enough to say that body and mind are mutually dependent and responsive to such an amazing extent that not an eyelid flickers nor does a muscle move nor an artery throb without the knowledge of the mind, and similarly not a memory stirs, nor does a thought strike, nor an idea occur without causing a reaction in the body. The effect of disease, of organic changes in the tissues, of exhaustion, of diet, of medicine, of intoxicants and narcotics on the mind, and of pleasure and pain, sorrow and suffering, emotion and passion, fear and anxiety on the body is too well known to need mention. The close connection between the two may with justice be likened to that existing between a mirror and the object reflected in it. The least change in the object is instantaneously reflected by the mirror and conversely any change in the reflection denotes a corresponding change in the object also.

In all temporal affairs affecting an individual at every moment of his existence, the correlationship and interdependence of the gross body and the ethereal mind is recognized and accepted without question; but strangely enough when dealing with spiritual matters this obviously unalterable rule determining the relationship of the two in the physical world is inexplicably lost sight of. Even eminent scholars, when discussing psychic phenomena of the most extraordinary kind, argue in a manner as if the corporeal frame which faithfully follows the law during their joint pilgrimage on the physical plane has no place in the picture from the moment of entry into the spiritual realms. Even after making full allowance for the miracles performed by them, the life stories of known saints, mystics, and prophets make it undeniably clear that the inviolable biological laws were almost as effective in their case as they are in the case of other human beings, and that they were as prone to hunger, thirst, and fatigue and as easy a prey to disease, senescence, and death as the other ordinary men of their time. Not one of them survived for a remarkably longer span of time than that normally allotted to mortals, say a few dozen years, to demonstrate conclusively the victory of spirit over flesh, nor did any of them completely conquer hunger, thirst and sleep or radically alter the predisposition of the body to age, disease, and decay. Most of them undoubtedly furnish unique examples of unparalleled courage and fortitude in adversity, extraordinary loftiness of character, unflinching adherence to truth, and other laudable virtues; but so far as this aspect of their existence is concerned, the histories of all nations contain numerous parallels in other departments of human endeavour in politics and war, art and literature, philosophy and science, discovery and invention, travel and adventure, even in robbery and piracy, of normal men and women who exhibited in an almost equally outstanding manner some or many of the noble traits characterizing the men of vision, without ever attempting to trace their sterling qualities to any supernatural agency or exceptional divine favour.

One can easily cite countless instances of the dominance of spirit over the frailties of flesh true of any nation and relating to any period of history. They are encountered daily, particularly in the humbler sectors of societies. Hence it would be a fallacy to assert that they are an exclusive feature of spirituality in the ordinary connotation of the term or that their occurrence in any way alters or nullifies the operation of the otherwise inviolable biological laws regulating the relation between the body and the mind. When even the flicker of a thought or the momentary sway of passion has a perceptible reaction on the body or a clearly noticeable effect on any particular organ, it is inconceivable that such abnormal and extraordinary states of mind associated with spiritual phenomena as are involved in the beholding of presences, hearing of unearthly voices, contemplation of enrapturing or awe-inspiring visions, entrancement and ecstasy, or any other form of psychical activity should not exhibit a corresponding physiological reaction in the body. It has been observed that at the time of psychic manifestations or physical phenomena in mystics or mediums, signs of faintness, partial or complete insensibility to surroundings, convulsive movements, and other symptoms of organic disturbance are frequently present. This fact alone should provide sufficient cause for questioning the attitude of those who accept the existence of the phenomena as a matter of course, as a perfectly legitimate activity of the mind alone, beyond the pale of organic laws, as also of those who as readily and as complacently deny their occurrence. It has become a common habit when dealing with abnormal manifestations of the mind to overlook the body and to treat such phenomena as more or less freakish occurrences, not amenable to ordinary biological laws.

In all probability there is a basic misconception owing to a wrong interpretation of religious doctrine or proceeding from superstitions, which allots to the cognitive faculty in man an entirely independent status utterly divorced from the body in respect to its supersensory and superphysical activity. It is under the influence of such erroneous premises that not infrequently even erudite men lend their support to dogmas crediting the human mind with unlimited powers even to the extent of comprehending the ultimate reality behind the visible universe, in its entirety or providing a suitable vehicle for its incarnation in human form. Bearing in mind the stupendous extent of the universe, the conception of the Creator becomes so staggering that it is utterly beyond the capacity of the human brain. Even the developed consciousness of an ecstatic, though itself an indestructible universal substance risen above the sense-bound human intellect, is utterly incapable of apprehending the real nature of its immeasurable source. Hence even in the highest condition of superconscious flight the most which renowned mystics have been able to say is too fragmentary and vague to justify the conclusion that what they perceived through supersensory channels was the reality in itself, and not merely a slightly brighter radiation from an extremely distant, unimaginable, conscious Sun, a closer proximity to which would mean instantaneous destruction of a frail receptive instrument like the human body, incapable of sustaining at its present stage of evolution anything but the tiniest measure of vital energy streaming everywhere through the Universe in incalculable abundance from that inexhaustible source.

Speaking more clearly, the transcendental state may be nothing more than a fleeting glimpse of a tiny fragment of the superconscious world illumined by the rays of a stupendous unvisualizable sun in the same manner as with our normal vision we see but a tiny portion of the gigantic physical universe around us. Since body is the vehicle and mind the product of the radiation filtering through it, animating its countless cells like a living electric current, vivifying the sensitive brain matter to a far greater pitch of vital activity than any other region, the whole machine can exhibit only a limited range of consciousness depending on the capacity of the brain and the efficiency of the various organs and parts composing it.

Because of the drastic restrictions laid on his sensual equipment and the extremely narrow bounds of his mental orbit, the average man, never in his life brought into contact with a state of consciousness distinctly superior to his own, is utterly unable to form even dimly a conception of a deathless, incorporeal conscious Energy of infinite volume, penetrative power, and mobility, able to act simultaneously in millions upon millions of living objects all over the earth, to say nothing of the unimaginably vast creation in other parts of the universe, to whose invisible activity he owes his own existence. The main stumbling block in the visualization of even a slightly higher plane of consciousness is the normally unalterable and limited capacity of the human brain, which in each individual is able to utilize only a specific quantity of life energy for the activity of the body and the mind. There is no known method by which the brain of a normal man can be made to overstep the boundaries set to it by nature, though it can be improved and sharpened with application and study, and made to accommodate more information and assimilate more facts, but with the exception of gifted individuals fashioned in a slightly different form, it cannot be made to transcend the limits of the native state of consciousness exhibited by it and to step into the next higher stratum, able to perceive what was imperceptible and to know what was unknowable before the transition.

The question to be answered is whether this transition from one sphere of consciousness to another can be effected and whether there are any authentic instances of it during recent times. The answer to the first part of the question is an emphatic 'yes'. The whole armoury of every system of Yoga, of every occult creed and of every esoteric religious doctrine is directed to this end. The only shortcoming, which makes the claim appear absurd and

fantastic to a strictly scientific mind, is that the biological process
by which the change can be brought about has not been explained
or probably even thought of under the false notion, already discussed, that the human mind can win entry to supersensory
realms without affecting the body in any way. Almost all the
methods in use from time immemorial for gaining visionary
experience or supersensory perception—concentration, breathing
exercises, postures, prayer, fasting, asceticism and the like—affect
both the organic frame and the mind. It is, therefore, but reasonable to suppose that any change brought about by their means in
the sphere of thought must also be preceded by alterations in the
chemistry of the body.

The ancient authorities on Yoga, though aware of the important role played by the physical organism in developing supersensory channels of cognition and fully conversant with the methods
for diverting its energies in this direction, were far more
interested in the spiritual than in the physical side of the science,
attached little significance to the biological changes occurring in
the flesh as compared to the resulting momentous developments
in the realm of mind. The general level of knowledge in those
days and the tendencies of the time also precluded the possibility
of such an investigation. Even the advocates of Kundalini Yoga,
starting with the discipline and purification of internal organs,
have failed to give that status to the corporeal frame as the sole
channel for success in Yoga, leading to transcendence, as it
deserved.

From the very nature of the exercises and the discipline enjoined, it should, however, be obvious even to the least informed
that the pivot round which the whole system revolved was the
living organism and it was to bring it to the required degree of
fitness that the initiates devoted precious years of their lives to the
acquirement of proficiency in maintaining difficult postures, in
the art of cleaning the colon, the stomach, the nasal passages and
the throat, in holding the breath almost to the point of asphyxia-
tion, and in other extremely hard, even dangerous, practices. In
the light of the facts mentioned in this volume, it is not difficult
to see that they are all indicative not only of a sustained en-

deavour to purify and regulate the system in order to adjust it to the heightened state of perception, but also of a preliminary arduous preparation of the body to bear safely a possible shock or excessive strain on the bursting of the vital storm in it, released to effect drastic organic changes, extending over years, and ending in death or immortality or only bitter disappointment at the close of a life spent in ceaseless striving and self-denial. It is, however, abundantly clear that all the exercises were directed towards the manipulation of a definite organic control-system in the body capable of bringing about the earnestly desired consummation by mysterious means even less understood now than they were in olden days.

Commentary to Chapters Seven, Eight and Nine

In Chapter Seven, the text takes up *prana* again, this time more metaphysically. In Chapter Eight, we come to another of the traditional problems associated with mystical experiences and that is the question of *secrecy*. Our author was strongly moved not to tell anyone of what he was going through, not even his wife. Again, this rigid secrecy is typical of one in the throes of a paranoid delusion. To open the secret is in a sense what we call 'reality testing'. If it were laughed at, argued away, diagnosed as sick, a whole world would collapse. But more, there is something in the nature of mystical experiences that demands secrecy, as if the archetype behind the events which are in process needs a certain tension in order for it to be fulfilled. The alchemists envisioned this secrecy in their image of the closed vessel. In many fairy tales the hero or heroine is ordered not to say anything until the ordeal is over. In the Greek religious mysteries the participants were threatened with death if they told what happened. Initiation rites also require sworn secrecy. Secrecy intensifies, allowing what is coming to fruition to swell and grow in silence so that later it can be brought forth and shown. Secrecy is the ground of revelation, making revelation possible; what happens

secretly in the wings, behind the scenes, makes possible the drama
when the curtains open and the lights go up. The urge to withhold
and keep back is part of being witness to the uncanny. What to
hold back, when to tell, whom to tell, how to tell, these questions
fraught with peril lie along the razor's edge between deluded
paranoid isolation and individual strength, between arrogant
private esotericism and uncertain loneliness of silence. Secrecy, as
well, gives individuality; what everybody knows is no longer
individual. Without our individual secrets we are only public
ciphers.

He tells us in Chapter Eight that 'at night I found myself looking with dread at horribly disfigured faces and distorted forms
bending and twisting into awful shapes. . . . They left me trembling with fear, unable to account for their presence.' The encounter with distorted human figures in a night-world seems another
authentic necessity. It is evidently so important that Homer,
Virgil and Dante describe similar phenomena in the descent into
Hades of their heroes. It is part of their journey. We find parallels
in analysis. After a certain integration has taken place, there sometimes occur dreams of a hospital ward with ill and maimed, or a
large photo of all the family members that oppresses the dreamer
thereafter for days, or one's early school class, or club, appear *en
masse* in the analyst's waiting-room. These shades too need transformation; they are parts that have not been redeemed despite the
integration achieved by the conscious personality and its ego.
Especially tormented in the Underworld are the unburied dead,
those configurations passed away or repressed out of awareness
but still not over and done with, hauntingly lingering at the
threshold. The manifestation of these 'awful shapes' reminds
heroic consciousness that there are still shadows in the cave even
if one has seen the light oneself. The psyche is separable; even if
'I' have moved, there are some tormented 'me's' left behind in
hell. In Greek thought the souls in Hades were regarded as moist,
preponderating in the wet element of generation; life-giving
moisture. Our author says these faces and figures eddied and
swirled using the language of water for their motions. Perhaps
these parts had not yet been through the cooking process, not yet

been volatilized, and so they may herald a new descent into hell's torment and drying fires.

At this time he notes that the 'current' seemed to have as its aim the *liver*. The liver has always been an important symbol in occult physiology. As the largest organ, the one containing the most blood, it was regarded as the darkest, least penetrable part of man's innards. Thus it was considered to contain the secret of fate and was used for fortune-telling. In Plato, and in later physiology, the liver represented the darkest passions, particularly the bloody, smoky ones of wrath, jealousy, and greed which drive men to action. Thus the liver meant the impulsive attachment to life itself. From this angle, the renewed interest in the liver by our author could predict a revivification of general activity.

But if the currents that run towards the liver (and heart, too) indicate emotional activity, what about the pull downward of the shapes in hell? The two tendencies—downward to the disfigured night-world and outward into activity—are not as contradictory as they seem. In neoplatonic thought the moist souls are precisely those which are still involved with the generative principle, the life-cycle of binding kleshas. The souls in Hades want blood and eat red-coloured food, i.e. they hunger for life. The activation of the liver may thus be seen as a movement towards feeding distorted fragments of unlived life that still longed to live, but which in the long run of any Indian spiritual discipline must be yoked to the single aim of 'pure cognition'.

Chapter Ten

I RETURNED to Jammu in a cheerful frame of mind, restored almost to my normal physical and mental health. The fear of the supernatural and antipathy towards religion that had been constantly present during the first few months had partially disappeared. I could not for a long time account for this sudden revulsion of what had been a deep-rooted feeling in me and even during the days of acute disturbance was surprised at this change in myself. It was not only because my irrepressible desire for religious experience had landed me in an awful predicament that I felt the fear and the aversion, but there seemed to have actually occurred an inexplicable alteration in the very depths of my personality, for which I was at a loss to assign a reason.

Devout and God-fearing until my abnormal condition, I had lost all feelings of love and veneration for the divine, all respect for the sacred and the holy, and all interest in the scriptural and sacramental. The very idea of the supernatural had become hateful and I did not allow my thoughts to dwell on it even for a moment. From a devotee I became an inveterate enemy of faith and felt seething resentment against those whom I saw going to or coming from places of worship. I had changed entirely, devoid completely of every religious sentiment, turned into a rank atheist, a violent heretic, the very antithesis of the religious and the spiritual.

In the early stages, desperately engaged in a neck and neck race, with death on one side and insanity on the other, I had neither the time nor the mental disposition to think seriously about this sudden disappearance of a powerful impulse which had dominated my thought from a very early age. As my mind grew clearer I wondered more and more at this quite unexpected alteration. When on the restoration of my general health, particularly the feelings of love, the distaste for the supernatural still persisted and I found myself empty of religious desire, as if washed clean of it, I became uneasy at the thought that it might not be Kundalini, considered to be the inexhaustible fount of divine love and the perennial source of spirituality, which was active in me, but some evil force of darkness dragging me towards the depths of irreligiosity and impiety. At such times the words of the Brahmin sadhu whom I had consulted during the preceding winter in a state of desperation always came back with an ominous significance. He had said slowly, emphasizing every word to make it sink deep into my terribly agitated mind, that the symptoms I had mentioned could in no way be attributed to Kundalini, the ocean of bliss, as she could never be associated with anything in the nature of pain or disturbance, and that my malady was most probably due to the vicious influence of some evilly disposed elemental spirit. I had been horrified at the words, which, spoken with certainty to a man fighting desperately with madness, spelled death for any spark of hope left in him; and they often came back to me in the darkest moments to shut out the last glimmer of reason still struggling for existence. With sanity restored, but still strangely altered by a strongly marked characteristic, the idea recurred with overwhelming force to harass me when I failed to find a satisfactory explanation for the change.

Shortly before coming to Jammu I had begun to feel vaguely the dim stirrings of the apparently dead impulse. This happened usually in the early hours of morning, immediately on awakening from sleep, as if the refreshed state of the brain afforded an opportunity to the vanished urge to make a shadowy appearance for a brief interval. At such moments my thoughts usually dwelt on the life stories of certain mystics whose utterances had once made a powerful appeal to me. I had wholly forgotten them during the preceding months and when recalled by accident the remembrance failed to evoke any warmth. I usually turned my thoughts to other things to avoid thinking of them. Now their memory returned as of old for a moment, the sweetness tinctured with a certain bitterness, for they had said nothing clearly of the dread ordeal which they too must have gone through in one form or another, nothing about the dangers and pitfalls of the path which they too must have travelled and which must be common to reach a goal open to all. But if they had suffered as I did or even a fraction of it, and come out of the tribulation to compose inspiring rhymes which had captivated my heart at the very first hearing, they were indeed worthy of the greatest homage, far above and beyond a man like me, shaken and shattered by the same ordeal.

A few weeks after my arrival in Jammu I noticed that the gap was quickly filling and that my religious ideas, sentiments, and memories were all reviving rapidly. I felt again the same deep urge for religious experience and the same all-absorbing interest in the supernatural and the mystical. I could again sit all by myself brooding on the yet unanswered problem of being and the riddle of my own existence or listen to devotional songs and mystical poetry with undiminished rapture from the start to finish without the least sign of disturbance or any symptoms of haunting terror. When it happened, the overhanging cloud of a malevolent spirit leading me towards degradation disappeared and my heart expanded in gratitude to the mysterious power working in me. It was only now that I really began to recognize myself, the being who about a year before had sat cross-legged in meditation, bent on invoking the supersensible, little knowing in his ignorance that the average human frame of today, emasculated by a faulty civilization and enervated by uncontrolled ambitions and desires, is not strong enough to bear the splendour of the mighty vision without long preparatory training, austerity, and discipline.

Slowly it began to dawn upon me that the torture I suffered in the beginning was caused by the unexpected release of the powerful vital energy through a wrong nerve, *pingala*, and that the hot blast coursing through my nerve and brain cells would have undoubtedly led to death but for the miraculous intervention at the last minute. Later on, my suffering was probably due, firstly, to the damage already sustained by my nervous system; secondly, to the fact that I was entirely uninitiated into the mystery; and thirdly and mainly, to the circumstance that my body, though above the average in muscular strength, was not sufficiently developed internally to withstand with impunity the sudden onrush of a much more dynamic and potent life energy than that to which the average human body is normally accustomed. I had experienced enough to realize that this powerful vital force, once let loose even by accident, cannot be restrained from carrying one onward and upward towards a higher and more penetrating consciousness for which it is the one and the only instrument. The awakening of Kundalini, it seemed to me, implied the introduction into the human body of a higher form of nerve force by the constant sublimation of the human seed, leading ultimately to the radiant transcendental consciousness aglow ever after in the transformed brain of successful initiates.

I speculated in this manner without being sure about the correctness of my surmises. I had undergone a singular experience, but how could I be sure that I was not the victim of an abnormal pathological condition, peculiar to me alone? How could I be sure that I was not suffering from a continuous hallucinatory affliction in this particular respect while normal in other ways, the unexpected result, in my case, of prolonged concentration and too much absorption in the occult? If I had within reach a recorded experience even distantly similar to mine or a really competent teacher to guide me, my doubts would have been resolved then and there, by which the whole course of my life might have been different and I might have been saved another equally long and equally awful period of agony, as the one I had just come through.

As I still failed to notice the development of any extraordinary talent or supernormal faculty, I continued to be tormented by serious doubts about the actual nature of the abnormality of which I was the victim. The ever-present radiation, bathing my head with lustre and glowing along the path of countless nerves in the body, streaming here and there in a most wonderful and sometimes awe-inspiring manner, had little in common with the effulgent visions described by yogis and mystics. Beyond the spectacle of a luminous circle around the head, which was now constant in me, and an extended consciousness, I felt and saw nothing extraordinary in the least approaching the supernatural, but for all practical purposes was the same man that I had always been. The only difference was that I now saw the world reflected in a larger mental mirror. It is extremely difficult for me to express adequately this change in my cognitive apparatus. The best I can do is to say that it appeared as if an enlarged picture of the world was now being formed in the mind, not enlarged in the sense of magnification by a microscope, but as if the world image was now presented by a wider conscious surface than before. In other words, the knowing self appeared to have acquired distinctly extended proportions.

It was at an early stage that I had become conscious of this inexplicable alteration. At that time I was not in a condition to give it serious thought and took it for granted that the change was brought about by the luminous vapour streaming into my brain. As already mentioned, the dimensions of the shining mist in my head varied constantly, causing a widening and shrinking of consciousness. This rapid alteration in the perceptive mirror, accompanied by an ever-present sense of deadening fear, had been the first acutely distressing and completely bewildering feature of my uncanny experience. As time wore on, the extension became more and more apparent, with less frequent contractions, but even in the narrowest state of perception, my consciousness was wider than before. I could not fail to mark this startling alteration in myself as it occurred abruptly, carrying me from one conscious state to another almost overnight. If the transition had taken place gradually, without the other accompanying factors like the radiating spinal currents and the extraordinary sensations that made the whole phenomenon so striking and bizarre, I might not have noticed the extension at all, as one does not notice the extremely slight daily changes in one's own face which immediately strike a friend after a long separation.

As the alteration in the state of my consciousness is the most important feature of my experience to which I wish to draw attention, having far-reaching results, it is necessary to say more about this extraordinary development, which for a long time I considered to be an abnormality or delusion. The state of exalted and extended consciousness, permeated with an inexpressible, supermundane happiness which I experienced on the first appearance of the serpent fire in me, was an internal phenomenon, subjective in nature, indicating an expansion of the field of awareness, or the cognitive self, formless, invisible, and infinitely subtle, the observer in the body, always beyond scrutiny, impossible to delineate or depict. From a unit of consciousness, dominated by the ego, to which I was habituated from childhood, I expanded all at once into a glowing conscious circle, growing larger and larger, until a maximum was reached, the 'I' remaining as it was, but instead of a confining unit, now itself encompassed by a shining conscious globe of vast dimensions. For want of a better simile, I should say that from a tiny glow the awareness in me became a large radiating pool of light, the 'I' immersed in it yet fully cognizant of the radiantly blissful volume of consciousness all around, both near and far. Speaking more precisely, there was ego consciousness as well as a vastly extended field of awareness, existing side by side, both distinct yet one.

This remarkable phenomenon, indelibly imprinted upon my memory, as vivid when recalled today as at the time of occurrence, was never repeated in all its original splendour until long after. During the following agonizing weeks and months there was absolutely no resemblance between my initial experience and the subsequent extremely disquieting mental condition, beyond the fact that I was painfully aware that an expansion had somehow taken place in the original area of my consciousness subject frequently to partial contractions.

At the time of my coming to Jammu I had gained my equilibrium of mind and soon after was restored fully to myself, with all my individual traits and peculiarities. But the unmistakable

alteration in my cognitive faculty, which I had noticed for some
time and of which I was constantly reminded when contemplating
an external object or an internal mental image, underwent no
modification except that with the passage of time the luminous
circle in my head grew larger and larger by imperceptible degrees,
with a corresponding increase in the area of consciousness. It was
certain that I was now looking at the universe with a perceptibly
enlarged mental surface and that, in consequence, the world
image which I perceived was reflected by a larger surface than
that provided by my mind during all the years from my childhood
to the time of the ecstatic vision. The area of my peripheral
consciousness had undeniably increased, for I could not be mistaken about a fact continually in front of me during waking
hours.

The phenomenon was so strange and so out of the ordinary
that I felt convinced that it would be useless on my part to look
for a parallel case, even if the weird transformation was because
of the action of an awakened Kundalini and not a unique abnormality affecting me only. Realising also the futility of revealing
this entirely out-of-the-common and unheard-of development to
others, I kept my secret strictly to myself, saying nothing of it
even to those most intimately connected with me. As my physical
and mental condition gave me no cause for uneasiness in any
respect, except for this inexplicable peculiarity, I gradually ceased
to trouble myself about it.

As already mentioned in an earlier chapter, in the initial stages
of my experience it appeared as if I were viewing the world
through a mental haze, or to be more clear, as if a thin layer of
extremely fine dust hung between me and the objects perceived.
It was not an optical defect, as my eyesight was as sharp as ever
and the haze seemed to envelop not the sensual but the perceptive
organ. The dust was on the conscious mirror which reflected the
image of the objects. It seemed as if the objects seen were being
viewed through a whitish medium, which made them look as if
an extremely fine and uniform coat of chalk dust were laid on
them without in the least blurring the outline or the normal
colour peculiar to each. The coat hung between me and the sky,

the branches and leaves of trees, the green grass, the houses, the paved streets, the dress and faces of men, lending to all a chalky appearance, precisely as if the conscious centre in me, which interpreted sensory impressions, were now operating through a white medium, needing further refinement and cleaning to make it perfectly transparent.

As in the case of enlargement of the visual image, I was entirely at a loss to assign a satisfactory reason for this whitish appearance of the objects perceived. Any change of time, place, or weather had absolutely no effect on the transformation. It was as apparent under lamplight as in the sun, as noticeable in the clear light of morning as at dusk. Obviously the change was internal and not subject to alteration by changed external influences. Surprised, yet mute, I continued to pass my days and nights at Jammu attending to my duties and minding my tasks as others were doing. The only plausible reason for this change in my cognitive faculty which I could think of was that the animating principle inhabiting the body was now operating the mechanism through an altered vital medium. This led to an alteration in the quality and behaviour of the nerve currents regulating the functions of the organs as well as in the quality of the sensory impressions and their interpretations by the observing mind. But all that had happened and was still happening was so unprecedented and incredible that I felt easier in mind in treating it all as an abnormality rather than as a natural growth governed by regular biological laws which ultimately it indeed proved to be.

In this manner a prey to doubts and uneasiness I continued to pass my time until one sunny day, when on my way to the office, I happened to look at the front block of the Rajgarh Palace, in which the Government offices were located, taking in my glance the sky as well as the roof and the upper part of the building. I looked casually at first, then struck by something strange in their appearance, more attentively, unable to withdraw my gaze, and finally rooted to the spot I stared in amazement at the spectacle, unable to believe the testimony of my eyes. I was looking at a scene familiar to me in one way before the experience and in another during the last few months, but what I now saw was so

extraordinary as to render me motionless with surprise. I was
looking at a scene belonging not to the earth but to some fairyland,
for the ancient, weather-stained front of the building, unadorned
and commonplace, and the arch of sky above it, bathed in the
clear light of the sun, were both lit with a brilliant silvery lustre
that lent a beauty and a glory to both and created a marvellous
light and shade effect impossible to describe. Wonderstruck, I
turned my eyes in other directions, fascinated by the silvery shine
which glorified everything. Clearly I was witnessing a new phase
in my development; the lustre which I perceived on every side
and in all objects did not emanate from them but was undoubtedly
a projection of my own internal radiance.

Chapter Eleven

ENTIRELY absorbed in the contemplation of the enchanting view, I lost all touch with my surroundings, completely forgetting that I was standing like a statue in the middle of a road thronged at that time of day with crowds of employees going to the Secretariat. Collecting my thoughts, like one suddenly awakened from a beatific vision, I looked around, withdrawing my glance with difficulty from the delightful scene. Many pairs of eyes from the rapidly moving crowd on every side looked at me in surprise, unable to account for my abrupt halt and subsequent immobility. Pulling myself together, I walked leisurely in the direction of the office, keeping my eyes on the building and the portion of the overhanging sky in front of me. Completely unprepared for such a development, I could not bring myself to believe that what I was gazing at was real and not a vision conjured up by my fancy stimulated to greater activity by the intriguing aureole, perceptible to me always around my head. I looked intently in front and around again and again, rubbing my eyes to assure myself that I was not dreaming. No, I was surely in the centre of the Secretariat quadrangle, moving slowly in the midst of a bustling throng hastening in all directions, like them in all other respects except that I was looking at the world with a different vision.

On entering my room, instead of sitting at my desk I walked out on to the verandah at the back, where it was my habit to pass some time daily for a breath of fresh air while looking at the fine view open in front. There was a row of houses before me edged by a steep woody slope leading to the bank of the Tawi river, whose wide boulder-covered bed glistened in the sun with a thin stream of water running in the middle, bordered on the other side by another hillock with a small medieval fortress on top. I had looked at the same sight almost daily in winter for several years and the picture of it was vividly present in my memory. During the past few months, when gazing at it, I found that it too had assumed grander proportions and had the same chalky appearance I had noticed in all other objects. On that memorable day when my eyes swept across the river bed to the hillock and from there to the sky, trying to take the whole panorama in one glance to make a comparison between what I was accustomed to see previously and what I perceived now, I was utterly amazed at the remarkable transformation. The magnified dimensions of the picture and the slightly chalky appearance of the objects were both present, but the dusty haze before my eyes had vanished and instead I was gazing fascinatedly at an extraordinarily rich blend of colour and shade, shining with a silvery lustre which lent an indescribable beauty to the scene.

Breathless with excitement, I turned my eyes in all directions, viewing each object attentively, eager to find whether the transformation was noticeable in all or whether it was an illusion caused by the particularly clear and sunny weather on that day. I looked and looked, allowing my gaze to linger for some time on each spot, convinced more firmly after each intent glance that far from being the victim of an optical illusion, I was seeing a brightly coloured real scene before me, shining with a milky lustre never before perceived. A surge of emotion too deep for words filled my whole being, and tears gathered in my eyes in spite of myself at the significance of the new development in me. But even in that condition, looking through tears, I could perceive trembling beams of silvery light dancing before my vision, enhancing the radiant beauty of the scene. It was not difficult to understand that, without my being aware of it, an extraordinary change had taken place in the now luminous cognitive centre in my brain and that the fascinating lustre, which I perceived around every object, was not a figment of my fancy nor was it possessed by the objects, but a projection of my own internal radiance.

Days and weeks passed without alteration in the lustrous form of sight. A bright silvery sheen around every object, across the entire field of vision, became a permanent feature of my being. The azure dome of the sky, whenever I happened to glance at it had a purity of colour and a brightness impossible to describe. If I had possessed the same form of sight from my earliest childhood I should not have found anything striking in it, treating it as the usual endowment of every normal man, but the alteration from the previous to the present state was so obvious, so remarkable, and so fascinating that I could not but be immensely moved and surprised by it. Examining myself closely for any other change in my sensual perceptions, I became conscious of the fact that there had occurred an amplification and refining of auditory sensations also, as a result of which the sounds heard possessed now an exotic quality and a distinctiveness that lent to music and melody a greater sweetness and to noise and clamour a more disagreeable harshness. The alteration was not, however, so marked and striking as the change in visual impressions until a few years later. The olfactory, gustatory, and tactile centres as well exhibited a peculiar sensitivity and acuteness, clearly perceptible, but in point of magnitude nothing compared to what had happened with my sight. The phenomenon was observable during darkness, too. At night lamps glowed with a new brilliance while illuminated objects glistened with a peculiar lustre not wholly borrowed from the lamps. In the course of a few weeks, the transformation ceased to cause me wonder or excitement, and gradually I came to treat it as an inseparable part of myself, a normal characteristic of my being. Wherever I went and whatever I did, I was conscious of myself in the new form, cognizant of the radiance within and the lustrous objectivity without. I was changing. The old self was yielding place to a new personality endowed with a brighter, more refined and artistic perceptive equipment, developed from the original one by a strange process of cellular and organic transformation.

Towards the middle of April that year, before leaving for Srinagar, I went to Hardwar with the sacred relics of my departed mother whom, to my sorrow, I had lost during the year preceding the experience. I had been to Hardwar once before on a similar errand after the death of my father. On this occasion all through the journey by rail and during the few days of my stay at Hardwar I was constantly reminded of the marvellous change in me. I travelled by the same route, saw the same stations, towns and sights, until I reached my destination and there also the same quaint streets and buildings, the same Ganges with its swiftly flowing sapphire water, the same bathing places and ghats thronged with pilgrims. They were all as I had seen them last but how different was the picture perceived by me on this occasion; every object now formed a part of a greatly extended field of vision in striking contrast to the previous one, the whole assemblage lit with a glitter like that of freshly fallen snow when the sun shines upon it. After performing the sacred rites, I returned to Jammu, refreshed by the change, more firmly convinced about the new development in me. Soon after, I left for Srinagar with my office as usual.

Years passed. My health and vitality were completely restored. I could read continuously for long periods without fatigue and even indulge in my favourite pastime, chess, demanding close attention for hours. The diet became normal and the only article to remind me of my experience was a cup of milk in the morning and another in the afternoon with a slice of bread. I could not, however, stand a fast with impunity, but if obliged to keep one was not seriously affected by it either. In spite of all these signs of normality, it was easy to perceive that mentally I was not the same old self. The lustre within and without became more and more perceptible with the passage of time. With my inner vision I could distinctly perceive the flow of lucent currents of vital energy through the network of nerves in my body. A living silvery flame with a delicate golden tinge was clearly perceptible in the interior of my brain across the forehead. My thought images were vividly bright, and every object recalled to memory possessed radiance in the same manner as in the concrete form.

My reaction to infection and disease was not, however, normal. In every illness the characteristic symptoms of the ailment, though present, were distinctly milder in nature and usually there was an absence of temperature. The rapidity of the pulse was the main indication of the indisposition, but it was seldom, if ever, accompanied by a corresponding rise in the heat of the body as normally occurs with disease. This peculiarity is as observable now as it was in those days. The only explanation for it that I can think of is that my highly nervous organism does not permit the flow of heated blood to the brain as a measure of safety to avoid injury to the now exceptionally sensitive cerebral matter, and adopts other devices to free the body from infection. I could not stand medication during illness or fasting and invariably resorted to dietetic remedies to get well.

I have said a good deal about the working of my mental equipment during waking hours without making any mention about its condition during sleep. The first time I became aware of an alteration in my dream consciousness was during the night in February 1938 when I passed the crisis, tasting sleep after several weeks of insomnia accompanied by a maddening mental condition. I fell asleep that night wrapped in a mantle of light perceptible in the dreams also. From that day extraordinarily vivid dreams became habitual with me. The bright lustre in my head, always present during wakefulness, continued undiminished during sleep; if anything, more clearly apparent and more active during the night than during the day. The moment I rested my head on the pillow and closed my eyes to invite sleep, the first object to draw my attention was the cranial glow, clearly distinguishable in darkness, not stationary and steady but spreading out and narrowing down like a whirlpool or swirling water in the sun. In the beginning and for many months it appeared as if a piston, working in the spinal tube at the bottom, were throwing up stream after stream of a very lustrous fluid, impalpable but distinctly visible, with such force that I actually felt my whole body shaking with the impact of the current to such an extent as made the bed creak at times.

The dreams were wonderful, and always occurred against a

shining background formed by the widespread luminous glow inside, which lent a strange phosphorescence to the dream images also. Every night during sleep I was transported to a glittering fairyland, where garbed in lustre I glided from place to place, light as a feather. Scene after scene of inexpressible glory unfolded before my vision. The incidents were of the usual character common to dreams. They often lacked coherence and continuity, but although strange, fanciful and fantastic, they possessed a visionary character, surrounded by landscapes of a vastness and magnificence seldom seen in real life. In my dreams I usually experienced a feeling of security and contentment with the absence of anything in the least disturbing or disharmonious, all blended into a sense of peace and happiness, which gave my dream personality a character so unique and alluring that I never missed having ten hours of rest and when distraught or dismayed during the day invariably sought the sanctuary of sleep to rid myself of worry and fear. I had never dreamt such vivid dreams before. They naturally followed the pattern of my new personality, and were woven of the same luminous stuff which formed the texture of my daytime thoughts and fancies. It was clear beyond a doubt that light not only pervaded my peripheral consciousness but had penetrated deep into the recesses of my subconscious being as well.

In course of time the idea began to take root in my mind that the enhanced activity of the radiant current during sleep was an indication of the fact that in some incomprehensible way the opportunity afforded by the passive state of the brain was being utilized for immunizing it and the complicated nerve structures to the action of the newly released dynamic force in place of the former less potent vital energy. But for years I was unable to guess what was happening inside me. I had come across vague statements in some of the ancient writings on Kundalini Yoga hinting at the transformative power of the divine energy. The hints were so obscure and so lacking in detail that I could not grasp how the human organism with an unalterable legacy of numberless hereditary factors stretching back for millions of years by which it is moulded into a certain shape, possessing a certain strictly circumscribed brain power and intelligence, could be rebuilt from within to a far different or higher type of cerebral activity, enabling it to transcend the limits prescribed by nature for it from birth. Taking into account the organic changes involved in a process of this kind, affecting simultaneously all constituents of the body and also the extremely delicate tissues of the brain and nervous system, the task of transformation envisaged in its true significance assumes such colossal proportions as to make it appear almost beyond the bounds of possibility.

But something wholly inexplicable was transpiring inside my body frame, particularly during the long period devoted to sleep, when my inactive will was powerless to cause any interference in the new immensely accelerated anabolic and catabolic processes in the body. That my whole system was functioning in an altered manner, forced to a far higher pitch of metabolic activity under the compulsion of the lustrous, vital, energy racing through my nerves, I realized immediately after the crisis. It was impossible to mistake the increase in the pulse rate and the greater activity of the heart during the first part of the night as well as the sudden undeniable alteration in my digestive and excretory functions. I could not disbelieve the testimony of my own senses for months and years and the evidence of those who surrounded and looked after me, nor can I mistrust the proof furnished by my senses now, as the apparently abnormal metabolic activity which started more than twenty-five years ago continues undiminished to this hour and, from all indications, will continue to the end. It is not necessary for me to array proofs in support of the startling disclosure I am making. That would make this work too lengthy and specialized. But any trained observer who has the least knowledge of physiology can convince himself of the fact in a day after kindling the sacred fire in himself.

The plan of this work does not permit me to describe in detail the constantly occurring physiological reactions and changes to which I was a daily witness, convincing me beyond doubt that my body was undergoing a process of purgation and rejuvenation side by side with some definite purpose entirely beyond my grasp. Otherwise there could be no other reasonable explanation for the feverish and sometimes even frantic activity continuously going on in my interior day and night, except that the organism as a whole was reacting to a new situation created inside by an altered activity of the vital organs, as happens in all pathological conditions to adjust itself to the changed environment within. Undoubtedly the disorder in my body was caused by the rapid passage of the luminous vital energy from cell to cell.

Under the action of a stronger current than that for which it was designed, any man-made mechanism, even a hundredth part as sensitive and intricate as the human frame is, would be wrecked or damaged immediately, but because of certain inherent qualities, developed by the human organism as a means of evolution, the sudden release of the serpent power, provided the blood is healthy and the organs sound, is not attended by fatal results in favourable cases because of safety devices already provided by nature to meet a contingency of this kind in individuals ready for the experience. Even in such cases it is essential that the energy be benignly disposed and that the subject take the necessary precautions to maintain the strength of the body and the balance of the mind during the subsequent period of inexpressibly severe trial. How far I was endowed with a constitution suited for the great ordeal I cannot say, but being an utter stranger to the science, taken unawares without the requisite preliminary course of physical and mental discipline, and a prey to adversity, I was buffeted unceasingly for many years partly because of my ignorance and lack of sufficient strength and partly because of the extreme suddenness and rapidity of the extraordinary development.

After the first most distressing period of trial I found in sleep the supreme healer for my physical and mental suffering during the day. There were unmistakable indications of abnormal activity in the region of Kundalini from the moment of my retiring to sleep until the morning. It was obvious that by some mysterious process the precious secretion of the seminal glands was drawn up into the spinal tube and through the interlinking nerves transferred into a subtle essence, then distributed to the brain and the vital organs, darting across the nerve filaments and the spinal cord to reach them. The suction was applied with such vigour as to be clearly apparent, and sometimes in the early stages with such violence as to cause actual pain to the delicate parts. At such times the ferment caused in the body resembled in effect the last minute frantic effort made for succour when a life is in imminent danger, and I, a dumb and helpless witness to the show, could not help but pass hours of agony thinking of this abnormal development in myself. It was easy to see that the aim of this entirely new and unexpected activity was to divert the seminal essence to the head and other vital organs, after sublimation, apparently to meet a contingency caused by a sudden disorder in any organ or a general discord inimical to the new development.

With the power of observation left to me even in the initial distraught condition of the mind, I could not fail to take notice of such a startling development in the sexual region functioning quite normally until that time. I could not fail to mark the agitated condition of the hitherto quiescent area now in a state of feverish activity and ceaseless movement as if forced by an invisible but effective mechanism, not in operation before, to produce the life fluid in superabundance without cessation, in order to meet the unending demand of the cerebral lobes and the nervous system. After only a few days of observation of this unmistakable organic phenomenon the idea dawned on me that I had unwittingly forced open a yet imperfectly developed centre in the brain by the long-continued practice of concentration, and that the abnormal and apparently chaotic play of vital currents which I clearly felt was a natural effort of the organism to control the serious situation thus created. It was also apparent that in this grave emergency the body was making abundant use of the richest and most potent source of life energy in it, the vital essence, always available in the region commanded by Kundalini.

I make but a simple statement of fact when I say that for years I was like one bound hand and foot to a log racing madly on a torrent, saved miraculously time after time from dashing to death against the many boulders projecting out of the swirling water on every side by just a narrow margin and in the nick of time, turning and twisting this way and that, as if guided by a marvellously quick and dexterous hand, infallibly correct in its movement. Often at night for years, when lying awake in bed waiting for sleep to come, I felt the powerful new life energy sweep like a tempest in the abdominal and thoracic regions as well as the brain with a roaring noise in the ears, a scintillating shower in the brain, and a feverish movement in the sexual region and its neighbourhood around the base of the spine, both in front and behind, as if an all-out effort were being made to fight an emergency caused by some poison or obstruction in the organism threatening the supersensitive and extremely delicate condition of the cerebrospinal system.

At such times I felt instinctively that a life and death struggle was going on inside me in which I, the owner of the body, was entirely powerless to take part, forced to lie quietly and watch as a spectator the weird drama unfolded in my own flesh. Nothing can convey my condition more graphically than the representation of Shiva and Shakti, pictured by an ancient master, in which the former is shown lying helpless and supine while the latter in an absolutely reckless mood dances gleefully on his prostrate frame. The self-conscious observer in me, the self-styled possessor of the carnal frame, now completely subjugated and pushed into the background, found himself utterly at the mercy, literally under the feet, of an awe-inspiring power indifferent to what he thought and felt, proceeding impassively to deal with the body as it chose without even conceding to him the right to know what he had done to merit the indignity. I had every reason to believe the representation was designed to depict a condition exactly similar to mine by an initiate who had himself passed through the same ordeal.

The utter helplessness of the devotee and his entire dependence on the mercy and grace of the cosmic vital energy, Shakti, when Kundalini is aroused, is the constant theme of hymns addressed to the goddess by eminent yogis of yore. As the supreme mistress of the body, she and she alone is considered to be competent to bestow on earnest aspirants (who worship her with true devotion, centring their thoughts and actions in her, resigning themselves entirely to her will) the much coveted and hard-to-attain boon of transcendental knowledge and super-normal psychic powers. All these writings assign to Kundalini the supreme position of being the queen and architect of the living organism, having the power to mould it, transform it, or even to destroy it as she will. But how she manages to do it, consistent with biological laws governing the organic world, no one has tried to state in explicit terms. Certainly it could not be done instantaneously, like a magical feat, setting at naught the law of causality in this one particular respect. In my opinion it is more reasonable to assume that even in those cases in which apparently a sudden spiritual development takes place there must occur gradual changes in the cells and tissues of the body for a sufficiently long period, perhaps even from the embryonic stage or early childhood, without the individuals ever coming to know what was happening in their own interior.

Commentary to Chapters Ten and Eleven

After the experience had calmed and his life returned to regularity, our author notes two remaining difficulties: he cannot read attentively for longer periods and he 'continued to have a fear of the supernatural'. In Chapter Ten he takes up this religious problem.

From the narrowly psycho-dynamic view, this *fear of the supernatural* is the result of repression. Anxiety is a manifestation in consciousness of a fear of a return of the repressed, in this case, of the unconscious itself. But, beyond this, we may also say that fear is the appropriate reaction after any trauma—the burnt child fears the fire. That this fear focused especially on the supernatural implies a new awareness of the unconscious, a new relation to it, a new orientation of consciousness towards whatever lies outside its ken. As modern readers we can identify with our author. Until his experience, and even in spite of a deeply religious attitude, our author was not afraid of the Gods or of the other world. He longed for it and worked daily to reach it. His religious attitude was comparable to the Western man's collective church-going belief. But now, having had a taste of this other world, he is in fear and trembling of anything which has to do with it. More, he is enraged by the usual sort of faith (people coming from places of worship, the usual pious literature, etc.). He finds himself 'devoid completely of every religious sentiment', and cannot understand this 'alteration in the very depths of my personality'. He is in a God-is-dead phase.

From the experience one gathers through working with Western practitioners of organized religion this turn of events is not unusual. A true face-to-face encounter with the numinous shatters all previous religious ideas. Sometimes analysis releases a genuine religious experience, and when it occurs in a clergyman, it seems to conflict with rather than support his previous training and system of beliefs. This is an astonishing state of affairs. Orthodoxy has always recognized this possibility and therefore warned dogmatically against individual experiences through visions and dreams. The mystic is not welcomed within the councils of collective religion, and one of the first acts of Jesus (cleansing the temple of money-changers) was performed in rage. Moses is moved by rage to smash the holy tablets, and the prophets—from the collective viewpoint—could also have been called 'devoid completely of every religious sentiment . . . rank atheists . . . violent heretics . . .'. Again, we have the psychological phenomenon that the greatest danger is not the opposite or contradiction of truth, but its nearest imitation. Pink sentimental religion threatens the real red thing more than does any antithesis.

The *alteration of his religious attitude* and his fear of the supernatural brought home to our author two lessons. First, a new appreciation of the values in this world (family, feeling connections, work and colleagues, health, the simple things); second, that the fear of the Lord is the beginning of wisdom. In other words, the fear of the supernatural has made him aware of his own natural limits. The other world has become terrifyingly, experientially real; he has felt its power, not just known of it from books and teachings. He becomes the '*homo religiosus*' through the very fear itself, which is nothing else than awe, the primary religious emotion.

Now he can say that the movement to the other world is not a one-step matter. It is not crossing a threshold from a smaller room to a larger just like that. This is an old debate in spiritual disciplines. Is enlightenment achieved step by step as a pilgrim climbs that mountain? Or is it achieved in a break-through flash of illumination? According to the proponents of the second view, the first is impossible since we cannot achieve the eternal through a process in time. Gopi Krishna's observation that crossing the threshold is not done in one step implies that he however inclines to the first view, that enlightenment has a process character.

Our text next describes the first major transformation: *the extension of consciousness.* This was first experienced as a halo or luminous circle around the head, at the beginning dusty, later cleared. Onians in his *Origins of European Thought* explains how the early idea of one's daimon or genius was imaged as a radiation around the head, and that seers could of course perceive this in another person. The Saint is painted with a halo, implying that sanctity has something to do with illumination, with altered consciousness.

He gives a clear account of this alteration. Consciousness and the 'I' are no longer identified. The ego 'instead of a confining unit, now itself encompassed by a shining conscious globe of vast dimensions'. He struggles with formulation, simile, metaphor— a common difficulty in the description of this phenomenon, since the formulator (the ego) cannot grasp the totality of the event. In a nutshell, 'There was ego consciousness as well as a vastly extended field of awareness, existing side by side, both distinct yet one.'

This formulation is valuable for modern depth psychology. In our therapeutic work we aim at ego-development, assuming that the development of ego and the development of consciousness are one and the same thing. Jung has shown that the ultimate development of the ego is its submission to, even immersion in, a field of wider psychic consciousness with many archetypal foci, much as Gopi Krishna describes the 'I' as immersed in the pool of light 'yet fully cognizant of the . . . volume of consciousness all around . . .'. The problem in modern depth psychology is: how do we combine the idea of ego extension and development with the idea of extended and developed awareness? I mean by this:

the two—ego and consciousness—are not the same; can they be developed independently of each other?

I think we come upon a main difference between Jungian analysis and all other forms of psychotherapy and also we come upon a major similarity between Jungian analysis and Eastern disciplines. An aim of individuation-oriented analysis is the development of consciousness. In this process the ego plays only one of the roles, since the consciousness of other archetypal components (anima/animus, shadow, mother and father imagos, and the self) is also an aim of the work. In contradistinction to other systems of therapy Jungian analysis may result in the extension of consciousness without any of the usual visible signs of ego-development. The balance is delicate indeed: too little ego and there is no observer, no central point; too little consciousness apart from ego and there is too little objective field of awareness apart from subjectivity, too little impersonal sensitivity and compassion. For Western analysts the distinction between ego and consciousness means a re-thinking of our therapeutic aims, especially those aims of contemporary 'ego-psychology'.

Alchemy gives us help in understanding the *whitening*. The 'silvery lustre', 'whitish medium', 'milky lustre', 'freshly fallen snow' are all terms we could as easily find in an alchemical text describing the wondrous appearance of the white phase. There, in alchemy, it occurs in the vessel and the language is chemical. They describe changes in which the substance so long worked over begins to whiten. (The earliest appearance of the white or anima phase, we may recall, came during the first burning fever reported in Chapter Four. There he catches sight of his small daughter, Ragina, lying in the next bed and considers himself through her eyes. He decides then not to treat himself from the outside [pouring cold water over his head] but to 'bear the internal agony' which then leads to the intuition of rousing the ida channel and cooling himself from within. It works. The fire gives way to a 'silvery streak' like the 'sinuous movement of a white serpent in rapid flight'. He then takes some milk and bread.)

Psychologically this phase was prepared already by the shift from pingala to ida, that is, the change from a masculine to a feminine channel, the activation of the unconscious feminine side of the personality, or archetype of the anima. Gopi Krishna recognizes that the Kundalini is a feminine force and he uses the image of the lively vital Shakti standing over the prostrate Shiva (who, by the way, in many pictures is passive but for his open eyes and erected penis). The shift from pingala to ida which our author takes up only in a physiological way means psychologically that the Shakti feminine power cannot be made to serve the masculine principle. The Goddess is not activated to serve the man, but the feminine force or anima must have its own channel of activity, and man is only an instrument through which this force manifests itself. So, artists and writers put themselves at the disposal of the feminine muse, that white Goddess, who shows herself, when beneficent, in beauty, love, and inspiration. Through the Goddess, as when a man comes under her spell by falling in love (the most common of all experiences of the archetypal anima), things are 'seen in a new light', one's 'senses are sharpened' and the push of pingala seems irrelevant.

The Kundalini as feminine force evidently required for our author a feminine channel, even if in some accounts of its rising it supposedly ascends through a central pathway, Sushumna. This feminine channel for the feminine force has a wide complex of meanings in Tantric thought just as it does in our notion of the anima archetype. Bharati (*The Tantric Tradition*, pp. 175-7) collects various meanings of the left artery or ida channel. Curiously, we find one of these meanings is 'the digestive power' hinting that by religious attention to his food intake and digestion Gopi Krishna may also have been paying homage to the anima. This corresponds with our ideas of the anima as intimately connected with the neuro-vegetative system. According to Bharati's translations the female pole can mean 'wanton woman' as well as 'nature' and 'intuitive wisdom', but also it can mean 'non-existence'. These aspects of the feminine are personified in Greek goddess figures where the not-being of Persephone is an essential part of her mother, nutritive nature, or Demeter, and where Aphrodite's wanton promiscuity finds place as does Athene's intuitive wisdom. This differentiation of the feminine is sorely lacking in our Judeo-Christian tradition which provides paltry examples of anima-consciousness, and these mainly secular and secondary.

In psychological practice, the white phase refers to that period where a new feminine principle seems to dominate consciousness. There is more fantasy, the dreams are more vivid, there is less purposeful worldly action, there is more slowness, gentleness, even cool remoteness. The long period of intense suffering, depression, and worry (the nigredo) seems to slip away into a world of moonlight where everything seems redeemed and it is enough to have a sweet simple smile of peace and wisdom. One is more receptive, impressionable, sensitive. A new form of love comes to life, which at first is still romantic and wrapped up with oneself. Above all, this white phase, once the regressive virginal aspects are recognized, offers the possibility of carrying the seeds for the future in patient pregnancy.

Alchemy too gives parallels to the phenomenon of improved *health*. The white phase was one of the pre-forms of the final Stone and as such was a pre-form of the elixir of health. Although not immune, our author writes that diseases now were 'distinctly milder in nature and usually there was an absence of temperature'. The idea that the Goddess in one form or another gives and takes away disease is widespread in India. In the West some go to the shrines of Mary for cures. Implied is the idea that a developed relation to the anima, to the feminine principle, is an essential ingredient for health or wholeness. The feminine as such is said to be the principle of nature and life to which we can hardly relate adequately until we have integrated that feminine part of our own selves. Gopi Krishna makes this a central point of his work, recognizing from the first that the Kundalini is feminine, a Goddess.

Chapter Twelve

Viewed in the light of the physiological reactions for which unmistakable evidence was furnished by my body every day, I had ample ground for the supposition that some kind of transformative process was at work in me, but I could not tell with what object. The most I could imagine was that I was gradually being led towards a condition of the brain and the nervous system which would make it possible for me to attain occasionally the state of extended consciousness peculiar to yogis and mystics in trance conditions. This did not mean that I had not an enlarged consciousness from the time of my first experience of Kundalini, which had caused me so much surprise and torture, and of which I was constantly reminded whenever my thoughts rested on myself; but the extension I had in mind was of a superior kind, signifying a complete negation of the ties that bind the spirit to the body, leaving it free to soar to superphysical heights and to return to the normal state refreshed and invigorated.

This was my idea of supersensible experience, gleaned from the scriptures, the stories of spiritual men and their own accounts of the ecstatic condition. Barring the blissful vision of extended personality which I perceived twice in succession in the very beginning, there was certainly no comparison between my now undeniably extended and luminous self, as securely bound to the body and the earth, as readily affected by physical needs and as strongly influenced by desire and passion, heat and cold, pleasure and pain as the common one, and the exalted, full of happiness, free-from-fear, immune-from-pain, and indifferent-to-death super-consciousness of the ecstatic. I was the same being mentally as I had been before; a man of common clay far below, intellectually and morally, the spiritual giants about whom I had read.

I missed no opportunity to study my symptoms critically and thoroughly. There was no other change save the unaccountable alteration in the nerve currents and the ever-present radiance inside and out. The lustrous visibility, which represented the latest phase in my strange development, had a heartening and uplifting effect upon me. This was indeed something that gave to my weird adventure a touch of sublimity. There could be no doubt now that I was undergoing a transformation, and although I had in no respect risen above the average, I had at least the consolation that in this particular I was nearer to the hallowed hierarchy than to the men of common calibre whom I resembled in every other way. But at the same time I could not shut my eyes to the glaring fact that the suffering I had undergone was out of all proportion to the results achieved, for which there was no explanation, save that either I had developed an abnormality or that the internal attempt at purification and transformation which began with the awakening had proved abortive in my case, and that consequently, perhaps as a result of inherent physical or mental deficiency, I had the unenviable position of being a rejected candidate—a 'Yoga Brishta'—one who had been tried and then given up as utterly unfit for the supreme state of yoga.

As years passed and I perceived no other indication of spiritual unfolding, or the growth of a higher personality endowed with superior intellectual and moral attributes, characterizing the blessed in whom Kundalini kindles the sacred fire, I was more and more led towards the disheartening conclusion that I was not provided with the essential mental and physical equipment. But as there was no decrease in the activity of the radiant force, I did not altogether cease to hope that perhaps the attempt would not go wholly for nothing, and that one day I might unexpectedly find myself favoured, if not to the maximum, at least to a noticeable extent.

Physically I became almost my old self again, hardy and tough, able to withstand hunger, the rigours of heat and cold, bodily and mental fatigue, disturbance and discomfort. The only thing I could not stand well was sleeplessness. It always caused haziness of mind and depression, which lasted for several days and did not wear off until the deficiency was made good by a longer period of rest during the day or night following the sleepless one. I felt on such occasions as if my brain had been deprived of its usual dose of energy which enabled it to maintain the extensive dimension to which it had now grown gradually during the years.

But there was absolutely no diminution in the activity of the radiant vital currents during sleep. My dreams, which possessed a highly exotic and elusive quality, were so extraordinarily vivid and bright that in the dream condition I lived literally in a shining world in which every scene and every object glowed with lustre against a marvellously luminous background, the whole presenting a picture of such resplendence and sublime beauty that without implying the least exaggeration I actually felt as if every night during slumber I roamed in enchanting empyrean regions of heavenly life. The last thing I remembered on waking suddenly from sleep was usually a landscape or a figure enveloped in a bright blaze of light in such sharp contrast to the encircling gloom which met me on awakening that it seemed as if a celestial orb shining brilliantly in my interior was eclipsed all at once, leaving me to my fate in utter darkness. The vivid impressions left by a well-remembered happy dream during a night lingered for the whole day, a sweet memory of what appeared to be a supermundane existence of a few hours, to be followed by that of another seen on the succeeding night as sweet and vivid as that on the previous one.

The magnificently brilliant effect present in the dreams was noticeable, though in a considerably diminished form, in the waking state also, but the sense of exaltation felt in the former was entirely absent. I distinctly experienced a partial eclipse of personality, a descent from a higher to a lower plane of being during the interval separating the dream state from wakefulness, and could clearly mark a narrowing down of the self, as if forced to shrink from a state of wide expansion to one of close confinement. There was undeniable evidence to show that the temporary transformation of personality apparent in the dreams was brought about by physiological processes which affected the whole organism, causing a heavy pressure on every part. During sleep my pulse rate was often considerably higher than during the day. I verified the fact frequently by putting my fingers to the pulse immediately on awakening at any time during the night. On numerous occasions I found it so rapid as to cause anxiety. The full and rapid beats clearly pointed to an undoubtedly accelerated metabolic process, to a quickly racing blood stream, to countless formations and alterations in cellular tissues, all affected by the vital current which swept like a storm through the entire organism with the obvious aim of refashioning it to a higher pitch of efficiency.

Lack of sufficient knowledge of physiology made it difficult for the ancient adepts to correlate the psychic and physiological reactions caused by the activity of Kundalini. I laboured under the same disadvantage, but on account of the fact that a superficial knowledge of every branch of science is an easily acquired possession in these days of research and publicity, and that I had ample opportunity to study my condition day to day for many years, it became possible for me to observe critically the effects of the sudden development upon my system and to draw tentative inferences from it.

I am irresistibly led to the conclusion that this extraordinary activity of the nervous system and brain is present in varying degrees in all cases of supernormal spiritual and psychic development, in a lesser measure in all cases of genius, in a still diminished form in all men of exceptionally high intellectual calibre, and in a morbid manner, when too violent and sudden or operative through a wrong nerve, in many kinds of insanity, neurosis, and other obscure and difficult-to-cure nervous and mental afflictions.

Kundalini, as known to and described by the ancient authorities, signifies the development, sometimes spontaneous and less frequently through special psycho-physiological exercises, of extraordinary spiritual and mental powers associated with religion and the supernatural. There can be no doubt whatsoever that the incessant, easily perceptible, rapid movement at the base of my spine, affecting the nerves lining the whole area, was an indication of the fact that, controlled by an invisible mechanism, a hidden organ had begun to function all of a sudden in the hitherto innocent-looking region, converting the reproductive fluid into a radiant vital essence of high potency which, racing along the nerve fibres as well as the spinal canal, nourished the brain and the organs with a rejuvenating substance out of reach in any other way. For a long time I laboured under the belief that the glow in the head and the powerful nervous currents darting through my body were all occasioned by the sublimated seed, but as time wore on I was forced to alter my opinion. The activity in the reproductive region was not the only new development that had occurred. A corresponding change in the brain and other nerve centres had also taken place which regulated the consumption and output of the new mechanism. After the crisis the luminous currents did not move chaotically but with definite aim and purpose which was clearly evident from the fact that the whole organism overcame the initial resistance of recalcitrant and inferior parts and began gradually to adjust itself to the new development.

On the strength of these and other facts I gradually came to the conclusion, which it shall rest with future investigators to confirm or disprove, that by virtue of the evolutionary processes still going on in the human body, a high-powered conscious centre is being evolved by nature in the human brain at a place near the crown of the head built of exceptionally sensitive brain tissue. The location of the centre allows it to command all parts of the brain and the entire nervous system with a direct connection with the reproductive organs through the spinal canal. In the common man the budding centre draws its nourishment from the concentrated nerve food present in the seed in such extremely limited measure so as not to interfere with the normal reproductive function of the parts. When completely built, the centre in evolved individuals is designed to function in place of the existing conscious centre, using for its activity a more powerful vital fuel extracted by nerve fibres from the body tissues in extremely minute quantities collected and rushed through the spinal tube into the brain. When accidentally the centre begins to function prematurely, before the nerve connections and links have been fully established and the delicate brain cells habituated to the flow of the powerful current, the result is likely to be disastrous. The delicate tissues of the body in that case are likely to be damaged irreparably, causing strange maladies, insanity, or death. In a grave emergency of this kind the only way open to nature to avoid a catastrophe is to use liberally the ambrosia contained in the human seed and to rush it in a sublimated form to the brain, the nervous network, and the main organs in order to provide the injured and dying cells with the most powerful restorative and food available in the body to save life.

The whole organism now begins to function in a most amazing manner which cannot but strike terror into the stoutest heart. Tossed between the old and yet incompletely built new conscious centre, the subject, unprepared for such a startling development, sees himself losing control of his thoughts and actions. He finds himself confronted by a rebellious mind and unruly senses and organs working in an inexplicable way, entirely foreign to him, as if the world, suddenly turned upside down, had dragged him to a topsy-turvy existence as weird and bizarre as the most fantastic dream. It is for this reason that the ancient teachers of Kundalini Yoga, taught by an experience extending for thousands of years, insisted on an exceptionally robust and hardy constitution, mastery over appetites and desires, voluntarily acquired control over vital functions and organs, and, above all, the possession of an inflexible will as the essentially needed qualifications in those offering themselves for the supreme undertaking of rousing the Shakti. An excellent condition of both body and mind, difficult to achieve in the unfavourable environment of modern civilization, is absolutely necessary in an enterprise of this nature to prevent the brain from giving way completely under the unbearable strain. It is not surprising, therefore, that any one who set himself determinedly to the hazardous task of awakening

Kundalini before her time was acclaimed a Vira, meaning a hero, and the practice itself designated as Vira Sadhana, or heroic undertaking, even by fearless ascetics themselves, indifferent to physical torture and death.

It should not be thought even for an instant that the alarming alteration in mental processes and the condition of the nervous system tending to produce a most stupefying and bizarre effect on even the most daring, persists for a short duration, only to be followed by a return to normality with a mastery over the newly developed powers. After the awakening, the devotee lives always at the mercy of Kundalini, wafted to a new state of existence and introduced to a new world as far removed from this one of rapid change and decay as reality is from a dream. The hypersensitive and critical condition of the nerves and the brain caused by the unceasing effort of the marvellous, invisible power to mould them to a higher and higher state of cognition, the possibility of injury and damage to the over-sensitive tissues, the process of repair and rejuvenation with the administration of nerve tonics and restoratives present in the system, and the tremendous strain on the excessively worked reproductive organs may continue undiminished for years. The only change is that with the lapse of time the individual becomes more and more accustomed to the play of the newly developed force in him and is able to regulate his habits and appetites according to the revised requirements of his system on the strength of the experience gained.

The time of sleep, when the body is at rest and the mind comparatively quiescent, provides the best occasion for the remodelling process to gather momentum by using the surplus energy, dissipated during the day in voluntary physical and mental activity, for reconstructive purposes. This results in a greater flow of the radiant vital energy into the brain with a corresponding amplification of the dream personality and other contents of the dream. The entire matter of the brain is invigorated with a copious flow of the subtle essence, abundantly supplied by the organs of reproduction, which makes it possible for the delicate tissues to maintain their activity at the pitch to which they are raised by the powerful vital current streaming into the cephalic cavity, in conformity with the needs of the newly opened centre of higher consciousness. The self-regulating mechanism of the body, trying desperately to adjust itself to the sudden development, lets no opportunity escape to bring about the necessary changes in the organism on every favourable occasion, in spite of the resistance offered, particularly when awake, by the ego consciousness which, acting during the day and dreaming during the night, tossed up and down like a cork floating on the surface of a billowy sea, remains entirely in the dark about the wonders enacted in its mortal mould.

My dreams had, therefore, a peculiar significance, and from the time of the awakening to the present day they have been no less an active and remarkable feature of my existence than the busy hours of wakefulness.

Chapter Thirteen

Except for the fact that it is attended by psychic manifestations of an extraordinary nature presenting an appearance of abnormality, the awakening of Kundalini is a perfectly natural biological phenomenon of an uncommon kind, demonstrable by any healthy human body on the attainment of a certain state of evolutionary perfection. The only peculiarity which gives it a semblance of the bizarre and the uncanny is the biological process which, set afoot, leads to the emergence of a conscious personality so superior and possessing such astounding, almost superhuman, attributes as to make the whole phenomenon appear to be the performance of a supernatural agency rather than the outcome of the operation of natural though as yet unknown biological laws. Those who possess an extensive knowledge of the animal kingdom know of numerous surprising instances of such extraordinary instinctive behaviour in certain lower forms of life as can aptly be classed as marvellous and even uncanny, but when corresponding gifts of an amazing nature, developed by the operation of yet obscure biological laws, are consciously exercised by a human being with a more elaborately fashioned brain and nervous system, the phenomenon is often regarded with suspicion and disbelief by the same observers who accept it unquestioningly in inferior forms of life.

To deny that the human body is capable of exhibiting an organic

activity that can sustain or lead to a consciousness of the supersensual type involves also the denial of some fundamental concepts of religion, of inspired prophet-hood, and of all kinds of
spiritual phenomena. If the human system is incapable of developing a brain and nervous activity expressive of a higher form of
consciousness than that which is common to all men, it is in that
case equally incapable of exhibiting super-ordinary mental faculties
and super-normal spiritual attributes, for the simple reason that in
all forms of life existing on earth there is an unalterable relationship between the organism and the level of consciousness; and
since it would be unscientific to suppose without demonstrable
proof that, of all living creatures, man alone forms an exception
to this rule, it will have to be admitted that an extraordinary
development of the human mind, radically different from or
strikingly above its normal range of expression, must necessarily
be attended by a corresponding change in or development of its
biological equipment also.

    The first pertinent question is likely to be how this alteration
and development takes place in the face of the fact that for any
such activity to be effective it must have existed as a continuous
evolutionary process for ages for which the human body, particularly the skull, provides no convincing proof, having exhibited
no marked variation for the last thousands of years conspicuous
enough to furnish conclusive evidence for a radical change in the
brain, the seat of its mental expression. If the answer to it be that
the alteration does not occur in the size or shape of the brain or
any other vital organ or in the body as a whole, but in the arrangement, quality, and composition of the constituents of the body in
respect of the extremely subtle life element present in every cell
and part of the organism, the point raised in the question would
cease to have any weight. The obvious reluctance of many otherwise highly intelligent minds to accord recognition to the validity
of spiritual experience and the reality of psychical phenomena is
due mainly to the inability of empirical science to grasp or
analyse the true nature of the life principle animating the cell, the
ultimate unit of all organic structures. At the present stage of our
knowledge the rousing of Kundalini provides the only possible

way to study the extraordinary behaviour and possibilities of the life element and the subtle biochemical medium by means of which it manipulates the organism and is able to augment or reduce its efficacy and power, leading to the bewildering diversity in intellectual acumen and spiritual insight of persons possessing approximately the same dimensions of the head and the same size and weight of the brain.

It is a great mistake to treat man as a completely finished and hermetically sealed product, entirely debarred from passing beyond the limits imposed by his mental constitution. There is a big gap between him and the most intelligent anthropoid apes, whose habits, it is said, he shared only a few thousand centuries ago, advancing in an inexplicable way beyond the mental boundary reached by the other members of that family. The cause of departure must have originated within, as external influences have no radically modifying effect on a mental compartment sealed by nature.

According to the popular beliefs in India, Kundalini is possessed of marvellous attributes. She is Para Shakti, the supreme energy, which, as illusive Maya, inveigles the embodied Jeeva into the mesh of transitory appearances, bound helplessly to the ever rotating wheel of life and death. She is the seductive female who lures him to the bed of enjoyment followed by procreation and pain, and she is also the compassionate mother who creates in him the thirst for knowledge and the desire for supersensible experience, and endows him finally with spiritual insight to lead him towards the realization of his own celestial nature. Amazing stories are current about the manner in which some very famous literary stars of India whose names are household words, became the fortunate recipients of her grace and from common men soared to unrivalled heights of poetic and literary genius almost overnight. They emerged as accomplished poets, rhetoricians, dramatists, and philosophers without the aid of teachers, without training, and sometimes without even the rudiments of education. There are also incredibly strange anecdotes of the marvellous psychic gifts showered by her on many exceptionally favoured devotees almost on her very first appearance before them in a vision, investing the hitherto unknown aspirants with such miraculous powers as enabled them apparently to defy at will some of the otherwise inviolable laws of nature.

Try as I might, I could not observe in myself the slightest sign of any such incredible development, and as year after year passed without bringing the least alteration in my mental or spiritual endowment, barring the luminosity and the widening of consciousness, I began to feel that the episode was over and the peculiarity in my mental make-up was probably all that I was destined to see of the supersensible in my life. I was neither happy nor dejected at the idea. The awful experience I had undergone and the terror that had haunted me relentlessly for months had had a chastening and curbing effect on my previous desire for supernatural adventure. The boundary line dividing the natural from the supernatural was not, I thought, negotiable by all and sundry; and as subsequent events clearly revealed to me, the narrow strip is so well protected that the cleverest man is sure to blunder in one pitfall or another unless guided at every step by a higher self-illuminating intelligence, which ceases to shine at the slightest tinge of impurity in the heart. The existence of a superintelligent internal monitor has been avowedly acknowledged by some very famous men of the world, both past and present, the monitor being none other than the mystic personality developed by Kundalini, imperceptibly active in them from birth.

After the incidents mentioned in the preceding chapters I lived an almost normal life for years similar to that of other men in all respects except for the ferment noticeable during the hours of sleep. The great increase in the metabolic activity of the body, resulting in more rapid heart action followed by lassitude in the mornings and the dynamic nature of my dreams, unmistakably pointed to the possibility that my system was being subjected to some kind of internal pressure which tended to accelerate the organic functions beyond the normal limit. On numerous occasions I was forcibly struck by the resemblance that I bore during those days to a growing baby, utterly unconscious of the great changes occurring in every part of the tiny frame tending to bring it by imperceptible degrees nearer and nearer to the massive proportions of manhood. I closely resembled one in the frequency of intake and more rapid digestion of food, quicker and more thorough elimination, longer periods of rest and sleep, and by an abnormal rapidity of the pulse, unaccompanied by fever or any other symptoms of illness. It was obvious that under the action of the transformed nervous energy my body functioned in a definitely altered manner in certain respects, forced to greater activity probably with some ultimate object in view which I could in no way guess at that time.

Apparently my body had become a target for invisible but superintelligent living forces which, using the surplus energy provided by my considerably enhanced intake and better assimilation of food, temperate habits, and frequently long periods of strict continence, were hammering away at my interior, bending and twisting the cells and organs to the required shape or the required degree of functional activity in order to make the whole system fit for the operation of a more potent life energy. The consistency in the symptoms and the mechanical regularity with which my body functioned under the action of the new vital current made it evident that even in its altered behaviour the organism was following a certain clearly marked rhythm, an essential characteristic of life in any form. This was a matter of great consolation to a man like me whose every night was a witness to strange, incomprehensible activities going on in his interior, as it tended to provide a proof for the fact that whatever transpired was taking place in accordance with certain biological laws to which the body was responding in an orderly systematic manner. Such would not be the case if an unnatural and chaotic condition had overcome the organism.

In the beginning I mistook the normal mode of operation of the new vital energy for a sudden disorder of the nervous system attended by malformation and erratic behaviour of the nervous currents. The descriptions contained in the ancient esoteric treatises on Kundalini represent the goddess as a stream of radiant energy ambrosial in effect, which, when roused by the power of concentration and pranayama, can be led gradually to her supreme abode at the crown of the head, there to taste the ineffable bliss of an embrace with her divine spouse, God Shiva, residing in the consciousness of the yogi. In the course of her ascent from her seat at the base of the spine to the crown, she, it is averred, waters with nectar the six lotuses flourishing at the six important nerve junctions on the cerebro-spinal axis, governing the vital and sensory organs which bloom at her approach, until she arrives at the thousand-petalled lotus at the top of the head and is absorbed in ecstatic union with her heavenly consort; when released from the chains which bind it to earth, the embodied consciousness soars to the sublime heights of self-realization, made aware for the first time after ages of bondage of its own ineffable, deathless nature.

At the time of her descent she repasses the lotuses, which droop and close their petals at her departure, until she assumes her original dormant state at the base of the spine, bringing down with her the temporarily liberated consciousness, adding link after link to the fetter which binds the attributeless, eternal substance inexorably to the flesh until the chain is complete at the last stage, when the yogi, coming down gradually from a condition of unutterable beatitude, awakes again to the world as embodied spirit, dominated by the senses, retaining only a brief but striking memory of its flight into the Infinite. The writings on Hatha Yoga contain graphic descriptions of these lotuses, their exact location, the number of petals on each, the name and form of the presiding deity, the letters of the Sanskrit alphabet associated with them, and the like. The students are enjoined to meditate on them in that form while practising Pranayama, beginning particularly with the lowest, or Muladhara Chakra, close to the abode of the goddess. The centres bearing the lotuses are called Chakras. Five of them are considered to be the centres of vital energy distinguished by thick clusters of nerves situated at different points along the spinal cord, which some modern writers identify with the various Plexuses. The sixth is said to be located in the brain at a spot corresponding to the point of junction of the two eyebrows and the root of the nose, and the seventh is in the cerebrum.

Biologically, a healthy human organism with an intelligent brain should provide at its present stage of evolution a fit abode for the manifestation of a higher form of consciousness than that which is the normal endowment of mankind in the present age. Its brain, nervous system, and the vital organs should have attained the state of perfection, according to the evolutionary standard, where a higher personality can step in without much commotion to take over control of the body. But ages of incorrect living in obedience to the dictates of civilization have played havoc with this most intricate machine, marring the growth of the organs and the efficiency of the nerves and loading the system with nervous poisons too subtle to be eliminated by the administration of drugs or other therapeutic agents. This is the main reason why the present-day human organism, instead of expediting the process, offers a strong resistance to its investiture with a more potent form of vitality, an essential preliminary to the installation of a higher personality. By no means known to science can this cleaning and remodelling of the body be done to make it fit for the transfer of power. All systems of Yoga aim at achieving this by overcoming these deficiencies. Kundalini is the mechanism as well as the motive force by which this biological trimming and remodelling is accomplished in the most effective manner, provided the system is not too much deteriorated either by its own defective mode of life or because of a retrogressive heredity.

The awakening being a rare but natural biological phenomenon it is futile to enter into a discussion of the reality of the lotuses, on which a good deal of emphasis has been laid by the ancient authorities. I did not come across any in the course of my own long adventure, not even a vestige of one in any part of the cerebro-spinal system. To assume their existence even for an instant in these days of physiological knowledge and research would mean nothing short of an insult to intelligence. In all probability their existence was suggested graphically to the disciples with colourful detail as an aid to concentration and to signify the location of the more sensitive and easier-to-effect brain and nerve centres, as well as to symbolize chastity; the lotus flower, unaffected by the condition of water in which it grows, has always served as an emblem of purity. By denying the existence of the lotuses and other accessories associated with them,

it is not intended in the least to undervalue or ridicule in any way
the colossal work done by the ancient masters, whose achievement in this insecure and inaccessible domain has been nothing
short of marvellous.

The idea of Chakras and lotuses must have been suggested to
the mind of the ancient teachers by the singular resemblance
which, in the awakened state, the lustrous nerve centres bear to a
luminous revolving disc, studded with lights, or to a lotus flower
in full bloom glistening in the rays of the sun. The circle of glowing radiance round the head, tinged at times with rainbow
colours and supported by the thin streak of light moving upward
through the spinal duct, bears an unmistakable likeness to a
blooming lotus with its thin stalk trailing downwards in water,
conveying to it the nutritive elements drawn by means of
innumerable root fibres, exactly in the same manner as the living
stalk of Sushumna supplies the subtle organic essence drawn from
every part of the corporeal frame by means of countless nerve
filaments to feed the Flame lit by Kundalini. It resembles in effect
a gorgeous lotus of extraordinary brilliance, having a thousand
petals to denote its large dimensions. In the absence of adequate
physiological information the old savants probably could not
seize hold of a better method, not only to indicate the position of
the nerve clusters which had to become seats of intense activity
simultaneously with the awakening, but also to prepare the uninitiated disciples for their subsequent brightly illumined lotus-
like appearance.

I have tried to make the point clear, as readers in the least
familiar with the writings on Kundalini are likely to be struck by
the singular absence of any reference in this work to Chakras and
lotuses, so lavishly dealt with in other books, that a whole literature has grown around them, detracting from the scientific value
of the actual phenomenon. I never practised yoga by Tantric
methods of which Pranayama, meditation on the nerve centres,
and posture are essential features. If I had done so with a firm
belief in the existence of the lotuses, I might well have mistaken
the luminous formations and the glowing discs of light at the
various nerve junctions along the spinal cord for lotuses, and in

the excited state of my imagination might even have been led to perceive the letters and the presiding deities in vivid form, suggested by the pictures already present in my mind. By the grace of the divine energy I was destined to witness a phenomenon of another kind, a unique phenomenon undoubtedly repeated many times during the past but in all probability seldom studied in detail and certainly never recorded in plain language free of unintelligible words and metaphors. Astounding as it may appear, I am convinced that an emphasis was designedly laid on great suffering to me particularly on such items of the experience as enabled me, though very imperfectly, to trace the biological processes responsible for the phenomenon. It is mainly because of this that I am in a position to adduce certain hitherto inexplicable facts, fully confident that the indistinct track, passing zig-zag through the thick undergrowth of superstition and ceremonial, now pointed out will with the labour of competent investigators soon lead to surprising developments and momentous results.

I was destined to witness my own transformation, not comparable in any way to the great transfigurations in the past, nor similar in point of results to the marvellous achievements of genius; but though simple in nature and ordinary in effect, a transformation nevertheless, attended all along by great physical and mental suffering. But what I witnessed and still witness within myself is so contrary to many accepted notions of science, at variance with many time-honoured dogmas of faith, and so antagonistic to many of the universally followed dictums of civilization that when what I have experienced is proved empirically there must occur a far-reaching, revolutionary change in every sphere of human activity and conduct.

What I realized beyond the least shadow of doubt is the fact, corroborated in part by ancient seers of many lands and more concretely by those in India, that in the human body there exists an extremely subtle and intricate mechanism located in the sexual region which while active in the normal man in the naturally restricted form tends to develop the body generation after generation, subject of course to the vicissitudes of life, for the expression of a higher personality at the end; but when roused to rapid activity, it reacts strongly on the parent organism, effecting in course of time subject again to numerous factors, a marvellous transformation of the nervous system and the brain, resulting in the manifestation of a superior type of consciousness, which will be the common inheritance of man in the distant future. This mechanism, known as Kundalini, is the real cause of all genuine spiritual and psychic phenomena, the biological basis of evolution and development of personality, the secret origin of all esoteric and occult doctrines, the master key to the unsolved mystery of creation, the inexhaustible source of philosophy, art and science, and the fountainhead of all religious faiths, past, present and future.

Commentary to Chapters Twelve and Thirteen

Unfortunately we do not have the content of his *dreams*. We are told only of their vivid intensity, their sweetness and sublime beauty, and the concomitant heightened physiological activity, especially sexual. As mentioned above, the vivification of imagination belongs to the white phase, to the activation of the anima. It is remarkable how differently his process moves compared with what goes on in a Western analysis. For us, beautiful dreams are not enough. They must be recorded, worked on, analysed, meaning extracted, integrated. For him, they needed only to be dreamt, felt, followed. Here we come to one of the ways consciousness and ego can be separated and developed independently. As long as we in analysis take up the dream in order to integrate it, we are extending the ego and identifying the extension of ego with the extension of consciousness. Our author did things another way. He let the ego sleep in its world of dreams; he observed merely what was going on, trusting (as one would in the white positive anima phase) and letting the process transform him. Rather than let his ego integrate the luminous other world, he let the luminous other world integrate him. His approach to greater awareness was just the reverse of what we assume in the

West. We work at it; it requires intense activity. Gopi Krishna slept!—but at the right time and in the right way. Compare St. Bernard's 'alive and watchful sleep' which 'enlightens the inward senses'.

There is probably a great deal more to the interrelation of *dreaming and sexual excitation* than we today understand. Freud was the first to see intuitively a connection between the dream world and sexuality. He caged his insight within a strained mechanical system, almost destroying its value, but if we let it take free flight again we can speculate along the lines of our author's observations.

Assuming with Jung and with Gopi Krishna that Kundalini is the instinct of individuation, this instinct will have at least a strongly sexual component, if not an erotic base. Assuming too with Jung and with Gopi Krishna that dreams play a major role in this process (mainly by preceding the level of awareness of consciousness), then we might speculate that what goes on in the dreams will be influenced by and reflect sexuality. Freud said this of course, but he did not see the purposeful individuating aspect. Worse, he reduced the dream to sexuality, whereas Gopi Krishna sees sexuality in the service of the dream. Recent research in the physiology of sleep shows penile erections synchronous with dreams. In general, during periods of dreaming there is erection; during periods of non-dreaming, there is detumescence. The experimenters speculate that the same biological system may be responsible for both activities. We would call this system the psychoid level; Gopi Krishna might call it Kundalini. Fantasy and sexual excitation seem to be two sides of the same activity. In Freudian psychoanalysis fantasy is to be reduced to its sexual origins so that sexuality can serve its ultimately extraverted biological purpose. In Kundalini Yoga, it would seem that sexuality is to be converted in order to feed its ultimately introverted biological purpose. Jungian analysis might be said to take a middle position; sexuality flows on a sliding scale, at one time expressed mainly in images, at another time mainly in actions. In all three views, the sexual permeation of the unconscious is clearly affirmed.

A direct connection between *brain and testicles* via the spine is a physiological axiom in Indian, Chinese, Tibetan, Arabic, and ancient Greek medicine. We have no modern anatomical evidence for this connection. Rather than dismiss the idea as superstition, we may reinterpret it as a psychological truth, i.e. between the two creative centres of man there is a direct relationship; man's backbone holding him upright expresses this relationship between the two poles of his force.

The sexual union between head and genitals experienced physiologically by our author is presented in alchemy as the conjunction of male and female opposites (King and Queen, Sun and Moon, red and white, etc.). Often the metaphor of brother-sister incest is used. Psychologically, this conjunction means the union with oneself, self-fertilization, self-generation, and self-creation. The intensive prolonged introversion of one's libido, the devoted love which one lavishes upon one's own psychic life, the joyful acceptance of all biological desire and sexual excitation as belonging to and furthering the process going on in the psychic, imaginative world, endowing one's own genitals with the sanctity of a God—all this is meant by the union of crown and seed. The actual moment of the inner conjunction is said to be comparable to orgasm (see Chapter Fourteen). From this comes the divine child, the second birth of the new man.

We are therefore not surprised to discover our author experiencing himself as a 'growing baby'. Again his experiences were not in fantasy images or dreams of birth and infancy (as we often find in analysis), but in the organic experience within himself of these changes. He lived through the archetypal experiences, naively, in the best sense of the word—simply, naturally, unaffectedly.

As our author says, in the standard works of Kundalini Yoga and Hatha Yoga, and Chinese Yoga as well, there are chakras, distinct centres of experience located in the body, each with an elaborate symbolism of colour, number, animal, God, element, and body organ or system. Gopi Krishna did not have these experiences, although he explains how it might be possible for one to have viewed the circles of light as petaled chakras. For him there were no lotuses. We are reminded of his suffering. However, the organic experiences he sensed do correspond with the emphasis in these yogic systems upon *physiological reality* and upon the changes in vital centres and organs expected once the Kundalini is aroused and the light or breath is in circulation.

The question arises: did these events actually take place in his body, in his cells, nerves, organs? Or did they take place in the yogic body? Bharati says (*op. cit.*, p. 291): 'The physical and the yogic body belong to two different logical levels.' The chakra system of the yogic body is not supposed to have any objective existence in physical space. Yet the psyche insists on this body language and body experience so that what is logically impossible is indeed psychologically not only possible but felt to be true. Thus for Gopi Krishna this question does not arise. His experiences were definitely physical and in his body, his flesh afire, his organs affected, his appetites altered. *Prana* connects the two levels, which are really but one identity which our minds divide into two logics. Physiologists—and there have been some—may examine the physical body during *samadhi* for traces of its alteration and thus may demonstrate the effect upon the physical body of changes in the yogic body. But the psychologist starts with the psychic data which follows Gopi Krishna's report: his physical body was for him the material place of projection of immaterial events and there in the 'body' they were experienced by the senses and felt to be 'real'. Evidently, there must be some *material place* for psychic changes: the object of art, the alchemical materials, the physical body. In our Western tradition we have come far in knowledge of the reality of the physical body, and are comparatively ignorant of the reality of the body of the imagination. We do not understand enough about the effects of the imaginal body upon our physiology, not only in psychosomatic symptoms, but in all illness and its treatment. Our author's account shows how intimately the two 'logical levels' merge in actual experience.

Because his report does not follow the standard examples of an ascent throught distinct chakras, it is just that more valuable. The alchemists too complained that the literature was obscure and useless: no one could learn how to make the Stone from anyone else. Each had to do the work alone. So, too, in analysis, no two processes move in the same way, produce the same patterning of symbols and motifs, yield the same emotional experiences. Each case is individual and each relationship between analyst and analysand is different. In this sense it is always a creative endeavour. One must make and follow one's own way. The archetype of individuation may be said to be single, its manifestations multitudinous.

Chapter Fourteen

I⊤ was my good fortune to have relatives and friends whose affection, loyalty, and help contributed to make the risky path I was traversing safe and smooth for me. My two sisters, their husbands, the father and brothers of my wife, and also my friends, few but sincere, surrounded me with affection and loyalty. My mother had died more than one and a half years before the occurrence and yet it was no less to her excellent upbringing than to the great devotion of my wife that I owed my survival. Among all my benefactors they stand out like two ministering angels, and the debt of gratitude for the unbounded love they bore me and the invaluable service they rendered I can never hope to repay in this world. It was my great good luck to have a mother whose kindness of heart, nobility of character, sense of duty, and purity were exemplary, and whose boundless love moulded my childhood and youth, exercising the greatest influence for good on my whole life.

Looking back now at the years which followed the awakening, I can affirm unhesitatingly that but for the robust constitution bequeathed to me by my parents and certain good traits of character inherited or learned from them, I could never have survived the ordeal and lived to relate it. Although for many years of my altered life I never breathed freely like a man sure of himself and of what he had to do, and I was at no time entirely without doubt about my condition, I managed by adopting an attitude of calm resignation to the inevitable and indifference to death, partly the effect of parental influence and partly cultivation, to keep my mind undisturbed even in grave situations. Often they were caused by my own neglect of the conditions regulating my peculiar existence, unavoidable due to the storm and stress of life, and sometimes by attacks of common ailments for each of which I had to discover and apply the treatment by trial and error suited to the changed reactions of my body.

An ordinary man in a humble walk of life, burdened with responsibilities, as I always have been and think myself to be, I never allowed any false idea about myself to take root in my mind after the new development. On the other hand, my absolute helplessness before the lately manifest power in me had the effect of humbling what little remnant of pride I still possessed. I attended to all my affairs in the same manner as I had always done before the change. The only thing to remind me of the internal upheaval was rigid regularity in diet and an adherence to certain other austere ways of conduct, which experience taught me to adopt in order to minimize resistance to the activity of the mighty energy at work inside me.

I lived outwardly a strictly normal life, permitting no one, save my devoted wife, to have the least glimpse into the mysterious happenings in my interior. Every year I moved to Jammu in winter with my office and to Kashmir in summer, in this manner to escape the rigour of heat and cold which might have proved injurious to the growth of the supersensitive tissues then in a state of development within. Gradually in the course of a few years my body attained a degree of hardiness and strength sufficient to withstand the effect of fasts, discomforts of travel, rigours of climate, irregularities in diet, overstrain, worries, and adverse circumstances which form an inevitable corollary to the struggle for existence.

I became almost my old self again, humbled and chastened by the experience, with a good deal less of ego and a great deal more of faith in the Unseen Arbitrator of human destiny. The only thing I was aware of was a progressively expanding field of consciousness and a slowly increasing brightness of the external and internal objects of perception, which in course of time brought the idea irresistibly home to me that though outwardly one with the restlessly active mass of humanity, I was a different being inside, living in a lustrous world of brilliant colour of which others had no knowledge whatsoever.

In mentioning apparently minor details I am influenced by the consideration that I should not omit any facts. Transformation of personality is fraught with risks, needing attention to every phase of conduct and careful regulation of activity. If all I have to relate was known but a few centuries earlier, the knowledge properly systematized and applied might have helped physicians to save many persons from the clutches of insanity.

It was my great ill luck not to have understood for many years what I have learned now after repeated bitter struggles. Side by side with the suffering, however, I have also tasted moments of incomparable happiness, supreme moments which liberally compensated me for long periods of pain and anguish, as the mere act of waking to reality instantaneously compensates a sleeper for the awful agony suffered in a prolonged nightmare.

About three years after the incidents narrated in the preceding chapters, I began to feel an irresistible desire for a more nourishing and substantial diet than that to which I had accustomed myself from the time of the awakening. The desire was more in evidence in winter when I was in Jammu than in the months of summer spent in Kashmir. Those were the closing years of the Second World War and the prices of commodities had risen enormously. Unable to assign any reasons for the sudden excess in a now otherwise normal appetite, I restrained the inclination because I considered it improper to give way to a desire which had something of a gourmand in it and also because our extremely limited means did not allow me the additional expenditure. Despite meagre resources our diet was sufficiently nutritious and balanced, including certain varieties of animal food, against which Kashmiri Brahmins as a community do not have any scruple. But the urge in me was not without good reason, and I had to pay bitterly for my short-sighted resistance to an impulse intended to expedite the process going on as strong as ever in my interior.

Soon after our annual move to Jammu in the month of November 1943 I received an invitation from my relatives in Multan to spend a few days with them during the ensuing winter. As it afforded me an opportunity to meet my cousins whom I had not seen for many years, I determined to accept the invitation and to go there during the Christmas holidays, extending the period by a few more days if necessary. That year, feeling particularly fit and strong, I left my wife at Srinagar and came alone to Jammu to stay with her brother, the municipal engineer of the town. He hired a building in an open locality on the outskirts of the town where, having a room all to myself and finding all my simple needs well provided for, I felt entirely at home, happy at the change and harbouring not the slightest suspicion that all my cheer would vanish in the horror of another awful trial.

I was happy to find myself in full possession of my normal health with a surplus amount of energy demanding an outlet. From early November I started taking easy physical exercises, beginning with the first grey streaks of dawn and ending with the sun just near the horizon, after which I had a cold bath and retired to my room for rest and study until office time. I do not know how it happened, but after only a few weeks of the programme the urge to take exercise partially disappeared, yielding place to a strong, almost irresistible desire for meditation. The glow of vibrant health resulting from systematic exertion made me feel reckless, and looking for an avenue to make the best use of my superb physical condition, I felt half inclined to yield to the impulse and try my luck again, swayed by the thought that with the experience gained and the immunity acquired by the organism I might succeed without encountering the mishap I had suffered last time. I had escaped by a miracle to pass years of uncertainty and suspense before I found myself again on firm ground. What an imbecile I was, I sternly told myself, not to profit by my previous extremely bitter experience and to expose myself again to the same ghastly battle the wounds of which were still fresh in my heart.

In spite of my sober reflections, in spite of myself, in spite of the suffering I had borne in consequence of it, I again began to meditate, starting from the early hours or dawn, losing myself in the contemplation of the wondering lustrous glow within, until the sun, risen high above the horizon, shone full in my room, indicating the nearness of the office hour. I began to practise from the first week of December; for a number of days in addition to the marvellous extension of personality and absorption in the enrapturing conscious glow that I had experienced on the first day of the awakening, differing only in the colour of the radiance, I felt a sense of elation and power impossible to describe. It persisted through the day and in my dreams to the hour of practice, and was replenished again the next morning to last for another day.

Astounded at the result of my effort, I increased the interval by beginning earlier, completely overpowered by the wonder and glory of the vision which, luring away my senses from the harsh world of mingled joy and pain, carried me to a supersensory plane where, caressed by lustrous waves of indescribable rapture, I found myself immersed in the boundless ocean of unconditioned being. It was indeed a marvellous experience, and I felt my hair literally stand on end when the stupendous vision wore its most majestic aspect. It seemed on every such occasion as if I or the invisible cognitive self in me, leaving its safe anchorage in the flesh, were carried by the strong outgoing tide of a lustrous consciousness towards an existence of such immensity and power as made everything I could conceive of on earth tame and trite in comparison: an existence where, untroubled by any idea of bondage or limitation, I found myself lost in an amazing immaterial universe so stupendous in extent, so sublime and marvellous in nature, that the human element still left in me, even when at the highest point of the experience, stared in amazement and trembled with awe at the mighty spectacle present before my internal eye. I was overjoyed at the glorious possibility within my reach now. There could be absolutely no doubt that I was the exceedingly fortunate possessor of an awakened Kundalini. It was only now that I could grasp the reason why in ancient times success in this undertaking was thought to be the highest achievement possible to man and why the followers of this path considered no sacrifice too much and no effort too great for the supreme prize attainable at the end. I now understood why

accomplished Yogis were always treated with the highest respect
in India and how adepts, who had lived long ago, even now commanded a homage and a reverence which have not fallen to the
share of any other class of men, including mighty rulers and
potentates. There was certainly no honour more signal or fortune
more precious than that which, without my asking for it, had
been bestowed on me.

But, alas, my good luck was exceedingly short-lived. After
only a couple of weeks I found that the ferment caused in my mind
by the breathtaking experience was so great that I could hardly
sleep for excitement and was awake hours before the time of
meditation, impatient to induce the blissful condition again as
soon as possible. The impressions of the last three days terminating
this extraordinary period of excursions into the normally for-
bidden domain of the supersensible are indelibly imprinted upon
my memory. Before losing myself entirely in the contemplation
of an unbounded, glowing, conscious void, I distinctly felt an
incomparably blissful sensation in all my nerves moving from the
tips of fingers and toes and other parts of the trunk and limbs towards the spine, where, concentrated and intensified, it mounted
upwards with a still more exquisitely pleasant feeling to pour into
the upper region of the brain a rapturous and exhilarating stream
of a rare radiating nerve secretion. In the absence of a more suitable
appellation, I call it nectar, a name given to it by the ancient
savants. All authorities on Kundalini Yoga are agreed about the
reality of the ambrosial current, which irrigates the seventh centre
in the brain at the moment of the union of Shakti with Shiva, the
superconscious principle behind the embodied self, and it is said
that the flow of the nectar into it or into one of the lower centres
on spinal axis is always accompanied by a most exquisite rapture
impossible to describe, exceeding many times in intensity that
most pleasurable of bodily sensations, the orgasm, which marks
the climax of sexual union.

On the last day of this unique experience I had no sleep during
the night. My mind was in a state of excitement and turmoil
with joy and exhilaration at this most unexpected and unbelievable
stroke of luck. I rose up at my usual time in a hurry and after

feasting my mental eye on the elevating beauty and grandeur that was now a reality for me, went to the market to make some purchases. I returned at nearly one o'clock in the afternoon in an unusual state of exhaustion which surprised me. I had not taken my breakfast that day and accordingly attributed my weakness to an empty stomach. The next day, the twenty-fifth of December, I had to leave for Multan by the morning train to see my cousins. I remained busy until evening, making preparations for the journey, and after dining at the usual hour retired early to bed. Only a few minutes after lying down the stark realization came to me that I had woefully blundered again. My head reeled, my ears buzzed with a harsh, discordant noise, and in place of the usual resplendent glow in my head a wide column of fire was mounting up, shooting out forked tongues of flame in every direction. Trembling with fear, I watched the awful display. Too late I understood what had happened. I had overdone the practice of meditation and strained my already over-stimulated nervous system to a dangerous limit.

It is needless for me to recapitulate all the incidents and details of the torture that I suffered again on this occasion for more than three months. Suffice it to say that after passing a terribly restless night I did not feel fit to undertake the long journey to Multan in the morning and was compelled to abandon the idea. Discarding meditation I again took all care to regulate my diet as I had done the last time. In a few days I noticed a slight relief in the tension in my head, but the insomnia grew worse and I became weaker every day.

Alarmed at my condition, my brother-in-law expressed his intention of writing to my wife to come to Jammu. It was the middle of January now and the winding mountainous roads from Srinagar were covered with snow, making travel extremely uncomfortable and even risky. Anxious to avoid her inconvenience as well as a shock, I dissuaded him from doing so hoping that the disturbance would cease after some time.

One day, finding that I was unable to rise from bed without assistance and losing all hope of survival, I yielded to the exhortations of my brother-in-law to send a telegram to my wife.

She arrived in all haste, half dead with anxiety, accompanied by her father and my younger son. Day and night without an hour's undisturbed rest for herself my wife waited on me, attending to my every need, trying to soothe by her presence the internal agony I was suffering, which she could not visualize in all its horror but the external indications of which she could see every moment without difficulty. My father-in-law, whose parental love and solicitude for me had impelled him to undertake the arduous journey to Jammu despite his age, was beside himself with grief and anxiety at my precarious condition, but restrained by a feeling of awe, which all those who surrounded me at the time felt in spite of themselves, he made no attempt to offer any suggestions or advice.

Alarmed by the seriousness of my condition and unable to think of any other way, as a last resort and without my knowledge they decided to take experienced sadhus and fakirs into their confidence. But all those who were brought to treat me expressed their inability to do anything. One of them, a venerable saint hoary with age, then on a visit to Jammu, whom thousands flocked to see every day, after listening to me attentively shook his head, saying that he had not heard of anything like it in his life and suggested that I should seek directions from the same teacher who had prescribed the practice responsible for the disturbance.

Growing more desperate with my progressively worsening condition, they ultimately approached a Kashmiri Sadhu staying at Lahore in those days and persuaded him to come to Jammu to see me. He stayed with us for some days studying my condition attentively. I had now grown extremely weak, almost exhausted, with spindle legs and emaciated arms, a skeleton with gleaming eyes, which made my wife wince every time she looked at me. For more than a month I had starved myself, subsisting on barely half a cup of boiled rice and a cup of milk two or three times a day. The poisoned condition of my nerves caused by acute digestive disturbances had translated itself into an ungovernable fear of eating because of a constant threat of dreadful consequence. I should have preferred not to eat anything at all, but knowing well that a completely empty stomach meant a dreadful death, in spite of the nausea and the revolt of my stomach, I used all my will power to perform the extremely unpleasant task.

Unable to penetrate the cause of my distemper, the learned sadhu, imputing my dislike for food to a whim, asked me to eat in his presence, directing that the full quantity I was accustomed to take be served to me. On his insistence I swallowed with great difficulty a few morsels more than my usual intake, washing them down with water to overcome the resistance offered by my throat. The moment I did so a sudden unbearable stab of pain shot across my abdomen and the area round the sacral plexus, attaining such an intensity that I fell prostrate, writhing and twisting, casting a reproachful look at the sadhu for thus subjecting me to torture by his ill-timed advice. Pale with mortification, he rose hurriedly and left the room. That evening he was attacked by a sudden sickness which kept him on his feet for the entire night without sleep, and he left the house in the early hours of the morning, attributing his own malady to the terrible power possessing me.

I recovered from the pain in a few hours without any serious after-effects, but the incident exposed the helplessness of my condition as being entirely beyond human aid and added immensely to the worry of my wife. Some days after the episode my son came into my room accidentally with a small plate of food in his chubby little hands. It was about noon. As usual I had taken a few spoonfuls of rice, my principal meal of the day, an hour before. The boy squatted down in front of me and began to eat, licking his lips and enjoying each mouthful in the manner of children. Unlike other times, the sight of food caused no revulsion, and as I watched the child eating with delight I felt the dim stirrings of hunger for the first time in weeks. In place of the usual bitterness I noticed a reawakened sense of taste in my mouth. I could have eaten a few morsels with appetite at that time, but the fear of the awful consequences which followed the slightest error in diet in that hypertense condition restrained me and I could not gather strength enough to take the risk and ask for something to eat. After only a few minutes the feeling disappeared and the old chaotic condition overcame me again.

Puzzled at the occurrence, which could not fail to strike me forcibly even in that distraught condition, I racked my brain to find a satisfactory explanation for the apparently trifling incident, full of the greatest import for me. Could it be, I asked myself, that the interval between the meals set by me was too long in my present debilitated condition? The next day I paid scrupulous attention to time, taking a few mouthfuls with a cup of milk every three hours, each time unwillingly and with fear gripping my heart. But I managed to carry out my purpose without noticing any adverse consequences, though there was no perceptible improvement either. I continued in this manner for a few days, but the condition of my brain was deteriorating and the convulsive movements of my limbs coupled with intensely painful sensations along the path of nerves, especially in back and abdomen, signified a serious disorder of the nervous system. I felt myself sinking and even the will to live which had sustained me so far appeared ready to give up the struggle as hopeless and to let the body drift to its doom.

After some days I noticed with a shock that I was slightly delirious at times. I had still enough sense to realize that if the condition worsened I was doomed. I had tried all expedients, used all my intelligence and exhausted all my resources, but had failed miserably to find a way out. Finally, losing every hope of recovery and apprehending the worst in a mood of utter depression, I prepared myself for death, resolved to end my life before the delirium of madness rendered the task impossible. Overwhelmed by the horror which surrounded me, I had now almost lost the power to think rationally or to exert my will to resist the dread impulse. Before going to bed that night I embraced my wife with enfeebled, palsied arms for a long time, noting with anguish her pinched face, and with burning tears in my eyes I resigned her to God, in pain at the idea of the inevitable separation ahead, leaving me no opportunity now to repay her with redoubled love for her unparalleled loyalty and sacrifice. Calling both my sons to me by name, I embraced them fondly, clasping each to my breast, entrusting them also to His care for ever and ever. With a wrench at the heart I remembered that I could not have a last look at my dear daughter, who was at Srinagar looking after the house.

Resigning her also to God and looking for the last time at her image in my mind, I recovered my breath and stretching my aching body on the bed, closed my eyes, unable to stifle the great sobs that shook my breast.

It took me some time to grow a little composed after what I had thought was my last adieu to my wife and children, believing death to be inevitable. Then I began to think seriously about my resolve. It was foolish to expect, I told myself, that if the malady were allowed to run its course I would have a peaceful end. Death would definitely be preceded by a raging madness which I had to avoid at any cost. Arguing in this manner I revolved in my mind the various methods within my reach to end my life, trying to select the one which was the easiest and the least painful, possible of execution by one in an extremely weak condition. I weighed the possibilities, passing now and again into a delirious condition, all the while tossing from side to side in the relentless grip of unconquerable insomnia. Hours passed and my agitated brain refused to come to a decision, passing from one hazy chain of thought to another, without the power to complete any. I cannot say how it happened that towards the early hours or dawn I passed into a sleeplike condition, the first in weeks, and for a brief interval dreamed a vivid dream in which I saw myself seated at a meal with a half-filled plate in front of me, containing boiled rice and a meat preparation common in Kashmir which I ate with enjoyment.

I awoke immediately, the lustre noticed in the dream persisting during wakefulness for some time. A sudden idea darted across my now almost delirious mind, and calling my wife to my side, in a weak voice I asked her to serve me nourishment every two hours that day, beginning early, each serving to include in addition to milk a few ounces of well-cooked, easy-to-digest meat. Following my muttered instructions to the letter, my wife with her own hands cooked and served the food to me at the specified intervals, punctual to the minute. I ate mechanically, my arms and hands shaking while carrying the food to my mouth, a clear indication of a delirious condition. I found it even more difficult that day to chew the food and swallow it, but managed to gulp it down with milk. After finishing the last meal at nine, I felt a slight relief. The tension grew less, yielding to a feeling of extreme exhaustion followed by a soothing wave of drowsiness until, with an inexpressible transport of joy, which made tears stream from my eyes, I felt blissful sleep steal upon me. I slept soundly until morning, enveloped in a glowing sheet of light as usual.

Chapter Fifteen

THE next day I reduced the interval to one hour, raising it to one-and-a-half hours after a week and adding in the course of this period fruits and a little curd to my diet. Gradually the signs of delirium vanished and the insomnia gave way to an excessive desire for sleep. I submitted willingly to the beneficial soporific influence day and night, awaking only at the time of eating in obedience to the gentle and cautious touch of my wife, who stayed in the kitchen all day preparing meal after meal and serving hot, appetizing dishes with a love and care which only a devoted wife can display. Thanks to her ministrations, stringent regard to time, and the excellence of the food, I began to grow in strength and in about two weeks was able to move from one room to another. After this period I prolonged the interval to two hours, thereby reducing to some extent the intake of food in a day.

Refreshed by sleep, my mind grew clearer, escaping by degrees the horror; in spite of the fact that the vital radiation had now assumed a colossal appearance, I began to feel a growing sense of confidence in myself and to hope that if nothing untoward happened I might pass the crisis with safety after all.

As if guided by a newly developed sense of taste I selected the constituents of every meal, rejecting this article and taking more of that, choosing a combination of acids and alkalis, sugars and salts, fruits and vegetables, in a manner that helped my stomach to digest the enormously increased mass under the stimulation of the new more powerful radiant current without any undesirable reaction. I was now passing through an experience as amazing and weird as any I had passed so far, utterly bewildered by the new direction taken by my singularly functioning organism. No man in his senses would believe such an abnormal performance of his digestive organs possible all of a sudden, turning one from a moderate eater into a voracious one; my stomach, working under the stimulation of a fiery vapour, consumed incredible quantities without causing the slightest adverse effect, as if licked up by fire. I had heard and read of yogis said to have commanded incredible powers of digestion, who could consume without ill effects prodigious loads of food with the aid of the luminous energy, but I had never lent credence to such stories. What I had disbelieved I now witnessed in myself, all the time overwhelmed with wonder at the powers and possibilities lying hidden in the body.

I was not so much alarmed by the voracity of my appetite as I was amazed at the capacity of my stomach. At the lowest computation I was consuming at least four times the amount of food I was used to before the occurrence. During the first week the quantity devoured must have been six times the normal amount. It was atrocious. The food disappeared in my stomach as if it had evaporated, no doubt sucked greedily by the hungry cells of the body. A disregard of time in eating was always visited with a sudden cessation of the desire for food and an absence of taste, aggravated at times to a feeling of nausea and utter dislike for any kind of nourishment. Experience had taught me that such symptoms indicate a poisoned state of nerves, an inevitable result of the awakening in the first stages, for which there is no known antidote except proper feeding in spite of the aversion, done in a manner as may be indicated by the habits and the condition of the system. One should take care to use only the best, most easily digestible, complete natural foods in such a quantity as can be readily tolerated at regular intervals, normally of not more than three hours. The availability of a nutritious diet in the stomach is essential in all normal cases and has, therefore, to be arranged with due care to enable the nervous system to rid itself of impurities.

At the present moment we are entirely in the dark about the nature of the subtle organic essence in the body which serves as nourishment for the ever-active nerves and the constantly fleeting nervous and thought energy. In the first stages of the awakening and until the system grows accustomed to the flow of the radiant current, the one and the only preservative of life and sanity is diet in right measure, correct combination, and at proper intervals. The whole science of Kundalini is fundamentally based on the assumption that it is possible for one to rouse to activity a mighty dormant power in the human body in order to gain freedom from sense domination for the embodied spirit, enabling it to soar unfettered to its celestial estate. The idea of stirring to activity a dormant vital force in the body, examined in the light of modern knowledge, can only signify the development or generation of a new type of vitality or life energy which clearly implies a recasting of the nervous system not possible without a biological evolution.

In the initial stages and later as well, nourishment suited to their appetite and constitution is taken by the initiates in surprising quantities as an offering to the power within. Aversion from food is a common feature in cases of a sudden awakening of Kundalini; the abrupt release of the new force and its stormy dash through the nerves causes acute disturbances in the digestive and excretory systems. The constant presence of the teacher for guidance at this critical juncture has, for this reason, always been considered essential, and not infrequently forced feeding is resorted to in order to preserve life when the disciple, completely unnerved by the weird developments in his interior, loses command over himself and is unable to muster enough strength of will to perform the act of eating in spite of the nausea and the chaos prevailing within. To avert disaster in acute conditions and to guard against the utterly unpredictable behaviour of the digestive and excretory organs after the awakening, the students of Hatha Yoga have to devote many years of their life to acquire the ability to empty the stomach and the colon at will to prepare for emergencies almost certain to arise sooner or later. Except for this, there can be no other meaning or utility, barring a cheap demonstrative or gymnastical value, in the elaborate and extremely difficult system of physical discipline and body control enjoined by all the exponents of this form of yoga as an essential prerequisite for those initiated into the final esoteric practices of the cult. The would-be aspirants have necessarily to attain proficiency in all preliminary exercises and methods of body control before embarking on the supreme but hazardous course of awakening the serpent.

We travelled to Srinagar in the beginning of April 1944. Owing to the joint efforts of my wife and her father and the pains taken by them to make every kind of provision for the two-day hilly journey, I reached Srinagar in my then extremely weak condition without mishap. There, surrounded by relatives and friends and nursed with assiduous care by my wife and daughter, I made rapid progress, gaining enough strength in a few months to resume my duties in the office. In the course of a year I grew hardy and strong, able to bear strain and fatigue, exertion and pressure, but I could not overcome the susceptibility of my system to digestive disorders in the event of unusual delay or irregularity in diet. I resumed my old habit of two meals a day, with a cup of milk and a slice of bread in the mornings and afternoons. By the end of the year my appetite became normal and the amount of food moderate, with a small measure of meat as a necessary ingredient. The lustrous appearance of external objects as well as of thought forms and the brilliance of dream images was intensified during the worst period of the last disorder and grew in brightness to such an extent that when gazing at a beautiful sunlit landscape I always felt as if I were looking at a heavenly scene transported to the earth from a distant elysium, illuminated by dancing beams of molten silver. This astounding feature of my consciousness, purely subjective of course, never exhibited any alteration, save that it gained in transparency, brilliance, and penetrative power with the passage of time and continues to clothe me and all I perceive in inexpressible lustre today.

Years passed without bringing any new development in me to

the surface. Whatever was happening was transpiring within, beyond my knowledge and away from the reach of my eyes. Failing to notice any other change in me except for the sea of lustre in which I lived, and sternly warned by the last awful episode to desist from invoking the supernatural again, I occupied myself fully with the world and its affairs in an attempt to lead a normal life. In 1946 in collaboration with a few friends and colleagues I started a movement for economic reform in all obligatory social functions in our community. I had become acutely conscious of the crushing load of misery and even infamy which a low-income family had to carry all its life, almost to the funeral pyre, for the transitory pleasure of excelling its neighbours in pomp and show, in the grandeur of a feast, in the richness of a dowry, or in other such items of social ceremonial, and wanted to create conditions that would make it possible for a man of modest means to escape the pillory which otherwise awaits him without injury to his self-respect or detriment to his position in society. We made the attempt, creating more enemies than friends, earning more censure than praise, and meeting more opposition than support, and finally had to desist.

In the summer of 1947 my daughter was married in an un-ostentatious manner in conformity with our reform scheme, the credit for which went not to us, but to her husband, a struggling young lawyer, orphaned at an early age and left without re-sources, who refused tempting offers of rich dowries to marry the dowryless daughter of a poor man. The alliance was proposed to his elder brother by a friend while I was at Jammu, and all I had to do was signify my assent to it. In this way in my peculiar men-tal condition nature spared me the ordeal of having to hunt in-definitely for a match for one who out of filial loyalty was as keen as I was myself to ensure that my principles in regard to dowry were not violated in any way.

In the autumn of the same year the peaceful valley of Kashmir was thrown into convulsions by a sudden raid from marauding hordes of frontier tribesmen, who, organized and led by trained martial talent, came down upon the defenceless Kashmiris, pillaging, raping, and killing indiscriminately, until almost the whole northern side of the valley shook with the lamentations of the bereaved and cries of the plundered and ravished. When the carnage was over and the invaders had retired after several scuffles with Indian forces, the members of our small band of enthusiasts, ready to devote their energies to a noble cause, threw themselves into the arduous task of providing relief to a large section of the ravaged victims.

That winter because of stormy conditions in many of the border districts of the state, attended by wholesale massacres and rape, the offices did not move to Jammu, and I therefore continued to attend to my duties at Srinagar, oblivious to the horror of the situation in the all-absorbing mission of service to which we had devoted ourselves. Entirely preoccupied with the task, I could not leave Kashmir during the winter of 1948 either and had to apply for leave of absence to complete the enterprise undertaken at a time when our own fate hung in the balance. During this interval momentous changes occurred in the political framework of the State. The hereditary ruler had to abdicate to make room for a people's government. This great upheaval brought in its wake countless smaller upheavals, bringing new values in place of the old and new ways of thought and action. The old order changed, as has always happened, often without effecting side by side the needed change for the better in human nature which, forgetting soon the lesson taught by a revolution, acts again in a manner that makes another upheaval inevitable after a time.

In November 1949 I again went to Jammu with the office. My wife chose to stay at Srinagar to look after the house and children. She had grown confident of my health and ability to look after myself in view of the endurance displayed by me during the past two years. My system had functioned so regularly that there had occurred not the slightest cause for any perturbation. On the other hand, I had found myself fully equal to and in fact took pleasure in the strenuous task of relieving the distress of hundreds of families taken by us upon ourselves, a mere handful of men without resources or influence, at a time of extreme tension and under rigorous conditions. I stayed at Jammu with an old friend who was good enough to place a room at my disposal. I was glad to accept his hospitality, offered with great cordiality and love, as it afforded me several facilities, especially the opportunity to be all to myself, absorbed in the contemplation of the luminous glow within which had begun to assume to some extent the enrapturing character of the vision perceived on the first day of the awakening.

Profiting by the awful experience I had undergone previously, I made absolutely no attempt to meditate as before. What I did now was quite different. Without any effort and sometimes even without my knowing it, I sank deeper and deeper within myself, engulfed more and more by the lustrous conscious waves, which appeared to grow in size and extent the more I allowed myself to sink without resistance into the sea of consciousness in which I often found myself immersed. After about twelve years a curious transformation had occurred in the glowing circle of awareness around my head which made me constantly conscious of a subtle world of life stretching on all sides in which I breathed, walked, and acted without either in any way affecting its all-pervasive homogenous character or being affected by it in my day-to-day transactions in the world. Speaking more clearly, it seemed as if I were breathing, moving, and acting surrounded by an extremely subtle, viewless, conscious void, as we are surrounded by radio waves, with the difference that I do not perceive or feel the existence of the waves and am compelled to acknowledge their presence by the logic of certain facts; in this case I was made aware of the invisible medium by internal conditions, as if my own confined consciousness, transcending its limitations, were now in direct touch with its own substance on all sides, like a sentient dewdrop floating intact in an ocean of pure being without mingling with the surrounding mass of water.

During the past months I had on a few occasions noticed this tendency of my mind to turn without encountering any barrier to its expansion within itself, extending more like a drop of oil spreading on the surface of water until, collecting myself with an effort, I came back to my normal state, itself more extensive by far than the original field of consciousness I had possessed before the awakening. I had not attached much importance to this phase, believing it to be an attempt of the mind to fall into reveries which, because of its luminous spaciousness, created the impression of further internal expansion without implying any additional change in my already peculiar mental condition. About a month after my arrival at Jammu I noticed that not only had this tendency become more marked and frequent, but the daily plunge into the depths of my lucent being was maturing into a great source of happiness and strength for me. The development was, however, so gradual and the change so imperceptible that I was led to believe that the whole occurrence was the outcome of the general improvement in my health due to the salubrious climate rather than to any new factor operating within me.

Towards the third week of December I noticed that when returning from these prolonged spells of absorption which had now become a regular feature of my solitary hours, my mind usually dwelt on the lyrics of my favourite mystics. Without the least idea of trying my skill at poetic composition, when not in an absorbed mood, I made attempts at it, keeping the mystical rhymes which I liked most as models before me. Beyond the fact that I had committed to memory a few dozen Sanskrit verses culled from the scriptures and a few dozen couplets picked up from the works of mystics, I knew nothing of poetry. After a few days of mere playful dabbling I became restless, and for the first time in my life I felt an urge to write verse. Not at all impressed seriously by what I thought was a passing impulse, I put to paper a few stanzas, devoting several hours every day to the task.

I wrote in Kashmiri, but after about a fortnight of daily endeavour I found I did not improve. The sterility of my efforts to write in verse, instead of dampening my spirits, urged me to greater efforts, however, and I devoted more and more time to what now became a regular, fascinating hobby for me. The standard of the compositions did not improve in the least, and I had often to labour for hours to complete a line and then longer to find another to match it. I never associated the new tendency with the mysterious agency at work in my body. But these unsuccessful attempts I was making at verse formation were a deliberately manoeuvered prelude to a startling occurrence soon after. I was being taught internally to exercise a newly developed talent in me about the existence of which I could have had no inkling otherwise; my crude attempts were the first indication of the schooling.

During those days an ardent member of our small band of zealous workers in Kashmir was on visit to Jammu. She came often to my place, usually to have news of our work at Srinagar about which I received regular reports from our Treasurer or our Secretary. One day I offered to accompany her home when she rose to depart, intending by the long stroll to rid myself of a slight depression I felt at the time. We walked leisurely, discussing our work, when suddenly while crossing the Tawi Bridge I felt a mood of deep absorption settling upon me until I almost lost touch with my surroundings. I no longer heard the voice of my companion; she seemed to have receded into the distance though walking by my side. Near me, in a blaze of brilliant light, I suddenly felt what seemed to be a mighty conscious presence sprung from nowhere encompassing me and overshadowing all the objects around, from which two lines of a beautiful verse in Kashmiri poured out to float before my vision, like luminous writing in the air, disappearing as suddenly as they had come.

When I came to myself, I found the girl looking at me in blank amazement, bewildered by my abrupt silence and the expression of utter detachment on my face. Without revealing to her all that had happened, I repeated the verse, saying that it had all of a sudden taken form in my mind in spite of myself, and that accounted for the break in our conversation. She listened in surprise, struck by the beauty of the rhyme, weighing every word, and then said that it was indeed nothing short of miraculous for one who had never been favoured by the muse before to compose so exquisite a verse on the very first attempt with such lightning rapidity. I heard her in silence, carried away by the profundity of the experience I had just gone through. Until that hour all I had experienced of the superconscious was purely subjective, neither demonstrable to nor verifiable by others. But now for the first time I had before me a tangible proof of the change that had

occurred in me unintelligible to and independently of my surface
consciousness.

Commentary to Chapters Fourteen and Fifteen

In his description of ecstatic samadhi, our author says he was
'living in a lustrous world of brilliant colour'. The extraordinary
visual experiences of colour and texture which are reported by
Huxley in *The Doors of Perception*, by those who have had LSD
visions, by Zaehner in *Mysticism—Sacred and Profane*, by Summers
in *The Physical Phenomena of Mysticism* confirm from different
angles that what our author experienced belongs to this path.
There are of course vast differences between the mysticism
'sacred' of our author and mysticism 'profane', by which, following Zaehner, I refer to technical chemical tricks 'to get an experience'.

Perhaps our contemporary greed to see (television, scuba-
diving, photography, nudity, sight-seeing, LSD and mescalin)
stands in place of the hunger of the soul for true visions. The prices
on the art market attest to what man is willing to pay for true
vision. Today the hungry eye wants the beatific vision; we would
see God's face, even if through chemical ecstasy.

Sacred mysticism recognizes the transformation of perception
not as a separate visual experience, a kick or thrill, but as the outcome of a state of being. In alchemy this stage was referred to as
the peacock's tail in which are 'eyes' unfurled amid some of the
most royally blazing colours known in nature. The Stone too was
known as the tincture, which stained and coloured any object it
contacted. The return of vivid colour follows the white phase.
Psychologically, it refers to the return of health and vitality, joy
in life, love for existence, the liberation of feeling beyond the
personal immediate surroundings, the extension of sensation beyond the senses to the spirit of nature itself; whereas the spiritual
world moves out from its shadowy existence as only a mental
phenomenon and takes on the colour of living reality.

Even in alchemy this stage was followed by a new *mortificatio*, a new disintegration. There, it is difficult to tell why; here, we are given an insight. Our author, in his honesty, writes: 'I was over-joyed at the glorious possibility within *my reach* now. There could be absolutely no doubt that I was the exceedingly fortunate *possessor* of an awakened Kundalini. It was only now that I could *grasp* the reason why . . . *success* . . . was thought to be the highest *achievement* possible . . . the *supreme prize attainable* at the end.' He compares accomplished yogis with 'mighty rulers and poten-tates'. It was an 'honour' that had been 'bestowed on me'.

The next paragraph begins: 'But, alas, my good luck was ex-ceedingly shortlived.' From my italics above, it becomes clear just why: he had fallen victim to a new inflation. Little wonder after that blaze that he did catch fire himself. So again an even worse purge, an even worse 'dying to everything' was necessary. (How necessary is suffering!) The peacock is also a symbol of vanity and pride; the tincture may stain the ego too, bringing to it the poisonous taint of revivified subjectivity, that this world I perceive is mine, my reward, given to me.

The peculiar physical experiences belong to the *death experience*, and similar fits of jerking uncontrolled movements are reported in medieval accounts where these motions were attributed to a plague of devils. The experience is one of dismemberment, dis-integration (attested to as well by the Shamans as an archetypal event in their process in individuation—see M. Eliade, *Shamanism, Archaic Techniques of Ecstasy*). Psychologically, the central system of will which has the ego as its core falls apart into autonomous complexes. One is no longer in control of oneself, and the autonomic nervous system dominates the habitual system identi-fied with the conscious will. One is indeed a victim of unconscious energetic centres, those devilish complexes, pulling every which way.

We cannot help but be enormously impressed with the over-whelming physical reality of Gopi Krishna's death experience. It confirms what I have tried to write about in my *Suicide and the Soul*, that only if the experience be totally convincing, totally 'real', can a convincingly real rebirth follow. Much as we may know this in advance, it is each time a terrifyingly threatening event—and it must be so, otherwise it would not carry the conviction of reality.

I am also enormously impressed that our author was saved by a dream, and such a simple one: a dish of *meat*. When he was first urged by an impulse to eat meat he disregarded the unconscious suggestion perhaps on doctrinaire grounds, still convinced that his mild diet was the right one and that his appetite was a sign of greed (whereas his true 'greed' was spiritual, as our italicized passages above show). This often happens in an analysis: the unconscious urges a step, an advance into health, which the conscious personality, still used to the limits of its neurosis, feels hesitant to make. But a forward step not taken when the time is there is the same as a step backward.

What does this meat mean? Is not meat a return to the human condition in its animal reality, the life of the blood, the instinct of involvement (hunting, struggling, killing)? Meat is the food of the hunter, warrior, chieftain. In alchemy it would belong to the symbols of the rubedo, the red king, of masculine emotional strength. It is also the final integration of the mother complex, eating her as body.

Subsequent to the acceptance of meat, Gopi Krishna returns to the world of action, as a 'chieftain', having organized a group for social work. He is thoroughly involved, not only with paper and ink as in his government office, but now on the plane of daily suffering—widows, refugees, war. The time of the *return* is traditionally critical. After the 'great liberation' how does one re-enter daily life? After such experiences how does one transfer the love and beauty and meaning to the other hours of the week? How does one bridge the gap between planes of being? If it is a narrow gate, an impossibly dangerous passage to cross the threshold into the releasing other world, how much more difficult to re-enter this known and confining world with all its pettiness and banal sorrows. For our author, the 'return' seems to have occurred quite naturally. (Of course, in one sense he did throughout keep one foot well planted in this world with job, family, and diet.) His crisis was less an externalized one: 'How do I enter society and the world of fellow-man bringing with me the gifts that I have been given?' His crisis came before, symbolized by the meat. Once that was eaten, his appetite 'returned' and with it re-entry into the world in a new way.

The natural and easy flow back into the world, spreading himself thin over the troubled waters of social reality, to calm, soothe, bind up, again has a striking resemblance to one of the last stages of alchemy. I refer to the image of 'oil'. He describes his expansion of consciousness to extend 'more and more like a drop of oil spreading on the surface of water'. The Stone was said to have an oily nature, easily melted but not to be evaporated, staining (as a tincture) all with which it came in contact. 'The development was gradual and the change so imperceptible' that he attributed it to general improvement rather than to a new principle at work. But just this imperceptible peaceful oozing rather than willing, this softening of friction rather than striving, this thick slowness which is yet lighter than water, is attached to it yet floats over it— just this is the fat and oil of abundance, the joy and compassion of full being.

Chapter Sixteen

AFTER escorting my companion to her destination I returned to my residence in time for dinner. All the way back in the stillness of a pleasant evening and the welcome solitude of an unfrequented path I remained deeply engrossed in the enigma presented by the vision and the sudden leap taken by my mind in a new direction. The more intently I examined the problem the more surprised I became at the deep meaning of the production, the exquisite formation, and the highly appealing language of the lines. On no account could I claim the artistic composition as mine, the voluntary creation of my own deliberate thought.

I reached my place while still deeply absorbed in the same train of thought and, still engrossed, sat down for dinner. I took the first few morsels mechanically, in silence, oblivious to my surroundings and unappreciative of the food in front of me, unable to bring myself out of the state of intense absorption into which I had fallen, retaining only a slender link with my environment like a sleepwalker instinctively restrained from colliding with the objects in his path without consciously being aware of them. In the middle of the meal, while still in the same condition of semi-entrancement, I stopped abruptly, contemplating with awe and amazement, which made the hair on my skin stand on end, a marvellous phenomenon in progress in the depths of my being. Without any effort on my part and while seated comfortably on a chair, I had gradually passed off, without becoming aware of it, into a condition of exaltation and self-expansion similar to that which I had experienced on the very first occasion, in December 1937, with the modification that in place of a roaring noise in my ears there was now a cadence like the humming of a swarm of bees, enchanting and melodious, and the encircling glow was replaced by a penetrating silvery radiance, already a feature of my being within and without.

The marvellous aspect of the condition, lay in the sudden realization that although linked to the body and surroundings I had expanded in an indescribable manner into a titanic personality, conscious from within of an immediate and direct contact with an intensely conscious universe, a wonderful inexpressible immanence all around me. My body, the chair I was sitting on, the table in front of me, the room enclosed by walls, the lawn outside and the space beyond including the earth and sky appeared to be most amazingly mere phantoms in this real, interpenetrating and all-pervasive ocean of existence which, to explain the most incredible part of it as best I can, seemed to be simultaneously unbounded, stretching out immeasurably in all directions, and yet no bigger than an infinitely small point. From this marvellous point the entire existence, of which my body and its surroundings were a part, poured out like radiation, as if a reflection as vast as my conception of the cosmos were thrown out upon infinity by a projector no bigger than a pinpoint, the entire intensely active and gigantic world picture dependent on the beams issuing from it. The shoreless ocean of consciousness in which I was now immersed appeared infinitely large and infinitely small at the same time, large when considered in relation to the world picture floating in it and small when considered in itself, measureless, without form or size, nothing and yet everything.

It was an amazing and staggering experience for which I can cite no parallel and no simile, an experience beyond all and everything belonging to this world, conceivable by the mind or perceptible to the senses. I was intensely aware internally of a marvellous being so concentratedly and massively conscious as to outlustre and outstature infinitely the cosmic image present before me, not only in point of extent and brightness but in point of reality and substance as well. The phenomenal world, ceaselessly in motion characterized by creation, incessant change, and dissolution, receded into the background and assumed the appearance of an extremely thin, rapidly melting layer of foam upon a substantial rolling ocean of life, a veil of exceedingly fine vapour before an infinitely large conscious sun, constituting a complete reversal of the relationship between the world and the limited human consciousness. It showed the previously all-dominating cosmos reduced to the state of a transitory appearance and the formerly care-ridden point of awareness, circumscribed by the body, grown to the spacious dimensions of a mighty universe and the exalted stature of a majestic immanence before which the material cosmos shrank to the subordinate position of an evanescent and illusive appendage.

I awoke from the semi-trance condition after about a half-hour, affected to the roots of my being by the majesty and marvel of the vision, entirely oblivious to the passage of time, having in the intensity of the experience lived a life of ordinary existence. During the period, probably due to fluctuations in the state of my body and mind caused by internal and external stimuli, there were intervals of deeper and lesser penetration not distinguishable by the flow of time but by the state of immanence, which at the point of the deepest penetration assumed such an awe-inspiring, almighty, all-knowing, blissful, and at the same time absolutely motionless, intangible, and formless character that the invisible line demarcating the material world and the boundless, all-conscious Reality ceased to exist, the two fusing into one; the mighty ocean sucked up by a drop, the enormous three-dimensional universe swallowed by a grain of sand, the entire creation, the knower and the known, the seer and the seen, reduced to an inexpressible sizeless void which no mind can conceive nor any language describe.

Before coming out completely from this condition, and before the glory in which I found myself had completely faded, I found floating in the luminous glow of my mind the rhymes following the couplet that had suddenly taken shape in me near the Tawi Bridge that day. The lines occurred one after the other, as if dropped into the three-dimensional field of my consciousness by another source of condensed knowledge within me. They started from the glowing recesses of my being, developing suddenly into fully formed couplets like falling snowflakes which, from tiny specks high up, become clear-cut, regularly shaped crystals when nearing the eye, and vanished so suddenly as to leave me hardly any time to retain them in my memory. They came fully formed, complete with language, rhyme, and metre, finished products originating as it seemed from the surrounding intelligence to pass before my internal eye for expression. I was still in an elevated state when I rose from the table and went to my room. The first thing I did was to write down the lines as far as I could remember them. It was not an easy task. I found that during the short interval that had elapsed I had forgotten not only the order in which the rhymes had occurred but also whole portions of the matter, which it was extremely difficult for me to recollect or supply. It took me more than two hours to supply the omissions.

I went to bed that night in an excited and happy frame of mind. After years of acute suffering I had at last been given a glimpse into the supersensible and at the same time made the fortunate recipient of divine grace, which all fitted admirably with the traditional concepts of Kundalini. I could not believe in my good luck; I felt it was too astounding to be true. But when I looked within myself to find out what I had done to deserve it, I felt extremely humbled. I had to my credit no achievement remarkable enough to entitle me to the honour bestowed on me. I had lived an ordinary life, never done anything exceptionally meritorious and never achieved a complete subdual of desires and appetites.

I reviewed all the noteworthy incidents of the last twelve years in my mind, studying them in the light of the latest development, and found that much of what had been dark and obscure so far was assuming a deep and startling significance. In the intensity of joy which I felt at the revelation I forgot the terrible ordeal I had passed through as also the gruelling suspense and anxiety that had been my companions for all the period. I had drunk the cup of suffering to the dregs to come upon a resplendent, never-ending source of unutterable joy and peace lying hidden in my interior, waiting for a favourable opportunity to reveal itself, affording me in one instant a deeper insight into the essence of things than a whole life devoted to study could do.

Thinking such thoughts I fell asleep at last, waking again in the luminous realm of dreams in which I had my abode every night. When I awoke in the morning the first recollection that came to my mind was of the transcendental experience of the previous evening. Even the fleeting memory of a superconscious flight into the wonderland of Infinity is transporting, surpassing anything we can think of or encounter in the physical world. Considering the stupendous nature of the vision it is no wonder that the ancient seers of India in constant communion with the transcendental reality regarded the world as no more than an inexplicable shadow, an impermanent, illusory appearance before an eternal, resplendent sun of indescribable grandeur and sublimity.

Every day during the next two weeks I wrote a few stanzas in Kashmiri that without exception dealt with some aspect of the unknown; some of them were definitely apocalyptic in nature. The verses occurred suddenly at odd times in the day or night, preceded by a voluntary pause on my part in the normal process of thinking. This preliminary cessation of mental activity was soon followed by a state of deep absorption, as if I were diving within myself to reach a certain depth where I could catch the vibrations of the message always expressed in poetry. The lines developed from an extremely subtle form, an invisible seed, and instantaneously passed before my mind as fully formed verses, following each other in rapid succession until the whole passage was completed, when I suddenly experienced a desire to withdraw myself from the state of semi-entrancement and return to normality.

On one more occasion during that fortnight I had the same transcendental experience as on the first day, tallying in almost all respects with the original one. I was sitting on a chair reading a piece written on the preceding day when, noticing the command,

I leaned back in the chair and closed my eyes in a mood of relaxation, waiting for the results. The moment I did so I felt myself expanding in all directions, oblivious to the surroundings, and enveloped in an immense sea of glowing radiance, entertained by a sweet internal cadence unlike any symphony heard on earth, drawing nearer to the supreme condition, until with a plunge I found myself detached from all belonging to the causal world, lost in the inexpressible void, a marvellous state of being absolutely devoid of spatial and temporal distinctions. I returned to my normal state after more than half an hour and during the few moments of transition found a beautiful composition waiting for cognizance by my mind, staggered by the extraordinary experience that it had just gone through.

After a fortnight the language changed and instead of rhymes in Kashmiri they occurred in English. The slight knowledge of English verse which I possessed was all confined to the study of a few selected poems forming a part of my school and college texts. Beyond that, having no inherent taste for poetry, I had never cared to read it. But I could easily perceive that the passage before me was similar to the poems I had read, but having no knowledge of the rhyme and metre of English poetry, I could not form any judgment about its excellence.

A few days after, the poems appeared in Urdu instead of in English. Having a workable knowledge of the former, I did not feel any difficulty in writing down the lines, but all the same many blanks were left which were filled only months later. Urdu was succeeded by Punjabi in a few days. I had not read any book in Punjabi but had learned the language by constant contact with Punjabi-speaking friends and associates during my several years' stay in Lahore as a school and college student. My surprise, however, knew no bounds when a few days later the direction came that I should prepare to receive verses in Persian. I had never read the language nor could I in the least understand or speak it. I waited in breathless expectancy and immediately after the signal a few Persian verses flashed before my mind in the same manner as the compositions in other languages. I had no difficulty in recognizing many Persian words and even the verse form of the lines. Kashmiri being rich in Persian words, it was easy for me to understand words already used in my mother-tongue. After a great deal of exertion and straining, I at last succeeded in penning down the lines, but there were many blanks and mistakes which could not be filled in or set right until long after.

The few short poems in Persian that I was able to jot down involved such a strenuous effort that after some days I was obliged to desist from the onerous task. I felt entirely exhausted and what was more serious, the unhealthy effect of the exertion and excitement elicited was becoming seriously apparent in the prolonged spells of restlessness preceding my sleep. Consequently I gave myself complete rest for more than a week.

After a short rest, feeling somewhat restored to health, I no longer felt it necessary to resist the impulse and submitted to the elevating moods at opportune times. One day when I had obeyed the unspoken direction for relaxing my mind to prepare myself for reception and had sunk deeply enough to reach the subtle emanations from the amazing conscious source within, yet tantalizingly out of my reach, I felt a thrill of deep excitement not unmixed with fear pass through every fibre of my being when the signal flashed across my now quiescent mind to make myself ready for taking down a piece in German. I came back from the semi-trance condition with a ferment in my mind, unable to reconcile myself to the idea that such a weird performance could ever be possible. I had never learned German, nor seen a book written in the language, nor to the best of my knowledge ever heard it spoken in my presence, and yet I was expected to write down a poem in it which in plain terms meant a complete negation of the time-honoured truth that language is an acquired and not inherited possession.

German was followed by French and Italian. Then came a few verses in Sanskrit followed by Arabic. Surely there could be nothing more convincing than the phenomena I had witnessed during the previous few weeks to bring the idea irresistibly home to me that I was in occasional contact with an inexpressible fount of all knowledge and that but for my inability to understand and transcribe, I could take down poetic pieces in most of the well-known languages of the earth. I felt wave after wave of conscious electricity pass through me replete with knowledge to which, because of the poor capacity of my brain, I could not have full access.

Language fails me when I attempt to describe the experience which off and on has all along since then been the most sublime and the most elevating feature of my existence. On every such occasion I am made to feel as if the observer in me, or speaking more precisely, my lustrous conscious self, is floating, with but an extremely dim idea of the corporeal frame in a vividly bright conscious plane, every fragment of which represents a boundless world of knowledge, embracing the present, past, and future, commanding all the sciences, philosophies, and arts ever known or that will be known in the ages to come, all concentrated and contained in a point existing here and everywhere, now and always, a formless, measureless ocean of wisdom from which, drop by drop, knowledge has filtered and will continue to filter into the human brain. On every visit to the supersensible realm I am so overwhelmed by the mystery and the wonder of it that everything else of this world, everything conceived by us of the next, every fact and incident of my life save this, every momentous event of history, every ambition and desire, and above all even my own existence, life and death, appear to be trite and trivial before the indescribable glory, the unfathomable mystery, and the unimaginable extent of the marvellous ocean of life, of which I am at times permitted to approach the shore.

Chapter Seventeen

THE daily dive into the conscious ocean to which I had now unexpectedly found access had a most exhilarating effect on my
mind. I was overwhelmed with wonder at the incalculable wealth
I had found within myself. The distracting anxiety I had felt and
the grave doubts I had entertained about my condition vanished
altogether, yielding place to a feeling of inexpressible thankfulness
to the divine power, which in spite of my ignorance, constant
resistance, many faults, frailties, and mistakes, had wrought with
matchless skill a new channel of perception in me, a new and more
penetrating sight in order to introduce me to a stupendous
existence.

In spite of all my efforts, the news of the strange psychic manifestations in me leaked out. My host, friends, and colleagues at
the office were struck by my altered behaviour and my constant
mood of deep absorption. Even if I had tried, I could not have
shaken it off, being myself entirely carried away by the wonder of
an occurrence beyond anything I could have imagined. I certainly
could not hide from my close associates a development that had
the effect of startling me out of my equilibrium. My host, uneasy
at my constant perambulations in a state of deep abstraction, almost to the point of being totally oblivious at times, grew positively alarmed at seeing my lights on at odd hours in the night and
finding me awake, writing in a mood of utter preoccupation.

Knowing of my mystical tendencies, he remonstrated with me gently under the misapprehension that my constant absorption and nocturnal exertions were a prelude to a complete renunciation of the world in order to take up a monastic life.

In the course of a few weeks, unable to resist the fascination of the newly found subliminal existence, I found myself powerless to come out of my contemplative moods. Except for a few hours of irregular sleep at night they were continuously upon me for the whole day, making it almost impossible for me to apply my mind to anything. I ate mechanically, almost as a child does in sleep, and when obliged to speak talked and heard like a man who is engrossed in watching a most fascinating drama enacted before him and returns laconic answers to the comments of those seated beside him, often without comprehending and remembering fully what is said. I went to the office more by force of habit than by choice or inclination. My whole being rose in revolt when I attempted to climb down from the ethereal heights of transcendence to the dry files lying unattended on my table. After some days the mere act of sitting in the cramped atmosphere of the room for hours became so unpleasant and oppressive that I proceeded on long leave, never to enter the premises again. I realized that the severance of my connection with the office would reduce my income to a great extent, but the urge in me to liberate myself from the bonds of servitude was too strong to be suppressed by monetary or wordly considerations.

In the meantime the strange news travelled through the town, and crowds of people called at my residence, attracted by the rumours of the miraculous development in me. Most of them came merely to satisfy their curiosity and to verify what they had heard, much as they would have gone to look at a freak or to watch the astounding performance of a conjurer. But few of them evinced any interest in the genesis of the change or the reason for the sudden manifestation. In a few days the rush of people became so great and continuous that from early morning to the hour of darkness I had not a moment to myself. Feeling that it would be discourteous to refuse interviews, and labouring under the notion that such an attitude on my part would be misconstrued as pride,

I bore the daily rush patiently at the cost of my mental peace, which ought to have been my primary concern in the initial stages of the new development. I was usually in an exalted state of mind throughout, and in the same condition talked to the people gathered round me, frequently passing into deeper moods under their looks from which I was often recalled to my surroundings by the entry of other groups. I greeted the eager crowds mechanically, barely mindful of what I said or of those who arrived and left during the day.

After a few days the strain became unbearable, and I began to feel its adverse effects on my health. The first indication of the trouble was a growing restlessness during nights, which soon assumed the state of partial insomnia. Instead of feeling alarmed at the reappearance of an enemy that had caused me so much agony in the past, I interpreted it as first sign of a liberated existence, of freedom from the domination of the flesh, considered to be an essential feature of true spiritual growth. Lacking the care of my wife, who with a woman's true instinct always exercised a strict supervision of my diet, I grew indifferent to food also, revelling in the thought that I had at last overcome a weakness which had compelled me to be too attentive to my nutrition and a slave to regularity. Gradually a feeling of detachment from the world began to take hold of me, accompanied by an increasing desire to break the chains that bound me to my family and to lead the life of a sanyasi untroubled by desire and unfettered by customs and conventions.

I had passed through a most strange experience which had culminated in a development entirely beyond my expectations and one which it was necessary to make known to others. It was therefore my duty, I argued with myself, to lead a life entirely free of the fret and fever of a worldly existence, devoted exclusively to the service of mankind, with the object of making known the great truth I had found. The only obstacle to the execution of this resolve, I thought, would be presented by the strong ties of affection which bound me to my family and friends and which, judging from my own past experience and inherent tendencies, would be very hard to break. But when I pondered more deeply on the issue and searched my heart for the answer, I found to my great surprise that the amazing experience I had now undergone had purged me clean of wordly love also, and that I could part from my family and friends forever without so much as a single look behind, to perform unhampered by any thought of family obligations the sacred task I eagerly wished to take upon myself.

But though I was afforded a glimpse into the state of mind and the motive power behind it that drove the prophets and seers of old to unparalleled feats of renunciation and asceticism, which appear beyond the capacity of the ordinary man, I was not destined to follow in their footsteps due to the extreme susceptibility of my system to disorder under the stress of unfavourable and rough conditions. There was a weak spot in me somewhere which often gave way under the rigour imposed by an ascetic way of life or continued irregularity in the matter of diet and sleep. I believe it is because of this vulnerability that I was able to trace the close connection existing between the body and the mind even in transcendental conditions of the brain which might not have been so clearly apparent to me otherwise.

For more than a month I lived in a state of triumph and spiritual exaltation which it is impossible to describe. During all this period my whole being was always pervaded by a distinct feeling that while moving, sitting or acting I was constantly encompassed by a stupendous silent presence from which I drew my individual existence. Frequently I had moods of deeper absorption when, speechless with wonder, I lost myself completely in the indescribable. These moods were attended occasionally by inspirational flashes towards the close. After the end of this period, owing to insufficient sleep and irregularity in diet, the feeling of exaltation and happiness, which had been present continuously, diminished perceptibly, and I again began to feel signs of exhaustion and at times even of uneasiness in my mind. I was roughly shaken out of this short-lived state of heavenly joy when one morning, rising from bed after a restless night, I found myself in the grip of acute depression which continued for the whole day, acting like a dip in ice-cold water on one in a state of inebriation. Startled out of my mistaken optimism and reprimanding myself sharply for the neglect, I forced myself to give immediate attention to my diet, and after some days noticed signs of improvement in my condition.

But my immoderate indulgence in psychic enjoyment, excessive mental exertion, and neglect of organic needs had, without my detecting it, depleted my vitality to an alarming extent, creating a poisoned state of the nervous system, which prevented me from noticing the extremely slow deterioration, in time to take appropriate precautionary measures. I had heard stories of men who, intoxicated with joy to the point of madness on their first glimpse of the supersensory state of existence after the awakening, had been so entirely carried away from earthly life that they found it impossible to come down to the normal level of consciousness in order to attend to the needs of the body; their spirits in unbroken ecstatic contemplation of the fascinating supersensual realm from the beginning to the end had departed the starved body without even once descending back to earth.

I immediately refrained from exhibiting myself before the curious crowds that came and went in an unending stream. Instead of encouraging the moods of intense absorption, always ready to settle upon me the moment my mind turned inwards, I deliberately avoided introversion, devoting myself exclusively to wordly trifles in order to allow a period of rest to the already overstimulated brain. It was about the middle of March, marking the beginning of spring in Kashmir, and I felt I should no longer delay returning to my home, my only asylum in times of distress, in order to submit myself to the affectionate care of my wife, my sole guardian during illness. Without losing a single day I journeyed to Srinagar by air, relinquishing forever the thought of roaming the earth in the traditional way to effect the regeneration of mankind, a fantasy in my case born from the desire for power, **the yearning** for mental conquest, which often accompanies the activity of Kundalini in the intellectual centre, causing a slightly intoxicated condition of the brain too subtle to be noticed by the subject himself or by his uninformed companions, however erudite and intelligent they may be.

At home I entrusted myself completely to the care of my wife, who from the absence of colour in my face and the look in my eyes, at once concluded that I was in a state of exhaustion and stood in urgent need of rest and recuperation. The news of my strange feats had travelled to Srinagar before me, and it became a difficult problem to prevent the crowds which assembled at my house from gaining access to me. After a few days I was able to devote several hours daily to meet the visitors without fatigue, and kept myself lightly engaged for the rest of the time to avoid the influence of contemplative moods which even now exercised such a fascination over me that I had to exert my will to the utmost to resist the temptation completely for even a day. In the course of a few weeks the crowds began to thin and ultimately ceased, allowing me more respite which coupled with the precautions taken in diet, helped me to overcome the deficiency caused by my own lack of restraint. But it took more than six months for me to be normal again and to attend my duties without losing myself all of a sudden in the rapt contemplation of an unconditioned existence.

By the time my leave expired I had made up my mind not to serve any longer. The way of escape from the sordidness and misery of the material world into the unutterable peace and tranquillity of the effulgent internal universe was too narrow and too risky to allow me to make use of it with a heavy load of wordly responsibilities upon my shoulders. In order to taste the fruit of true spiritual liberation, it was necessary for me to free myself as far as possible from the chains that bound me to the material world. The secluded corner of a busy office room, throbbing with noiseless activity and tense with subdued excitement was not a place where a man now constantly preoccupied with the unseen, could pass several hours at a stretch always at the call of others, without running the risk of serious injury to his mental health. There were other reasons too, which precipitated my decision to sever my connections entirely with the office. The change of Government had brought in its wake a host of burning problems all demanding immediate solution. They had to be handled, and handled carefully at a time when the whole country was in a state of ferment caused by a wild scramble for power and

possessions on the one side and the efforts made to avert deprivation and dispossession on the other. Our office could not escape
the general commotion visible everywhere, and soon its atmosphere grew charged with mutual suspicion to an extent that for a
man in my condition it was positively dangerous. Accordingly I
applied for premature retirement which, after the usual formalities
was ultimately sanctioned.

I was now free to pass my time as I pleased, untroubled by any
thoughts of how to find my way out of the ever-present official
dilemmas and the constant conflicts between my conscience and
the wishes of my superiors. After an absence of many months,
during which there had literally occurred a world of difference in
me, I again joined the staunch group of friends who had kept our
movement alive during the interval. I again participated in their
activities, which were now directed towards providing amenities
for the utterly destitute widows in our society or towards re-
moving the barrier of public opinion against the remarriage of
those of them who were agreeable to it, in this way mitigating to
some extent the suffering of many subjected to inhuman treatment in the name of religion and caste by their own families.

In spite of the deep desire of every member of the little group
to confine their activities to the mission of service, they were
drawn unwillingly into the troubled waters of political rivalry
and ambition by constant opposition, aimed at forcing their
allegiance. In the course of a few years it was made difficult for
them even to carry on the humanitarian work in which they were
engaged. But determined to persist they managed to continue
their activities in a restricted form, always anxious to steer clear
of rival political groups angling for their support.

During the critical years that followed my first experience of
the unseen, the work centre of our group served for me the twofold purpose of providing congenial occupation without any cur-
tailment of my freedom, and also a fruitful and healthy hobby
for my leisure. I had for the first time tasted the joy of a new
existence and it maddened me to an extent I could not believe
possible, creating a feeling of estrangement from the world and
an aversion towards the things of life as if I were a captive in an

alien land impatient to break away from the prison but unable to do so. I might have turned a recluse to assuage the fire of renunciation kindled in me but for the constant touch with suffering and misery and the slender chance I had of alleviating it. My active participation in the charitable endeavour, though extremely limited in scope, conduced to some extent to keep me normal with enough attachment for the world to combat the morbid escapist tendencies that had developed in me. The rest was accomplished by my wife, whose immense love, unremitting attention to my smallest need, and constant care made me so dependent on her that the idea of residing in solitude, away from her even for a short time, appeared too formidable to be possible of execution by one in such an extremely delicate and peculiar state of health as I was.

From the very beginning of the new development, many persons prompted by desire or driven by necessity came to see me with an ulterior object in view. They waited for hours, seeking an opportunity to talk to me alone about the purpose of their visit. During the earlier period, when the crowds showed no sign of diminution and I was generally in an elevated and far-from-communicative mood, they came several times in succession until able to snatch a few minutes of private conversation with me. For most of them I had attained a state of authority, of command over the subtle forces of nature, able to do and undo things, competent to alter circumstances, to change the destiny and modify the effect of other people's actions and conduct. They allotted to me a position of suzerainty, of close intimacy with the Almighty, with powers to defy the laws of nature and to interrupt the march of events by merely a gesture or an effort of my will. I heard their stories in silence, touched at the scenes of human misery and tales of harrowing grief which they narrated. Some were destitute, some unemployed, some childless, some involved in litigation, some hopeless invalids, some in the grip of reverses, some entangled in domestic troubles, and so on. They expected me to intercede with fate on their behalf to rid them of their sorrows and to free them from their difficulties against which they were powerless to battle, and were eager to catch at every passing chance, holding the slenderest ray of hope as a drowning man catches at a straw. They were all of them afflicted, frustrated, or disillusioned men and women for whom life was a bed of thorns.

The general belief among the masses about psychics and men of vision, stretching back to prehistoric times, credits them with amazing supernatural powers. The impression is that they possess a mysterious link with or control over subtle, intelligent forces of nature and command over the elementals and spirits. I could not escape the consequences of this conception, and no amount of denial and argument on my part was effective in carrying conviction to people not only deeply steeped in the superstition from early childhood but also forced by exceedingly painful situations to be eagerly on the lookout for a supernatural source to extricate them from their difficulties. Not a few of them, ascribing my honestly expressed inability to help them out of their afflictions to reluctance on my part to do anything, behaved like children, imploring my assistance with folded hands and tears in their eyes. The sight of tears and manly voices husky with emotion left me powerfully affected, as shaken with grief as they were.

These afflicted men and women who came to me for a miraculous escape from their ills were mostly the victims of social injustice, and my heart went out to them in sympathy. In their position I, too, might have acted in the same manner. My utter inability to relieve their distress added so greatly to my sorrow at their misery that, unable to bear it, I sometimes had to seek the sanctuary of my deeper being to gain assurance and strength to overcome it. I consoled them as best as I could, and often they went in a more peaceful frame of mind than that in which they had come, leaving me restless and unsatisfied, heavy with their grief, vividly conscious of the fact that forming as we do the tiny individual cells of a mighty organism, we share alike the sorrows and misery existing in the world; but debarred from realizing it by the wall of ego segregating each cell from the rest, we feel happy and proud at acquisitions often purchased at our own cost, which we mistakenly believe has been paid by others.

While there is a solid foundation for the venerable belief which attributes transcendental powers to visionaries, the popular idea has persisted through centuries that those possessing the power are in a position to set aside the laws of nature and to change the ordained course of events. This idea rests on an incorrect evaluation of the position and also on an unhealthy attitude towards the problems of life. The development of a supersensory channel of knowledge for the perception of subtle realities beyond the reach of senses and reason is not intended to supplant but rather to aid the rational faculty in the management of temporal affairs rigidly ruled by temporal laws. The psychic and even physical powers possessed by prophets and seers are merely in the nature of a manifestation, an emblem of sovereignty bestowed by nature. In the circumstance the application of the extremely rare spiritual endowments to the solution of the day-to-day problems of man's physical existence, for which intellect is the proper instrument, would be no less irrational than the utilization of the quality of heaviness in gold for the purpose of crushing stones with it to provide material for roads. The curative and other powers sometimes exercised by mystics and saints never went beyond the sphere of individual application, and it was left for men of genius who brought vision to the aid of intellect to devise universally efficacious remedies for scourges like smallpox, and to make other discoveries in the physical realm, a task which was neither accomplished by nor fell in the province of prophets and visionaries.

As time wore on and I firmly refused to be tempted into making a vulgar exhibition or impious use of the priceless gift which heaven had bestowed on me, there occurred a perceptible thinning in the number of supplicants who came purely with the object of a miraculous redress, and ultimately they ceased altogether. I scrupulously adhered to a normal mode of life, performing all the duties incumbent on me as the head of a family, and in my dress, manner, and behaviour displayed not the slightest deviation from the pattern which I should have followed in the usual course. This made most of the people, who in the beginning had evinced the deepest interest in my astounding performance, revise their opinion and regard the development as either freakish, disappearing as mysteriously as it had come to pass, or as an ab-

224   *Kundalini*

normality that subsided of its own accord with the passage of time. In the course of a few years the incident, after existing as a nine-day wonder, was almost forgotten and is now seldom mentioned save by traducers, who refer to it as an incontestible proof of my eccentric disposition when they wish to run me down.

In view of this experience I wonder at the inability of the mass mind to move out even an inch beyond the accustomed rut. Barring not more than half a dozen people in all, the thousands who came to see me evinced not the least curiosity to know how the develpment had occurred and what the mystery was behind the surprising manifestation. If in the beginning, side by side with the manifestation, I had started to talk and whisper in a mysterious manner and edited recondite volumes for mystified readers to pore over, each at liberty to draw his own meaning from the vague expressions and obscure passages, instead of making a plain, unambiguous statement of facts, and had followed the same principle in my dress and behaviour, the interest and curiosity created would have increased enormously, at least for a period, securing me not only popularity but money as well at the cost of truth.

Chapter Eighteen

In the course of time I came more and more towards the normal, while retaining the heightened state of consciousness inviolate, and descending mentally from a state of intoxication to one of sobriety. I became more keenly conscious of the fact that though my psycho-physiological equipment had now attained a condition that made it possible for me on occasions to transcend the boundary rigidly confining the mental activity of my fellow beings, I was essentially in no way different from or superior to them.

Physically I was what I had been before, as susceptible to disease, decay, and age, as liable to accident and calamity, as prone to hunger and thirst as I always had been, a normal man in every other way save the alteration in the mental sphere, which by bringing me on occasions nearer to sober metaphysical realities, as astounding and remote from our ordinary conceptions as light is from darkness, had a curbing effect upon the frivolous and vain tendencies of my mind. I had in no way overcome the biological limitations of my body, in no manner exceeded the measure of its endurance and physical capacity, or attained any miraculous powers to defy the laws of nature. On the other hand, my system had grown more delicate. I was the same man, now advanced in age, who had sat for meditation on the memorable day when I had my first experience of the superphysical, with the difference that since then my brain has been attuned to finer vibrations from the unimaginable conscious universe all around us, and has in consequence acquired a deeper and more penetrating inner vision. Except for the alteration in the vital current and certain peculiar biological changes there was no distinctive external feature to mark me out from the rest. The moods of deep absorption, leading to the indescribable super-condition on occasions, became a normal feature of my existence. I lost touch with it, however, during intervals of illness and in the debilitated condition of the system which followed in its wake.

The transcendental experience has been repeated so often that there is no room for doubt about its validity, and it tallies so clearly with the descriptions left by mystics and yogis as to yield no possibility of mistaking it for any other condition. The experience is genuine beyond question, but there is a difference in my recognition of it as compared to that accorded it in the past. The variation lies in treating the manifestation not as a mark of special divine favour, vouchsafed to me in particular or earned by me as a reward for merit, but as an ever-present possibility, existing in all human beings by virtue of the evolutionary process still at work in the race, tending to create a condition of the brain and nervous system that can enable one to transcend the existing boundaries of the mind and acquire a state of consciousness far above that which is the normal heritage of mankind at present. In other words, instead of believing that the experience, in spite of its marvellous and sublime nature, denotes a subjective apprehension of ultimate reality, complete and whole, it represents to me an upward climb from one rung of the ladder of evolution to another.

To me there appears to be no reason to attribute the phenomenon to the direct intervention of Divine Will, irrespective of physical and spiritual cosmic laws. The progress made by man during the aeonic cycle of his evolution could not be accidental, nor could his transformation be effected without divine guidance and favour at every step. It would be little short of ridiculous to assume that he is dearer to God now than he was a million years ago, and is entitled at present to special favours withheld at that time. Unless we eliminate Divinity altogether from creation or at least from the whole scheme of organic evolution, there is no alternative but to accept the origin and subsequent development of the latter from the first stir of life in the primordial state to the emergence of man as being due entirely to the operation of Divine Will acting through eternal laws, obscure and unintelligible to us at present. The distance left behind by man on his ascent from the lowland of instinct to the height of a rational being was as essential a lap of his journey as that now in front of him from the state of an earth-bound mortal to the heaven-kissed peak of godhood. The former owed its origin as much to Divine Will as does the latter, both dependent for success on the proper observance of still obscure cosmic laws.

There is a law at work even in such cases where the manifestation is sudden, following extraordinary spiritual striving and penance, or without it, or there occurs to all appearances a miraculous intervention at a critical moment, as happened in my case more than once, for which there is absolutely no explanation and no alternative except to treat the phenomenon as an act of divine grace. I do not know whether it was owing to the nature of the manifestation or to the fact that I was vouchsafed the privilege while leading the normal life of a householder without any previous indoctrination, religious bias, or monastic mental discipline, but the fact remains that from the very start an inborn conviction gradually gathered shape in my mind that what I experienced in the transcendental state is but the next higher phase of consciousness which humanity is destined to acquire in course of time as its normal possession, aspiring again to a still more sublime form impossible even to conceive of at present.

Warned by the ill effects that followed my excessive absorption in the superconscious at Jammu, I tried and gradually succeeded in exercising restraint and moderation on the supersensory activity of my mind by keeping myself engaged in healthy temporal pursuits and the work of the organization. The exhausting mental effort needed for the reception of compositions in languages other than those known to me was too high a price to be paid for a performance which at the most had only a sensational or surprise value for others. I found in the course of time that only a slight knowledge of a language was sufficient to enable me to receive passages in verse without straining the memory or causing a harmful fatigue of the sensitive brain. Perhaps because of the possibility of injury, due to the strenuous ment.¹ exertion required in the reception of unknown languages, this phase of the newly developed psychic activity ceased after a while. Passages in the known languages continued to come off and on, especially during the three months of winter, when probably owing to a greater adaptability to cold than to heat my system can sustain the higher moods more easily than in summer. But whether summer or winter, it is essential for the supersensual play of my mind that the body be in normal health, entirely free of sickness and infection.

The luminous glow in the head and cadence in the ears continue undiminished. There is a slight variation in the lustre as well as in the quality of the sounds during bodily or mental disturbance, which clearly indicates at least as close a relationship between the now highly extended consciousness and organism as existed between the two before the awakening. My reaction to infection and disease is slightly different; first, an utter absence of or only a slight rise in temperature during illness, with an abnormal rapidity of pulse, secondly, my inability to undergo a fast with safety. It appears that the drain on the vital fuel in my system to feed the ever-burning flame across the forehead is too excessive and the reserve of energy too small to allow it to carry on the highly increased vital activity for lengthy periods without replenishment. This susceptibility of the organism might be because of the tremendous strain borne or even slight damage sustained by my nervous system on more than one occasion, owing to my unconscious violation of the conditions governing my new existence, or to the inherent weakness of some vital organ, or to both. For this reason in any disorder of the system I have to be extremely careful about diet and regularity.

Apart from the crises I had to face in the spiritual domain, fate had destined me for no less severe trials in the temporal sphere as well. The severance of my connection with the office resulted in the reduction of my income by one half, on which I had to maintain myself and my family. I was in too delicate and precarious a condition both mentally and physically for years to allow me to take up any occupation to augment my resources requiring sustained attention and labour. I needed freedom and rest to save myself from a mental disaster in that extremely sensitive condition of the brain. During this very period the prices of commodities soared, making it impossible for us with our small income to make ends meet. Far from stretching my hand to anyone for help, I did not even allow the least indication of our crushing poverty to leak out. I had no brother or uncle from whom to expect assistance. My poor father-in-law, always solicitous for my welfare, was shot dead by the raiders at the time of their incursion in 1947, and his eldest son was held captive at Bunji where he underwent great hardships for more than a year before securing his freedom. His younger brothers had their own hands full trying to retrieve the ruined fortune of the plundered and ravaged family. My two sisters, both extremely kind and affectionate to me, were themselves caught in economic distress and for years could not extricate themselves sufficiently to plant their feet on firm ground again.

The chilling wave of penury which submerged us swept over almost all the families closely bound to us in ties of kinship and there could be no possibility of support from any side. Even if there had been, I should have been the last person to avail myself of it. Although we suffered terribly, not the least gesture was made to anyone for help. Compared to pre-war prices, the cost of food had risen many times as the result of inflation apparent everywhere. The whole salary I received from the office before my retirement, even if doubled, could not have enabled us to meet the needs of our small family in the face of the high rise in prices, and even in the normal course would have entailed financial difficulties. But with the income halved, the cost of living at least fourfold, and the unavoidable demand for a more nutritious and hence more costly diet for me with absolutely no other source of income and no possibility of one, placed me in an indescribable predicament at a time when I was mentally in a precarious condition.

The struggle lasted for nearly seven years. Only the heroism of my wife saved my life. She sold her ornaments and denied herself to the limit to provide the indispensable articles of food needed for my use. I was utterly powerless to prevent her from doing so and had to continue as an impotent witness to her sacrifice. She was the only person who knew all about my condition, and, without in the least understanding the real significance of the development, tortured herself to save me from the pain of violent bodily disorders which invariably followed in the wake of a marked irregularity or deficiency in diet. On no less than three occasions during this period I came back from the jaws of death, not because of any caprice of the mighty energy now inhabiting my body, or owing to any deliberate omission on my part, but because of grinding poverty, lack of amenities, insufficient and unsuitable diet, which in spite of the heroism of my wife and the sacrifice of my two young sons, who often insisted on surrendering a part of their own share to me, could not be what it should have been because of the utter inadequacy of our finances. On such occasions, lying in a state of utter exhaustion on the sick bed, I wondered at the stupendous mystery of fate which allowed one destined to reveal a mighty secret to be distressed and tortured for the lack of a few coins which flowed in streams on every side and were scattered right and left by many on trifles every day. But even in the most gloomy conditions an unshakable conviction always persisted in my mind like a solitary star, gleaming faintly in an otherwise darkly threatening sky, that I would somehow survive the crisis and live to place in the hands of mankind the great secret on which depended the future safety of the race. It was mainly because of this inward strength, which no external source could infuse in me, that I was able to put up a strong resistance even in the most desperate situations with no possibility of help from any earthly source.

The evil effects of these serious breakdowns in health, the unavoidable result of destitution, lasted for several months each time and once for nearly two years. During such periods until the body regained the depleted store of vital energy, I lost the sublime moods and for part of the time even suffered from disquieting mental symptoms. But there was no diminution in the vital current or in the radiant halo around the head even in the weakest conditions. The violent reaction of my system to any default on my part, which impeded in any way the action of the processes going on inside, especially any laxity in the matter of nutrition, was clearly understandable. It is necessary for any natural transformative tendency to be effective that it should be attended by a biological activity directed to that end, and for any biological activity to be operative, food in sufficient quantity and wholesome form is an indispensable and primary requirement. If it is obligatory for an athlete to adhere to certain rigid rules of conduct, to have regular hours of rest and a balanced diet, how much more necessary it is for one whose entire organism is in a state of feverish activity, akin to the exertions of an athlete during intensive training, to be cautious in all these and other respects in order to save his system from irreparable harm. The process at work in him is not merely aimed at building the arm, leg, and chest muscles, but more importantly directed at the development of the brain and nerves, the main channels of life, hammering away at them and all the vital organs day and night, while the owner, in the present state of our knowledge about the mechanism, remains entirely in the dark about the form of conduct he must pursue and the precautions he must take to save himself from injury more imminent and far more serious than that which an athlete would suffer by a similar neglect.

But for the care taken of me by my mother in my childhood and youth, under adverse circumstances and in the grip of poverty, and thereafter by my wife through all the critical phases of my transformation and all the vicissitudes in my life to this day, I could never have emerged from the terrible ordeal alive and intact. Were it not for the colossal self-sacrifice of my wife and the anxious care lavished by her on me every day for more than twenty-four years, counting only the period after the manifestation, I would not be alive now to write these lines. Whenever I tried to visualize how I should have acted in her position if our roles had been reversed under similar circumstances, in spite of all my experience of the supersensible and my claim to supersensory knowledge, I have been humbled by the thought that I would have failed miserably to emulate her in the performance of all the tiresome, yet essential, tasks which she carried out serenely and conscientiously for years.

Perhaps no one who reads this account would be as surprised as I am myself at the marvellous ingenuity of nature and the wonder she has hidden in the frail frame of men, which, through the clay binding him to earth, allows his spirit to soar unfettered to giddy heights to knock for admission at the portals of heaven itself. Like a small child for the first time venturing outdoors and finding himself on the shore of a billowy ocean, casting one look at the familiar cottage behind and another on the stupendous sight in front of him, I feel utterly lost between the two worlds in which I live . . . the incomprehensible and infinitely marvellous universe within and the colossal but familiar world without. When I look within I am lifted beyond the confines of time and space, in tune with a majestic, all-conscious existence, which mocks at fear and laughs at death, compared to which seas and mountains, suns and planets, appear no more than flimsy rack riding across a blazing sky; an existence which is in all and yet absolutely removed from everything, an endless inexpressible wonder that can only be experienced and not described. But when I look outside I am what I was, an ordinary mortal in no way different from the millions who inhabit the earth, a common man, pressed by necessity and driven by circumstances, a little chastened and humbled—that is all.

The one really remarkable change I perceive in myself is that, not by my own effort but by what at present I can only call grace, as the result of a day-to-day observable but still incomprehensible activity of a radiant kind of vital energy, present in a dormant form in the human organism, there has developed in me a new channel of communication, a higher sense. Through this extraordinary and extremely sensitive channel an intelligence, higher than that which I possess, expresses itself at times in a manner as surprising to me as it might be to others, and through which again I am able on occasions to have a fleeting glimpse of the mighty, indescribable world to which I really belong, as a slender beam of light slanting into a dark room through a tiny hole does not belong to the room which it illuminates, but to the effulgent sun millions and millions of miles away. I am as firmly convinced of the existence of this supersense as I am of the other five already present in every one of us. In fact on every occasion when I make use of it, I perceive a reality before which all that I treat as real appears unsubstantial and shadowy, a reality more solid than the material world reflected by the other senses, more solid than myself, surrounded by the mind and ego, more solid than all I can conceive of including solidity itself. Apart from this extraordinary feature, I am but an ordinary human being with a body perhaps more susceptible to heat and cold and to the influence of disharmonious factors, mental and physical, than the normal one.

The truthful, unembellished account of a normal life unfolded in these pages, before the sudden development of the extraordinary mental and nervous condition already described is, I believe, sufficient to provide ample corroboration for the fact that initially I was no better and no worse as a human being than others and did not possess any entirely uncommon characteristics, such as are usually associated with men of vision, entitling me to special divine favour. Also that the final exceptional state of consciousness, which I continue to possess now, did not appear all at once, but marked the culmination of a continuous process of biological reconstruction covering no less than fifteen years before the first unmistakable sign of a new florescence. The process is still at work in me, but even after an experience of more than twenty-five years I am still lost in amazement at the wizardry of the mysterious energy responsible for the marvels which I witness day after day in my own mortal frame. I regard the manifestation with the same feelings of awe, adoration, and wonder with which I regarded it on the first occasion, the feelings having increased in intensity and not diminished as is generally the case with material phenomena.

Contrary to the belief which attributes spiritual growth to purely psychic causes, to extreme self-denial and renunciation, or to an extraordinary degree of religious fervour, I found that a

234   *Kundalini*

man can rise from the normal to a higher level of consciousness by a continuous biological process, as regular as any other activity of the body, and that at no stage is it necessary or even desirable for him either to neglect his flesh or to deny a place to the human feelings in his heart. A higher state of consciousness, able to liberate itself from the thraldom of senses, appears to be incompatible, unless we take the biological factors into account, with a physical existence in which passions and desires and the animal needs of the body, however restricted, exist side by side. But I can say confidently that a reasonable measure of control over appetites coupled with some knowledge of the mighty mechanism and a befitting constitution proved a surer and safer way to spiritual unfoldment than any amount of self-mortification or abnormal religious fervour can do.

I have every reason to believe that mystical experience and transcendental knowledge can come to a man as naturally as the flow of genius, and that for this achievement it is not necessary for him, save for well directed efforts at self-ennoblement and regulation of appetites, to depart eccentrically from the normal course of human conduct. Whether the transformative process is set in motion by voluntary effort or is spontaneous, purity of thought and disciplined behaviour are essential to minimize resistance to the cleansing and remodelling action of the mighty power on the organism. The subject must emerge normal in every way from the great ordeal, metamorphosed but mentally sane and with unimpaired intellect and emotion, to be able to evaluate and taste in full the supreme happiness of an occasional enrapturing union with the indescribable ocean of consciousness in the transcendental state, by marking the difference between the frail human element in him on the one hand and the immortal spirit on the other. It is only in this way that the incomparable bliss of liberation can be realized, because unconditioned existence being beyond the pale of enjoyment or its opposite, the actual enjoyer in the egobound conditioned human creature, is the visionary and no other.

Commentary to Chapters Sixteen, Seventeen and Eighteen

Verse comes naturally to those seized by what Plato called 'mania' or divine frenzy. Shakespeare in one phrase joins 'the lover, the lunatic, and the poet'. Lovers compose poems; mystics (the prophets, Blake, John of the Cross) use the verse form; haiku and Zen go together; and even some alchemists recounted their experiences in poetry. Those in analysis frequently find that only verse is suitable for giving form to what is going on—and this expression has nothing to do with art. Characteristic of verse is rhythm, the use of words for sound as well as sense, the symbolic cluster of meaning, brevity and intensity. Verse has a ritualistic aspect. It is language as revelation, as pure symbol; echoed in it is the primitive throb of the dance, the ritual chant, and the nonsense of the child. It would seem to be the true language of the spirit.

That his verse came in many tongues is a fact not unknown to parapsychological research. In trance states there are mediums who do speak in foreign tongues, even converse in languages they do not consciously know, nor have ever learned. These cases of glossolalia are evidence for what Dr Ian Stevenson, who is the pioneering contemporary investigator in this field, calls reincarnation. Gopi Krishna would not deny this idea, but he finds another ground. His ability is owed less to a former incarnation than to his contact with the supersensible world through which all can be known. The great experience is set in paradoxes. This is typical of the indescribability of the highest mystical experiences. It is both 'nothing yet everything', 'immeasurable', 'yet no bigger than an infinitely small point', 'infinitely large and infinitely small at the same time'. This is the Atman, bigger than big and smaller than small. From the topological view of the psyche, the ego focus is identified with its objective psychic ground. This totality is of course spaceless, timeless, extending everywhere unendingly and eternally present, in so far as the human personality when released of its limitations of circumstance is part of the same matter, the same energy, which makes up the whole universe. That especially the categories of spatial size are used for this description (rather than say categories of motion, nature, time, love, etc.) reflects the difficulties inherent in ego formulations of such experiences. The ego is bound to its body and this body has its definite spatial limits. Grand as we may imagine ourselves to be, we are but minute figures in a vast Chinese landscape, and placed not even in the centre of the picture. Transcendence of ego limitations is therefore presented by the ego primarily as a leap out of its spatial limitation given by the body's pounds and inches. (Distorted forms of this discrepancy between ego experience and body limitations can be found in every depression and inflation, when one feels smaller than small, or bigger than big.) I would also hazard the guess that space is the category appropriate to intuition (extension of vision, light, all-encompassing) and there-fore preferred by intuitive types, which I assume Gopi Krishna to be partly on the basis of our author's own admittedly obsessive (at times) preoccupation with diet, body, sensation and health, and his difficulties in regard to the factual order.

The experience itself was ushered in with 'a cadence like the humming of a swarm of *bees*'. The 'bee-loud glade' is a favourite image in poetry and comes in mythology as well as in the Bible. But we must remember, in our text we are not dealing with images as in a Western individuation process reflected mainly in dreams, but with *lived* experiences. The whitening, the meat, the baby, the oil, were all *actualities* for our author. Because of this, we may gain some insight from his experiences into why the bee is a widespread symbol of natural wisdom. In addition to its natural intelligence and social organization used often as a meta-phor for society, its conversion of nature into culture (honey and wax), its dancing, mating, feeding, building rituals, its death sting, its orientation ability—the bee sound (just as the numinous sound of the lion, the gander, the bull, etc.) evidently occurs, if we follow our text, at a special moment in the liberation experience. Perhaps it is the sound of a strata of instinctual earth wisdom, deeper than our mammalian blood, representing a spontaneous flight, wild yet ordered, of the collective spirit beyond personal individuality. The Pythian oracle spoke from such depths. Her psychic state was that kind of mania which Plato terms prophetic and which belongs to the God, Apollo. Her answers were in verse, 'some even maintained that the hexameter was invented at Delphi' (E. R. Dodds, *The Greeks and the Irrational*, Chap. 3 'The Blessings of Madness', *vid.* Notes and References). 'Pythia' refers to 'Python', the snake that Apollo killed and who resided in that place. She was, in other words, the daimon of the snake itself, the serpent power now in female form giving utterance to its wisdom. Supposedly, the serpent's bones and/or teeth were used for her oracles. And: she was described in the Homeric hymn to Hermes as a 'delphic bee' (Kerenyi, 'Gedanken über die Pythia'). Quite possibly, Gopi Krishna's experience of the bee-sound in connection with his prophetic verse corresponds with the actual experience of the Pythian oracle so that through his account some light is shed on that ancient enigma.

After this last, highest encounter, the return itself is threatened. He abandons his work, identifies for a time with the *image of the holy man*, feels purged 'clean of worldly love', and is ready to follow the traditional pattern of mystic seer, wandering, devoted only to the spirit. He views his attachment to the world as a weak spot in his system, but as we see later he is then reconciled with this attachment and in the last instance realizes its positive value.

The *alternation of his states of consciousness* throughout the years, especially the loss of heavenly joy time and again, is also described by the alchemists. They said the Stone must be coagulated and dissolved again and again. The more it alternated between these opposites the more valuable it became. This lesson is hard to learn, for after every peak experience one wants to 'hold it', and after each valley experience one feels guilty, lost and humiliated.

Again we have evidence that the development of ego and the development of awareness are separate matters. His external ego situation in fact deteriorated in that he no longer had a job and was reduced to living upon the sacrifices of his wife, nor did he feel himself to be of any use even in the realm of therapy with all those who came with problems. Straightforwardly he tells the limits of the enlightened one: such a one may be of value in teaching or helping others who are on the same path, but he is not a miracle man. To assume this role would be to misuse the experiences. This keeps our author from being a fraud and mountebank. He remains aware of his human limits, and he chooses to remain within those limits.

By giving credit to his wife he acknowledges an archetypal aspect of this path. It is not taken alone; there is always the 'other'—master, disciple, pupil, sister, wife, friend, beloved—who is the silent partner, who represents the human love and care, who carries the other side, gives encouragement by believing, and is the mortal twin to the immortal urge.

It could be argued again that this dependence upon his wife and family, his precarious health and his general ineffectiveness as both householder and as healer negates all that has happened, so that it becomes merely a psychic aberration. He admits that were it not for his mother and his wife, he would have died long ago. So what has this twenty-five years of ordeal really achieved? What positive results give evidence of the Great Liberation? Is he not just where he started: in the mother-complex, a victim of mother-matter, passive, delicate, dependent? How these destructive negative thoughts must have tormented him—or would have tormented his counterpart in the West.

However, within his tradition, this dependent relation to the Mother archetype is inevitable. Ramakrishna for example was always the devotee of the Mother, while the Indian Holy Man is ever her son in the sense of drawing sustenance from life and earth which is the cow that must never be harmed. Only in the West is this attitude questionable, for we tend to view negatively the realm of the Mother and to call that inevitable dependency upon the material limits in which we are set a 'complex.' We in the West are often too quick to condemn the 'Mother' thereby cutting ourselves off from our own ground. Our author is neither paralysed by his passivity nor rebellious against it, and so he cannot be said to be caught in a complex. Rather, he lives the opposites. On the one hand he is involved in the bold spiritual adventure, requiring the masculine virtues of endurance, courage and individuality, while on the other he acknowledges without shame his weakness, sensitivity and physical limitations. He accepts the feminine root, not only of the Kundalini, but of life itself, thereby showing us a positive relation to the maternal archetype.

At the end of Chapter Eighteen, there is a passage which conveys what we might call his *declaration of faith*, remarkable for its simplicity. 'I found that a man can rise from the normal to a higher level of consciousness by a continuous biological process, as regular as any other activity of the body, and that at no stage is it necessary or even desirable for him either to neglect his flesh or to deny a place to the human feelings in his heart.' The same credo could apply to analytical psychology with a few exceptions. Rather than 'biological' we might refer to the process as 'psychological'. We might interpret 'flesh' and 'feelings' with more liberality so as to include more shadows of the body and the heart. We might raise a question about the continuity of this process, since it also seems to have a discontinuous aspect that works by leaps and jumps and that devolves backwards on to itself. It can even devour itself so that the accomplishments of one phase of life may all be consumed in later errors. Our psychological process is definitely not progressive, ever upward and ever better, much as we idealize it and much as older people are obliged to believe. Jung gives us models for the completeness of consciousness, but these models are to be found more in his books than in his disciples. But then Gopi Krishna too points the way in his own person and his writings, not through training others. However, for our psychology the overriding importance in his credo is its emphasis upon an instinct of individuation (which as I said Jung called the Kundalini) and the process character of consciousness. This implies that something is meant with our psychic lives, our souls, and that this urge of meaning is a regular (continuous) function of our bodily nature. It is possible to each and it does not deny the world and its life.

Chapter Nineteen

CONSTITUTED as I was by nature no manifestation of the ordinary kind, whether in the form of entrancement accompanied by visions and ecstasy or in the shape of suddenly awakened psychic powers, could have brought absolute conviction to me, silencing the low, insistent voices of innumerable doubts that have to be satisfied now in the light of modern knowledge before the existence of the spiritual world and the possibility of development of a higher state of consciousness in a normal man can become acceptable to a strictly rational mind. Such an explanation must appear as convincing to the anthropologist as to the man of God and as reasonable to the psychologist as to the student of history. The answer that ultimately came to me, after about half-a-century of waiting and watching and but a little less than a quarter century of suffering, with a startling thoroughness, which is characteristic of all universal laws, at last succeeded in stilling the stubborn doubts one by one with a workable solution of the greatest problem of all time facing man. It needs now but the labour and sacrifice of other able men from this and the coming generations to make it the principle of the exact science, that will have to come to it for inspiration and guidance, for the first time made aware of the purpose and goal of human existence towards which as one they will have to strive.

Without pride of achievement, without the least pretension to any divine office, I humbly submit, on the strength of knowledge gained, that religion infinitely more than that it is or has been supposed to be, is in reality the expression of the evolutionary impulse in human beings, springing from an imperceptibly active though regularly functioning organic power centre in the body, amenable to voluntary stimulation under favourable conditions. Further, that the transcendental state of which as yet only a faint though unmistakable picture is available from the descriptions furnished by visionaries is the natural heritage of man, with all his feelings and desires, only refined and restrained to act in consonance with the needs of a higher kind of perception. Also, that the happiness and welfare of mankind depend on its adherence to the yet unknown laws of this evolutionary mechanism, known in India as Kundalini, which is carrying all men towards a glorious state of consciousness with all their capacities to act, love, and enjoy intact, enhanced rather than diminished but functioning in subjection to a cultivated will, in obedience to the dictates of a properly developed conscience and in accordance with the decrees of a correctly informed intellect fully aware of the goal in front of it.

From my own experience, extending to a quarter of a century, I am irresistibly led to the conclusion that the human organism is evolving in the direction indicated by mystics and prophets and by men of genius, by the action of this wonderful mechanism, located at the base of the spine, depending for its activity mainly on the energy supplied by the reproductive organs. Though not in its general application as the evolutionary organ in man, but in the individual sphere as the means to develop spirituality, supernormal faculties and psychic powers, the mechanism has been known and manipulated from very ancient times. When manipulated and roused to intense activity by men already advanced on the path of progress and subject to numerous factors, especially favourable heredity, constitution, mode of conduct, occupation and diet, it can lead to most remarkable and extremely useful results, developing the organism by general stages from its native condition to a state of extraordinary mental efficiency, conducting

Kundalini

it ultimately to the zenith of cosmic consciousness and genius combined.

Civilization and leisure, divested of the glaring abuses that have crept into both due to ignorance and a fundamentally wrong conception of the goal of human life, are but means to this important end. Crudely planned and wrongly used at present, they will necessarily have to pass through a process of refinement when the goal is clearly established. All great sages and seers of the past and all great founders of religions, whether guided intuitively by evolving life itself or led by observation, have consciously or unconsciously laid emphasis mostly on only such traits of character and modes of conduct as are definitely conducive to progress. The highest products of civilization, prophets, mystics, men of genius, clearly indicate the direction and goal of human evolution. Studied in the light of the facts mentioned in this volume they will all be found to have common characteristics. The motive and guiding power behind them in all cases without exception is Kundalini.

Studied critically from this angle, the ancient religious literature of India, the esoteric doctrines of China, the sacred lore of other countries and faiths, the monuments and relics of prehistoric culture, with variations owing to the level of development, environment, and the habits and customs of the people, will all be seen pointing unmistakably in the same direction. Extensively in India, to a lesser degree in China, and to some extent in the Middle East and Greece as well as Egypt, the methods to activate the mechanism in order to develop supernormal mental faculties and spiritual powers were known and practised centuries before the Christian era. In India its ability to confer genius was recognized and consciously availed of for its pragmatic value. There is sufficient material available in the sacred books of my country to corroborate these assertions in almost every respect. The doctrine of Yoga, one of the greatest products of sustained human endeavour extending to thousands of years, owes its origin to the possibility existing in the human organism of remoulding itself at the initiation and with the cooperation of the surface consciousness to a higher state of functional and organic efficiency, tending to bring it closer and closer to the primordial substance responsible for its existence. This possibility cannot be accidental, present in some and not in others, nor can it be merely an artificial product of human effort entirely divorced from nature. It must exist as a potentiality, naturally present in the human body, dependent for its effective materialization on laws and factors not yet properly known or understood.

The awakening of Kundalini is the greatest enterprise and the most wonderful achievement in front of man. There is absolutely no other way open to his restlessly searching intellect to pass beyond the boundaries of the otherwise meaningless physical universe. It provides the only method available to science to establish empirically the existence of life as an immortal, all-intelligent power behind the organic phenomena on earth, and brings within its scope the possibility of planned cultivation of genius in individuals not gifted with it from birth, thereby unfolding before the mental eye of man avenues and channels for the acceleration of progress and enhancement of prosperity which it is impossible to visualize at present. But the heroic enterprises can only be undertaken by highly intelligent, serene, and sober men of chaste ideals and noble resolves. The experiment is to be made by them on their own precious flesh and at the present moment at the risk of their lives.

When conducted by the right type of man on proper lines and with due precautions, partly explained in these pages and partly to be explained in other works, the experiment will surely be successful, in a few cases sufficient to demonstrate the existence of the mechanism leading after the awakening to divergent results. The reaction created in the system may subside after a while, fizzling out like an ignited match without effecting any noteworthy alteration in the subject, after existing as a remarkable and weird biological phenomenon for months, open to observation and capable of analysis and measurement; or it may after varying periods lead ultimately to permanent injury, either mental or physical, or death. In the last and really successful case the transformative process generated may lead to that sublime state which carries the erring mortal to superphysical heights in joyous proximity to the everlasting, omniscient, conscious reality, more wonderful than wonder and more secret than secrecy, which as embodied life manifests itself in countless forms—ugly and beautiful, good and bad, wise and foolish, living, enjoying, and suffering all around us.

The experiments, besides providing indisputable evidence for the existence of design in creation, would at the same time open to view a new and healthy direction designed by nature for the sublimation of human energy and the use of human resources, frittered away at present in frivolous pursuits, debasing amusements, and ignoble enterprises unsuited to the dignity of man. The knowledge of the safest methods for awakening Kundalini and their empirical application on themselves by the noblest men physically and mentally equipped for it, will yield for humanity a periodic golden crop of towering spiritual and mental prodigies who and who alone in the atomic and post-atomic age will be able to discharge in a proper manner, consistent with the safety and security of the race, the supreme offices of the ministers of God and the rulers of men.

It is not difficult to see that at present there exists a greater menace to the safety of mankind than any it has faced before. Though that may not assume the terrifying danger of wiping off every trace of civilization from the face of the earth, it is yet likely to cause widespread havoc, loss of millions of lives, untold misery and suffering it has never experienced so far, to humanity inured to hardship and accustomed to catastrophes. It was a riddle to me why the world situation should wear such a threatening aspect in an era of popular rule, of unprecedented prosperity, unparalleled advance in all branches of knowledge, widespread education, freedom of thought and above all, nearly complete command of the earth's resources. What tiny screw was loose in an otherwise perfect machine which created such a disturbance as threatens to rend the whole complicated mechanism in pieces? But when the answer came I at once saw light where there had been complete darkness before, and in that light the mighty scroll of human destiny unfolding itself allowed me a glimpse into man's past and future. I thus came to know why his efforts to amass wealth finally go to feed dissipation, why his attempts to raise empires lead always to invasion, and why his endeavours to gain power end invariably in dissension. All that knowledge pointed to but a small screw in the human organism which, neglected so far, exercises the same effect on the rise and fall of men and of nations as the hairspring has on the accuracy of a watch.

A host of highly important issues, demanding urgent attention, is bound to arise when it is established that an evolutionary mechanism, ceaselessly active in developing the brain towards a pre-determined state of higher consciousness, really does exist in man. It is not difficult to form an idea of these issues whereof the most vital, namely the direction of the evolutionary impulse, the biological factors at work and the mode of conduct, necessary for individuals and societies to facilitate the process of transformation, need immediate clarification to prevent all of them, at present entirely in the dark about the goal ahead, from pulling in a direction contrary to that designed by nature. Such a conflict cannot but result in a gigantic tussle in which, after prolonged suffering and grief, the party vanquished and injured, as can be readily understood, will be only man.

It is easy to see that a clearly discernible alteration is occurring in the extremely delicate fabric of the human mind, which we are apt to attribute to change of times, to modernity, to progress, to freedom, to liberal education and to a host of other relevant and irrelevant factors. When closely studied, the change, although in part brought to the surface by any or several of these factors, in reality springs from the hidden depths of personality, from the foundations of life. The variation, though extremely slight, could not occur at once, but must be the cumulative effect of imperceptible changes that have been going on in the extremely complicated psycho-physiological organism of man through centuries of a civilized existence, in some ways incompatible with evolutionary laws. For the proper growth of man on which depends the safety and happiness of the individual and mankind, it is essential that his mental content show a harmonious and appropriate blending of emotion, will, and thought, and that there be a concordant development of the morals and intellect. If this does not come to pass and there is a disproportionate preponderance of one with the underdevelopment of one or both of the others, it is a sign that the growth is abnormal and as such can never be conductive to happiness or to the progress of the race.

The present disquieting world situation is the direct outcome of such an inharmonious growth of the inner man. By no exercise of the intellect and by no artifice can mankind escape the penalty it has to pay for continued violation of evolutionary laws. Although unperceived yet because of absolute ignorance about the all powerful mechanism, Kundalini discharges as important an office in shaping human destiny and in the spiritual and mental development of man as the reproductive system does in propagating the race. The time is near when the mechanism will make its existence felt by the sheer force of inexplicable concomitant factors, which are not amenable to any other solution. Only the progressive sphere of human knowledge must first widen to an extent to make detection of the lacunae existing in the current explanations possible to the intellect.

In the present era of unprecedented technological development and of high explosives powerful enough to wipe out large cities in a moment, the least vagarious tendency of the mind in the leaders of men, especially in those holding seats of power, is fraught with the gravest danger for the race. A single unpremeditated act or an unforeseen chain of circumstances, reacting on ethically inferior minds, however dominating intellectually, can give off the spark that might suffice to reduce whole portions of the smiling garden of humanity to mounds of virulent ash. Consequently so long as the basic facts about mind are not known and science does not come in possession of effective techniques to control inherent propensities, which, present in men holding positions of authority, can cause havoc on a global scale, mankind will continue to bide precariously on the top of a sleeping volcano liable to violent eruption at any time.

The only sure safeguard against the now constantly over-hanging threat of an annihilating war is comprehensive knowledge of Kundalini. I feel it is the unseen hand of destiny, which in spite of my limitations, drives me to present a demonstrable religious truth of paramount importance that can save humanity at this crucial time, when it is drifting helplessly towards the greatest disaster it has ever suffered, all because of its utter ignorance of the laws of the mighty mechanism operating in the system of every member of the race.

The only source of strength I possess is my absolute conviction of the correctness under all circumstances of the disclosures I am making about Kundalini. I feel completely sure that the main characteristics of the awakening described in this work, the results defined, and ultimate consequences foretold will be fully established by experiment and by corroboration from unexpected sources, partly before the end of this century and mainly in the centuries to come. I am also certain that the disclosure of a mighty law of nature, that could well have remained shrouded in mystery for a long time yet without anyone being able even to make a guess at it, is in the nature of a divine revelation. I was led to the knowledge of this momentous truth step by step by the action of a superphysical energy upon my system, shaping it by degrees to the required state of nervous efficiency, as if to be instructed in the ancient science I was destined to make known in a verifiable form suited to the tendencies of the age.

One may ask how all that I can say will have such an effect on the world as to succeed in creating the mental climate that will remove the threat of wars, usher in an era favourable to the establishment of a universal religion, a new world order and a one-world government, with the demolition of racial and colour barriers and the introduction of other much-needed reforms conducive to the unhindered progress and uninterrupted happiness of mankind. The answer is simple, so simple perhaps that many may find it hard to reconcile its apparently ordinary character with the colossal nature of the transformation it is expected to bring about. All the changes I have mentioned will be brought about by the simple device of demonstrating empirically the alteration wrought in the human organism by a voluntarily awakened Kundalini. In every successful experiment the results would be so positive as to leave absolutely no room for doubt and so astounding as to demand immediate revision of some of the most firmly

established scientific theories and concepts of today, leading in-
evitably to the transference of the world's attention from purely
materialistic objectives and projects to spiritual and psychical
problems and pursuits.

The fortunate man in whom the divine energy is benignly disposed from the beginning, possessing the psychical and biological
endowments, which as far as I have been able to judge, predispose
him to a favourable termination, will after varying periods normally extending to years show remarkable developments, both
internally and externally, so startling and, judging from the preva-
lent notions of great thinkers, so unexpected that they are sure to
strike with overwhelming effect not only the subject himself but
also the trained scientist engaged in the observation of the phenomenon. Inwardly the man will bloom into a visionary, the
vehicle of expression of a higher consciousness endowed with a
spiritual or mental sixth sense; outwardly he will be a religious
genius, a prophet, an intellectual giant, with bewildering ver-
satility and insight, completely altered mentally from what he was
before the experiment. In exceptional cases, and such instances
will occur in the era to come when more facts become known
about the mode of operation of the mighty power, the favoured
mortal may develop into a superman, capable of prodigious
spiritual, mental, and physical feats, a source of ever-present awe
and wonder to the multitudes and of inspiration and guidance to
others already firmly planted on the path but not destined to reach
his heights. Most of the successful hierarchs will sooner or later
find access to the eternal repository of infinite wisdom to bring in
inimitable language inspired messages suited to the need for the
enlightment and guidance of mankind.

Only a few successful experiments would suffice to convince
the world of the validity and the natural character of the phenomenon. The results obtained will furnish the evidence necessary
to find out the nature and purpose of the religious impulse in men,
reveal the mysterious sovereign power from which prophets and
sages drew their authority and inspiration, disclose the source of
genius, lay bare the secret fount of art, and above all make known
the immediate goal destined by nature for humanity, which it

must achieve at any cost to live in peace and plenty. On the empirical side the effects will be uniformity of symptoms, regularity and ordered sequence of the biological processes, clearly observable day to day for years, indicative of the action of a superior form of vital energy in the organism, resulting finally in the complete alteration of personality and development of superior mental faculties. This cannot but lead irresistibly to the conclusion that by the operation of some extraordinary biological law yet entirely unknown to science the human organism can complete within the period of a few years the evolutionary cycle needed for its ascension to the next stage, requiring in the normal course of events enormous spans of time for the completion of the process.

The paramount importance of the issues raised by this psycho-physiological phenomenon, viewed in the perspective of the modern scientific trend, cannot be exaggerated. The emergence of a consciousness of the transcendental type at the end of a certain period, the inevitable result of the awakening of Kundalini in all successful cases, provides incontrovertible evidence for the fact that the regenerative force at work in the body is at the very beginning aware of the ultimate pattern to which it has to conform by means of the remodelling biological processes set afoot.

The existence of an empirically demonstrable power in the system not only fully aware of all the perplexing psycho-physical intricacies of the organism but also capable of reshaping it to a far higher pitch of organic and functional activity so as to bring it in harmony with the demands of a higher state of consciousness can have only one meaning: that the evolutionary force in man is carrying him towards an already known, and predetermined, state of sublimity of which humanity has no inkling save that provided by the religious concepts of prophets and visionaries.

The inquiry is not to be approached in a spirit of conquest or arrogance with the intent to achieve victory over a force of nature, which has characterized man's approach to the problems of the material world, but rather with humility, in a spirit of utter surrender to Divine Will and absolute dependence on Divine Mercy, in the same frame of mind one would approach the flaming sun. There is no other way save this open to man to arrive at the solution of an otherwise impenetrable mystery of creation, no other way open to him to find out what path has been aligned for his progress by nature, no other way for him to know and recognize himself, and no other way to save himself from the awful consequence of conscious or unconscious violation of the mighty laws which rule his destiny. This is the only method to bridge the gulf at present yawning between science and religion, between warring political ambitions and ideologies, more deadly than the most virulent disease and more awful than all the epidemics combined, between religious faiths, races, nations, classes and finally between men. This is the immortal light, held aloft by nature from time immemorial to guide the faltering footsteps of erring humanity across the turns and twists, ups and downs, of the winding path of evolution, the light which shone in the prophets and sages of antiquity, which continues to shine in the men of genius and seers of today, and will continue to shine for all eternity, illuminating the vast amphitheatre of the universe for the marvellous, unending play of the eternal, almighty, queen of creation, life.

Commentary: Conclusion

All the Gods are within. This message is given by Heinrich Zimmer in his paper 'On the Significance of the Indian Tantric Yoga'. Within may mean within the psyche, within the body, within the collective unconscious. Gopi Krishna makes it explicit that what happened to him was not an act of God, person-to-person as for instance such mystical experiences might have been taken by a medieval Christian. It did not come from without but from within. The incarnation of these Gods within is a terrible task, as our text has shown. 'Whoever is near unto me is near unto the fire' is an apocryphal saying of Jesus. How are we to understand this incarnation? How are we to read the purpose of these events? What do the Gods and Goddesses want with us?

So many questions flood in—metaphysical, historical, religious—
that a psychologist is unable to cope. We can only turn to the
case at hand. Our author knows what the Goddess wants of him
and the publication of this book is part of the purpose of that
which he has been driven and led to incarnate.

The instinct of individuation, as the evolutionary energy in
man, is given to every man. Our author's experiences, he tells us,
are possible in varying forms to everyone. Furthermore, they are
teleologically meant for everyone. Our task is to incarnate the
Gods within. Having seen this as the result of decades of wrestling
with himself and these Gods, he can give us a golden vision of how
things not only might be, but are meant to be. Can we blame him
for this vast speculation; is not this the stuff of prophecy and vision
and is not our age deaf and dry to just such calls? The relation of
the one who sees the shadows as shadows to those still in the cave
is an archetypal problem. Our author has grasped the dilemma
and spoken out. Our author does not believe that it is enough for
the mystic 'to work out his salvation with diligence'; he feels a
call to call others. In this respect he is not to be regarded as a
mystic nor is this an account of an 'experience' of which we have,
due to drugs, more and more at hand from every side. He pre-
sents himself as a modern teacher and scientific inquirer into a
realm that has been neglected and covered over with accounts of
'mystical experiences'. He does not want us to take this material
as another variety of religious experience but as the very meaning
of human life itself.

The experience of himself as only a vessel through which the
wind of human history blows and from which the call to others
sounds is entirely in keeping with his point of view. As Professor
Spiegelberg points out, Gopi Krishna never felt that what took
place was personally his. From the beginning he was a mere
instrument; therefore, at the end, he is merely a mouthpiece of a
vaster truth. The degree to which the ego personality takes part
in these collective unconscious events determines their final shape.
In the West, the mystic or artist to whom the extraordinary
happens hammers the impersonal into personal form and presses
his own vision upon archetypal patterns. The specific absence of

personal form, the characteristic of impersonality, is the mark of the East. Yet, Gopi Krishna's biography is personal and it is just this which makes it unusually contemporary and accessible. Just because this book from another culture is so accessible it meets us more than halfway, addressing to each reader a question about the nature of man. His question is the fundamental one. What could be more important to inquire about than the nature of man, his psyche, his spirit, his body, and the purpose of his consciousness?

Note

In addition to the works mentioned within the context of the Commentary, I would refer the reader to the *Collected Works* of C. G. Jung, Volumes 11, 12, 14, and 16 in particular. Very valuable also is a collection of excellent studies (among them Zimmer on Tantric Yoga) called *Spiritual Disciplines* (Papers from the Eranos Yearbooks IV), New York and London, 1960. For psychological background material I read Jung's 'Seminar on Kundalini Yoga' and his 'Lectures on the Process of Individuation', both unpublished and privately circulated.

Botorp, Hemsö,   J.H.
Summer, 1965.
(Revised *idem*, 1969)

Other Books by Gopi Krishna

The Awakening of Kundalini. New York: E.P. Dutton & Co., 1975.
Toronto: F.I.N.D. Research Trust/Kundalini Research Foundation,
1989.

Biblical Prophecy for the Twentieth Century. Toronto: New Age
Publishing Ltd., 1979.

The Biological Basis of Religion and Genius. New York: N.C. Press,
Inc., 1971, and Harper and Row, 1972. London: Turnstone Press,
1973.

Dawn of a New Science. Part I. New Delhi: Kundalini Research &
Publication Trust, 1978.

From the Unseen. Kashmir: Gopi Krishna, 1952. F.I.N.D. Research
Trust/New Concepts Publishing, 1985.

Kundalini: The Evolutionary Energy in Man. London: Vincent Stuart
& John M. Watkins, 1970. Boston & London: Shambhala, 1985.

Kundalini for the New Age. New York: Bantam Books, 1988.

The Present Crisis. New York: New Concepts Publishing, for the
Kundalini Research Foundation, 1981.

The Riddle of Consciousness. New York: Kundalini Research
Foundation, 1976.

The Secret of Yoga. New York: Harper and Row, 1972.

Secrets of Kundalini in Panchastavi. New Delhi: Kundalini Research &
Publication Trust, 1978.

The Shape of Events to Come. New Delhi: Kundalini Research &
Publication Trust, 1979.

*Three Perspectives on Kundalini: The Real Nature of Mystical
Experience, Reason and Revelation, Kundalini in Time and Space.*
Toronto: F.I.N.D. Research Trust/Kundalini Research Foundation, 1991.

The Way to Self-Knowledge. Toronto: F.I.N.D. Research Trust/New
Concepts Publishing, 1985. Toronto: F.I.N.D. Research Trust/
Kundalini Research Foundation, 1987.

What Is and What Is Not Higher Consciousness. New York: Julian
Press, 1974. Toronto: F.I.N.D. Research Trust/Kundalini Research
Foundation, 1988.

The Wonder of the Brain. Toronto: F.I.N.D. Research Trust/Kundalini
Research Foundation, 1987.

Yoga—A Vision of Its Future. New Delhi: Kundalini Research &
Publication Trust, 1978.